WARM BREAD
and honey cake

home baking from around the world

WARM BREAD
and honey cake

Gaitri Pagrach-Chandra

Photography by Vanessa Courtier

INTERLINK BOOKS

First American edition published in 2010 by

INTERLINK BOOKS
An imprint of Interlink Publishing Group, Inc.
46 Crosby Street, Northampton, MA 01060
www.interlinkbooks.com

Design and layout © Pavilion, 2010
Text © Gaitri Pagrach-Chandra, 2010
Food photography © Vanessa Courtier, 2010
Other images © see acknowledgements on page 320
Americanized text © Interlink Publishing, 2010

Commissioning editor: Emily Preece-Morrison
Designer: Louise Leffler at Sticks Design
Cover design: Georgina Hewitt
Photographer: Vanessa Courtier
Home economist: Jane Suthering
Prop stylist: Wei Tang
Copy editor: Caroline Curtis
Proofreader: Alyson Silverwood
Indexer: Patricia Hymans
Production: Rebekah Cheyne
Americanization: Sara Rauch
Food consultant: Hiltrud Schulz

ISBN 978-1-56656-792-3

10 9 8 7 6 5 4 3 2 1

Reproduction by Mission Productions, Hong Kong
Printed and bound by 1010 Printing International Ltd, China

To request our free 48-page full-color catalog, please call us toll-free at 1-800-238-LINK,
e-mail us at info@interlinkbooks.com, or visit our website at www.interlinkbooks.com

CONTENTS

FOREWORD

Born in Crabwood Creek, in what was then British Guiana, I come from a Hindu Brahmin cultural background. My childhood was a privileged colonial one, spent on a series of sugar plantations in Guyana. My father worked for Bookers, who owned the plantations, continuing as a consultant long after retirement. As a child, I traveled extensively with my parents and sister, and I continue to enjoy doing so. From high school, I went to university in Canada, where I double majored in Political Science and Spanish. I spent a year in Salamanca, Spain, and met my Dutch-Jewish husband in the cheerful bustle of student activities in that city. We subsequently settled in the heart of Holland and I soon slipped into place in village life.

Baking has always been my passion, from the time when I made my first Bakewell tart at school. I was never allowed to get in the way in the kitchen at home except to bake the occasional cake, and I've been making up for that ever since!

My childhood prepared me well for my present life. For many people, their childhood seems gilded in retrospect. Mine, though, really was 24-carat gold. I grew up in multi-racial Guyana at the end of the colonial period and witnessed independence, and my life was slightly schizophrenic in a very normal kind of way. We lived on a sugar plantation in one of about 15 spacious dwellings that housed a mixture of local and expatriate families. This handful of men managed the plantation, which offered employment to thousands and contributed significantly to the local economy. We ran, swam and played with great abandon in our own little world while high chainlink fences and token security officers guarded our Westernized existence.

Then there was my other life: visits to my grandparents in their respective villages. My paternal grandfather was a *pandit* (Hindu priest), a village notable in a rural Indian society that still set store by ancient caste and hierarchical systems. He and my grandmother lived close enough for frequent afternoon visits. Some distance away, my mother's family lived in crumbling semi-feudal splendor in a village my great-grandfather had nostalgically named Bengal. The family as good as owned the village and its surrounding rice fields and coconut walks, and practically every house held an abundance of cousins, aunts and uncles. Indian clay ovens were as familiar to me as high-tech electric cookers, and it was as natural to sit at a crystal- and silver-laden dining table, eating what passed for sophisticated Western fare, as it was to attend a village wedding, sit cross-legged on the floor and use my fingers to tuck into the spicy vegetarian meal contained in the lotus leaf "plate" on my lap.

Later, I went to school in the capital: first a Protestant school, then a Catholic convent. Mass and hymns so modern that one hardly dared call them that, accompanied by the guitar strumming of the girls, became a regular part of my school life, while my home life still included the tinkling of tiny bells, sacred ghee-fed fires and Sanskrit chanting. Years later, it became equally natural to stand up for the *Amida* or join in the *Shema* in a liberal synagogue in Holland.

Growing up like this has left me easily able to adapt, and given me a sponge-like ability to absorb all kinds of facets of any culture, without quite knowing how. I am also marked by an insatiable curiosity and craving for even more cultural wealth. For me, food has always been one of the most enjoyable paths to other societies. A trip to another country automatically means eating local food and visiting groceries and markets, and I am very fortunate in having good friends on several continents with similar interests, so I often get an insider's view. I invariably try to recreate in my own kitchen whatever it is I have eaten, and have always been an avid collector of cookbooks, especially baking books.

The frustration when recipes fail to live up to my expectations always drove me to make alterations. It was not long before I began to compose my own, writing them down in a tattered, batter-splattered notebook that bore the grand title "Gaitri's Baking Journal" – itself a source of hilarity to my children. Every time I baked something, I made notes about how it turned out, and any changes, substitutions or different methods were duly recorded.

Missing the flavors of my childhood and wanting my family to know them, I started badgering friends and relatives for recipes. Their usually vague instructions as to amounts and methods were jotted down in the trusty Journal, allowing me to experiment. I learned to make Black Cake by phone, along with Chinese Bean Cakes, Azorean Honey Cake and many others, and while I already knew the basics of *roti*-making, I bullied my mother into demonstrating the finer points every time she visited. And the more I baked, the more I wanted to perfect this recipe and tweak that one, so there was always an abundance of baked goods in the house. Fortunately, there was no shortage of eaters, and nothing was too strange for my family and friends to taste. Indeed, they developed into a very critical tasting panel, and thanks to their comments, the "Baking Journal" eventually became a book – this one.

Gaitri

INTRODUCTION

Treasured memories are infused in homemade breads, cakes, and pastries. I can hardly remember a time when they have failed to lift my spirits in some way. Post-colonial plantation life in Guyana was characterized by a sense of Britishness that was enhanced by the presence of a large number of expatriate families in the otherwise small and isolated community. It found its chief expression in food, and teatime was a favorite part of the day. Sometimes this was no more than a hurried cup of tea in the kitchen with a pastry or a buttered slice of homemade bread; at other times, it was a lavish spread on a cool veranda.

If our own house had meager offerings that afternoon, it was quite normal for us children to head for a friend's house with richer pickings. Depleted tea tables were no obstacle to enjoyment. We simply made our way to the kitchen and adopted such well-feigned looks of starvation that it took a very hard-hearted cook not to respond with a plateful of fresh cake, coconut roll, pine tarts, cheese rolls or patties. With all the cunning of street urchins surviving on our wits, we soon knew whose cook made what best, and we weren't averse to cajoling our chosen target into making her specialty for us.

Later, at school, Fate gave me her seal of approval. Food and Nutrition was an optional subject, and as well as a written examination, there was a practical one. The various topics were handed out at random, and as we started opening them the Cookery Room was filled with muted cries of satisfaction and smothered groans of disgust. I read mine and hugged it gleefully to my chest. Not for me a request to prepare an evening meal for a young family with a laboring father, or a resident grandfather and a nursing mother – or any such mundane silliness. My slip said simply: Demonstrate the uses of raising agents. Even before I began, I could smell and taste the shrimp pizza, scones with clotted cream and chocolate cake.

Moving abroad, out of the reach of friendly cooks, I started experimenting – and swiftly came to the conclusion that baking is the most pleasurable of all culinary branches. One of the most enjoyable aspects is that, apart from daily bread, there is no real pressure to do it. This contributes to the general feeling of pampering that is generated by home-baked treats. It is something one does for the sheer joy of it, and the possibilities are endless. There is something to grace any occasion or suit any mood, including a potentially bad one. What better way to relieve stress than by pummelling the daylights out of a lump of yeast dough? And how soothing it can be to relax with some music, while patiently putting together a batch of dainty tarts or pastries. And there is the satisfaction that comes from pouncing on a quick and simple recipe, knowing that a minimum of effort will produce a much-appreciated treat.

Being a passionate baker myself, I enjoy the process of creation as much as the final reward of eating it. And so, in a way, I have made a rod for my own back. My family feels very hard pressed if they aren't kept supplied with home-baked goodies; friends and neighbors are only too happy to help with any leftovers; and local raffles and charity events all make demands from time to time. Pride, pleasure, nurturing, caring – all these, and many other positive emotions, find expression in home baking.

I hardly need tell you that store-bought articles, packed with additives and excessive amounts of salt, sugars and fats, cannot in any way compare with what you can produce in your own kitchen. The mere aroma of baking can transform the smallest, coldest, untidiest house into a warm and inviting home. Never hesitate to bake simply because you live and eat alone or because your household is tiny. Think of the simple and sincere pleasure and gratitude that the gift of even a single slice of homemade cake or bread can elicit – and if there are not enough recipients for your bounty, there is always the freezer.

With this book, I would like to share my enjoyment with you. Whether you are a novice or seasoned baker, you should be able to find something here that will get your fingers itching to bake. I have tried to cater for all levels of proficiency and for a variety of tastes. This is not an encyclopedic collection of recipes: you won't find puff pastry or muffins, but you will find an ingenious Chinese method of layering pastry and dainty little steamed rice cakes, as well as European classics that are too good to be left out. Most importantly, I hope you'll find new inspiration.

There is a wide selection of cookbooks available on almost all aspects of baking, and I feel no need to cover well-trodden ground. But there is one aspect that I feel has been neglected: ethnic baking, which so richly deserves to be drawn out from the shadows. True, one sometimes finds a good recipe tucked away at the back of a book on a particular cuisine, but many fantastic recipes never leave their region of origin, let alone make their way into print.

Inevitably, any collection of recipes will have a personal flavor and many of those included here are old family favorites. These have been joined by newer acquisitions, some of which are the result of visits to like-minded friends all over the world. I have also adapted the recipes of professional bakers, to suit the home baker. My choice is by no means random and I am particularly keen to highlight both similarities and differences, as well as to demonstrate the way that food changes character as it travels from its place of origin to fresher pastures. Explore the story of baking, and it is not long before snippets of world history come to the fore. Take the Indian flatbreads that crossed the seas to the Caribbean with indentured laborers; or the Spanish *Ensaimadas* that took on a new identity when they came into contact with Filipino flavors; or the New World's reinvention of a Roman favorite, the cheesecake. And then there are those items that have not traveled so well: baklava in immigrant communities abroad is a pale copy of the succulent sweets so lovingly

created by Turkish bakers from the finest ingredients. For this reason, I have devoted an entire chapter to Leaf & Thread Pastries (pp. 262–311).

This book features general chapters on Ingredients & Equipment (pp. 12–39) and the following chapters deal with a specific topic, each one beginning with tips and methods relevant to the subject. Do take a little time to read this information; it may tell you something you might otherwise have overlooked.

The most important piece of advice I can give you, though, is simple: read through the whole recipe before you start to bake, and make sure that you have all the necessary ingredients and equipment to hand.

Happy baking!

Above: Pulse-cake makers, c. 1890 (watercolor on paper), Punjabi School.

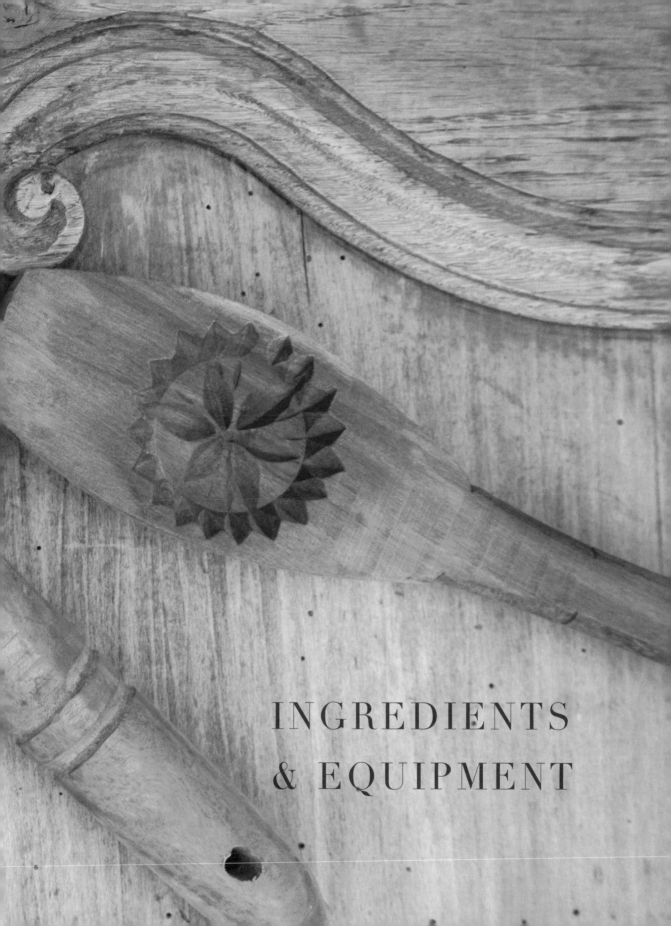

INGREDIENTS
& EQUIPMENT

SUGAR AND SWEETENERS

Sugar is important in baking for more than one reason. It is obviously used for its sweetness but it also has the ability to trap air and therefore lighten the texture of baked goods. In addition, it provides an appetizing color because it caramelizes when subjected to high temperatures.

I would be lying if I said that beet sugar is the same as cane sugar. The chemical composition, nutritional aspects and baking results may be equivalent, but for me there is also an emotional aspect. Having literally grown up in Demerara within the sight and smell of sugar cane in its various stages, I can tell you that cane sugar has an aroma that is definitely lacking in its beet counterpart. As children, we would make excursions (often semi-illicit) to the sugar factory and taste our way through the production process, from sweet and refreshing cane juice to fragrant yellow crystals. When I first came to live in the Netherlands, I kept on throwing away freshly opened packets and buying new ones, only to have to throw those away as well. It wasn't until my husband asked why there was always so much sugar in our trash can that I managed to figure out what was wrong: the absence of the accustomed appetizingly syrupy scent had convinced me that the sugar was spoiled. From that day on, I have kept vanilla pods (beans) in my sugar canister in a desperate attempt to force some semblance of flavor into it. If you decide to perfume your beet sugar similarly, do let the people in your house know what you have done. I shall never forget my husband's agonized yell that there were slugs in the sugar, the first time he saw the chopped-up pods nestling cozily between the crystals.

Granulated sugar is an all-purpose cooking and table sugar. It is refined sugar with a coarse structure. **Superfine sugar** is similar to granulated sugar, but it has a much finer structure with smaller crystals. It takes its name from the fact that it used to be sprinkled from a sugar caster, a practice popular in the past, when sugar was also used as a table condiment. This is the baker's favorite sugar since its structure allows it to dissolve more readily, making it easier to cream with butter, for instance. **Confectioner's sugar** is ground to a powder and a proportion of cornstarch is often added to prevent lumping. In baking, confectioner's sugar tends to be reserved for making meringues, creams and frostings, or cookies with a very fine texture. If you were to follow the same cake recipe using first granulated sugar, then superfine sugar and, finally, confectioner's sugar, the result would reflect the type of sugar used. Granulated sugar would produce a coarser structure with large air pockets; superfine sugar would produce more even-sized pockets; and confectioner's sugar would produce a cake with a fine but rather compact texture.

As far as the **brown sugars** go, many people are inclined to believe that brown is healthier than white. That is true only if the brown sugar really is a semi-refined product and not simply cheap white sugar colored by molasses, which unfortunately is often the case. The best, but most expensive, of the soft brown sugars is **muscovado**, a semi-refined cane sugar that comes in varying degrees of darkness. It is moist and in its darkest state it has a powerful taste and smell of molasses. There are other more neutral soft sugars on the market, and these are excellent for baking. **Demerara (raw brown) sugar** is a golden cane sugar with a coarse and hard structure and is the product of the first crystallization so that it still has natural molasses clinging to it. Originally from the province of Demerara in Guyana, it is now made in many other countries and the name is used to denote its type rather than origin. It has a marvelous flavor, but is best sprinkled on food for added crunch or used in recipes where it must first be dissolved; it takes ages to cream. **Brown superfine sugar** is also sold, often made from demerara-type sugars that have been ground to the required fineness. These are easier to cream.

More exotic kinds of sugar, such as **jaggery**, can also be made from sugar cane and sugar palms. The flavor and color will vary, depending on the base material. It is a cruder form of sugar, and is made and used primarily in India and the Far East. In Indonesia and Malaysia, it is called **gula jawa** or **gula melaka** and its consistency varies from a thick syrup to compact, hard cakes. The cakes can be crushed, and the result looks like granulated sugar. It is not really suitable for baked goods made by traditional Western methods, but it is very flavorful in local rice-based delicacies. **Panela** and **piloncillo** are Latin American variants and are usually made from sugar cane.

Molasses is a by-product from refining cane sugar. This substance, so prized when subtly present in other sugar products, can be overwhelming on its own and is mainly used in combination with sugar. It makes delicious spice cakes and is sometimes used to give color to fruit cakes. It adds flavor and moistness to some breads.

Honey is one of the oldest sweeteners known to man. It was used in ancient forms of baking and primitive confections and is still very much in evidence today in some spice cakes and specific types of confectionery such as nougat. It is available in countless varieties, from clover to orange blossom to Australian eucalyptus, and each has its own specific flavor characteristics. In appearance, it varies from yellow paste to amber liquid and the latter is generally used in baking.

FLOUR, MEAL AND STARCH

Flour provides the body of breads and cakes and forms the backdrop for the other ingredients. **Wheat flour** is most commonly used for baking and is valued for its neutral taste. Always take care to use the flour specified in the recipe because it will have been chosen for particular properties. In other words, flour types are not necessarily interchangeable, and substituting one for the other can have very unexpected results. Bear in mind, too, that no two countries produce the same flour, whether or not they cultivate the same kind of wheat. Climate and soil play important roles as well as the season in which the wheat is planted. Hard spring wheat, for instance, is planted in spring and is stronger (in other words, harder) than hard winter wheat planted in autumn. Flour goes stale after a few months, especially whole-grain flours. Always store your flour in an airtight bag or canister and be sure to observe the manufacturer's guidelines regarding shelf life.

Bread flour is the product of hard wheat and is used for baking bread. It has great powers of absorption and a high gluten content that allows the crumb to stretch without breaking as it expands. It needs to be kneaded very well in order to develop the gluten.

The soft **pastry flour** so loved by American bakers is not widely available outside the United States. It is ideal for cakes because it can support all the fat, sugar and moisture necessary to produce a moist, tender-crumbed cake. Note that products sold in Europe as cake flour are not the same; many contain a raising agent, cornstarch and flavoring. American pastry flour will give good results only in recipes compiled specifically for its use. None of the recipes in this book call for pastry flour.

All-purpose flour is used in most of the recipes in this book. It is a blend of varying proportions of hard and soft flours, making it suitable for many ends – as its American name suggests. When a raising agent is added, it becomes **self-rising flour** and some brands may also contain salt. In general, I prefer to use all-purpose flour and add the correct amount of baking powder and salt needed, as these can vary.

Bleached flours are flours that have been treated with chlorine or similar substances. Freshly milled flour contains pigments that give it a yellowish tinge, and bleaching whitens it. Bleaching also ages flour artificially, and flour needs to be aged to strengthen the gluten and improve baking qualities. Rather than storing it and allowing it to mellow naturally, chlorine dioxide is added.

Whole-wheat flour contains a high percentage of bran because the entire wheat berry is milled instead of just the endosperm. Bran content and coarseness may vary. Whole grains are generally held to be a healthier alternative, but this is debatable because the amount of extra nutrients absorbed by the body is so negligible that it can make little difference. What is true is that whole-wheat products cleanse the digestive tract, as they contain indigestible fibers. As a rule, the gluten content is lower in whole-wheat flour than white flour. Its shelf life is also more limited.

Semolina is coarsely milled durum wheat, one of the hardest types. Milling fragments it into particles of varying size. Finely ground, it turns into durum flour, which is the best flour for making pasta. The particles are sold as fine, medium and coarse semolina and are used in many Middle Eastern cakes and pastries. Semolina absorbs moisture while holding its shape very well and retains some bite even after being cooked, adding texture to baked goods.

Rye is a less demanding crop than wheat and can be grown in poorer soil and colder climatic conditions. Often stigmatized as a peasant food, rye flour is used in many excellent breads from northern Europe. In its coarsest form, it makes hearty pumpernickel-type breads, and in its finest milling, it is a crucial contributor to the texture of the famous Dutch spice cakes. Rye flour gives bread a moister and looser texture than wheat flour. Because of its low gluten content, it is often mixed with wheat flour in varying proportions depending on the desired result. Some supermarkets and most health food stores sell it. The finest milling – whole grain or otherwise – is needed for the recipes in this book.

Cornmeal is ground maize and is available in coarse and fine millings. It has been used for thousands of years in South and Central America. The Maya and Aztec Indians prepared a wide variety of breadlike products from cornmeal and developed a clever technique known as nixtamalization. The procedure involves soaking the grain with lime or wood ash, which softens the outer skin, making it easier to grind, and also enhances the nutritional value, reducing the risk of diseases such as pellagra. North American Indians used a similar method with wood ash. Cornmeal is not often nixtamalized outside Latin America. The fine type of cornmeal used for making polenta is suitable for the recipes in this book.

Cornstarch and **potato flour** are the starch that has been extracted from these plants. They contain next to no gluten and are often used in cake-making to "cut" other flours, reducing the gluten content and so producing a shorter and more tender crumb. They are very rarely used on their own except as thickeners for sauces. Cornstarch is not to be confused with cornmeal, which is milled from the whole kernel.

Rice flour is ground from rice grains and has a sweetly aromatic taste. There are various kinds, each with the specific properties of the rice from which it has been milled. Glutinous rice flour will therefore give a sticky result and a non-glutinous one will yield a looser result, more comparable to wheat flour. Always use the type that is specified. If the package simply says "rice flour" and you have bought it in a

Western supermarket, it is generally safe to assume that it is the more neutral non-glutinous kind.

FATS

Butter tenderizes cakes and breads and also adds flavor. My recipes all use **unsalted butter**, sometimes called **sweet butter**. Butter was originally salted to improve its keeping qualities and many people have acquired a preference for it, finding sweet butter too bland for their palate. However, the salt content can vary from brand to brand, so it is best to use unsalted butter for baking. Butter is made by skimming cream off milk, and then churning it until the solids and liquids separate. The solids form butter and the thin, tart liquid that remains is traditional buttermilk. The solids, with a fat content of about 80%, are either packaged as they are, or salted first. The water content hovers around 16%, but this can vary a little and can be influenced by seemingly remote factors such as animal fodder and grazing conditions.

Manufacturers have been inducing us for years to believe that **margarine** is a healthy substitute for butter. Ordinary margarine has the same number of calories as butter and a similar fat content; diet margarines may vary. Impartial surveys have shown that margarine is not the wonder product it is often thought to be, and it is certainly not risk-free in terms of health. Butter gives a far superior flavor and I use it almost exclusively.

Ghee, or **clarified butter**, is a favorite in Indian cooking and can be bought in tins from ethnic grocers. In the Middle East and North Africa, a similar product is known as **samn**. It can easily be prepared at home. To make it, butter is melted and the froth is skimmed off. The yellow liquid under the froth conceals a milky layer that leaches out as it cooks. This thin, milky fluid is discarded after the yellow part has cooled and solidified into ghee. Ghee will keep for far longer than butter, especially if salt is added. As it is almost pure milk fat, with very little excess moisture, it cannot be used interchangeably with butter unless specifically indicated in the recipe. "Vegetable ghee" is simply margarine by another name, so steer clear of it.

Lard is rendered pig fat. Its high saturated fat content has reduced its popularity considerably in recent years in favor of fats perceived to be lighter, such as butter and margarine. It is used in some traditional breads and pastries and, handled correctly, can produce a wonderful texture. Lard is often described as bland, but this is a matter of opinion: I find that the flavor almost inevitably dominates the recipe in which it is used. It can also cause allergic reactions in some people, and for these reasons I prefer to substitute butter in my recipes.

Vegetable shortening is a smooth white substance made with partially or completely hydrogenated oils. It has no obvious flavor of its own and simply borrows some from the other ingredients. Although it has good creaming properties, it is not a fat I choose to use in cakes. However, I do use it in a few instances when the authenticity of a recipe requires it.

Oil (preferably a neutral-tasting one like corn, sunflower or peanut) is fine in many flatbreads and a few breads, but it does not have a beneficial effect on cakes. It lacks creaming qualities and produces a close texture. However, olive oil is used in some Mediterranean cuisines to make cakes. The flavor can be a bit too powerful for the purpose, and a Spanish tip is to heat the oil with some lemon peel and then leave it to cool before baking with it. Obviously, using a neutral-tasting oil neatly circumvents this step.

CREAM

Cream is skimmed from the top of milk and its main use in baking is for fillings and glazes. It is available in varying percentages of fat, all suited to a particular purpose. **Light cream** has a minimum fat content of 18% and is generally used in its existent state over fruit and puddings and in beverages. **Whipping cream or heavy cream** contains 30–40% fat, enabling it to be whipped; the higher the fat content, the better it whips. When chilled heavy cream is whipped, the fat globules expand and stick to each other. If the fat is not cold enough, it will be too soft to support the surrounding foam, and the cream will collapse. If cream is overwhipped, it will separate, leaving globules of butter floating in milky liquid. Once the whisk starts to leave trails in the cream, you must be vigilant, as the process speeds up considerably from this point and even a few seconds can make a difference. The right stage to stop is a matter of personal preference and varies from soft to stiff peaks. There is usually a choice between **pasteurized** and **sterilized** or **UHT** (ultra heat-treated) cream. The former has a simple fresh taste and can be found in the refrigerator section. UHT cream has a slightly sweet flavor, the result of some caramelization during the heat treatment. It is sold in small boxes straight from the shelf and does not need to be refrigerated, making it a handy cupboard standby. However, it must be chilled well before whipping, for the reason given above.

Crème fraîche is a lightly fermented cream with a thick consistency and a fat content of at least 30%. It can be used as it is or sweetened or flavored in some other way – for instance, with a few drops of rum. It makes an excellent accompaniment to many cakes and desserts and can be used in some cooked fillings too.

Sour cream was traditionally precisely what its name implies: cream left to sour naturally. Nowadays, bacterial cultures are introduced into light cream to produce a thick and slightly tart cream. It is used in a host of savory dishes and is the cornerstone of many Central European cuisines, Hungarian prominent among them. It is also an excellent addition to some kinds of pastry.

Kaymak or **qymak** is a thick cream used in several countries, including Turkey, the Balkans and Afghanistan. Its consistency has often been compared to English **clotted cream**. The basis varies from buffalo to cow's and goat's milk, and in the Balkans it is generally salted and stored, to be used later as a cooking medium as well as in many sweet and savory dishes. Afghans enjoy it floating on a special cup of tea or as a treat eaten with freshly baked bread. In Turkey, it is greatly prized in sweets and a sweet dish may be garnished with a dollop of *kaymak*, much as whipped cream or crème fraîche is used in the West. It is also used in many kinds of baklava, both as filling and garnish. It is a specialist dairy product best left to experts to produce since it is made by boiling, simmering, skimming and then chilling milk or a mixture of milk and cream – a process that takes several hours, if not days. In the Netherlands and Germany, where there are large Turkish immigrant populations, there is a proliferation of small ethnic groceries that sell, among many other interesting things, tins of *kaymak*. Middle Eastern grocers in larger cities around the world will probably stock it too. Failing that, use crème fraîche. It gives excellent results for the recipes in this book.

YOGURT

The word "**yogurt**" has been borrowed from the Turks and they are likely to have been instrumental in its introduction to Western Europe. Yogurt was originally a product that was made and eaten in central and western Asia and the Balkans, and is now enjoyed all over the world. Though most often made from cow's milk, it can be made from several kinds of milk – including sheep, goat, water buffalo, mare, camel and even yak – often reflecting regional preference and local availability. To produce yogurt, specific bacterial cultures are introduced into whole or skim milk and the mixture thickens as it ferments. It is used in varying consistencies; it can be diluted to make refreshing drinks such as *ayran* and *lassi*, respectively Turkish and Indian. It is also used in a variety of savory and sweet dishes, from soups to desserts. When well strained, it forms a soft cheeselike product. The texture and consistency of yogurt sold in Western countries vary considerably, from thin and easily poured to thick and firmly set. Many commercially produced yogurts are thickened with gelatin. This type of yogurt is not suitable for the recipes in this book as the consistency is artificially induced and will break down on cooking. Try to get a thick, naturally set kind such as **Greek** or **Greek-style yogurt** that has had much of the liquid strained out to produce a texture similar to crème fraîche.

SOFT CHEESES

Cream cheese is the mainstay of many cheesecakes. It was the serendipitous creation of two American dairymen who were, apparently, trying to reproduce French Neufchâtel cheese. Its rich taste and texture caused them to call it "cream cheese" and it was marketed under the brand name that is still synonymous with the product across the globe.

Quark is a moist, soft curd cheese with the color and consistency of very thick yogurt. It is usually made from skim milk, but cream is sometimes added to make a richer version. A great favorite of the Germans, it is the basis of their deliciously light *käsekuchen*, or cheesecakes. Its popularity is spreading: already available in most European countries, it is becoming easier to find in North America. Similar cheeses are made in the countries of Central and Eastern Europe. There is no real substitute; ricotta can be used, but the texture and flavor will change.

Ricotta is a soft, crumbly Italian cheese made from the whey left after the production of some other types of cheese. A coagulant is added to this whey to encourage it to produce a second lot of curd. It is used in sweet and savory fillings for Italian dishes, and makes beautifully textured cheesecakes.

MILK

Milk (usually dairy milk from cows) is generally used to moisten dry ingredients. **Raw milk** is untreated milk straight from a primary source and should be boiled to make it safe to use, unless you are absolutely positive that it has come from a healthy cow on a clean farm. It is becoming increasingly difficult to buy raw milk, as regulations are constantly being changed. Most milk is sold as a **pasteurized** product; it is heated briefly to destroy bacteria and must be kept refrigerated. Pasteurized milk is available as **whole milk**, with a fat content of 3–4%; as **2% milk** with a fat content of 2%; and as **skim milk** with a fraction of a percentage of fat. **Sterilized** and **UHT** (ultra heat-treated) milk are subjected to prolonged heat treatment, which lengthens their shelf life and makes refrigeration unnecessary. Pasteurized milk has a fresher, more natural taste than UHT milk, which is sweeter due to the slight caramelization that takes place when it is heated. I use 2% milk for everyday purposes, including baking, but do feel free to substitute whole milk if you prefer. I don't recommend skim milk for baking unless absolutely necessary for health reasons.

Evaporated milk is subjected to even more rigorous heat treatment than ordinary sterilized milk. About half of its water content is evaporated, making it a very concentrated product that should be diluted before use. While not common in most Western countries, it can be a godsend to people living in remote areas or those who have to cope with primitive refrigeration. Like the other types, it is also available in whole, 2% and skim versions.

Condensed milk has a reputation for being a socially inferior product used only by colonials and yokels. Those who are prepared to put aside such preconceptions will discover that it can greatly enhance a number of dishes, including cheesecakes and ice creams. It is made in a manner similar to evaporated milk but sugar makes up almost half of its weight. Condensed milk is almost always sold in its whole milk form.

Powdered milk is made by extracting virtually all of the liquid present in milk. It is usually reconstituted before use, but nowadays it is a popular ingredient for bread machine loaves and is often added in its dry form. As it is almost fat-free, skim milk powder will keep better than the whole milk variant. None of the recipes in this book require powdered milk, but it can be used when fresher types are not readily available.

EGGS

Eggs not only aerate a cake by trapping air when beaten, they also hold the other ingredients together because they coagulate when heated. Hens' eggs are by far the most popular, mainly due to their availability. Free-range eggs tend to have more flavor and a more attractive yolk color than battery eggs. In my recipes, I use medium eggs, called standard in many countries. They weigh 1¾ oz on average. In general, an overall difference of a few ounces will not spoil the result, so I specify a weight only where absolutely necessary – in meringues, for example. Always use eggs at room temperature. If you forget to remove them from the refrigerator in time, put them in a bowl of very warm water for a few minutes. Cold eggs are one of the main culprits in curdled mixtures.

RAISING AGENTS

The texture of a cake or bread depends to a great extent on the raising agent and it need not always be a tangible substance; rubbing fat into flour, for instance, introduces air into pastry and similar mixtures, lightening them without substantially increasing the volume. In other cases, a different application of an ingredient already present can make a huge difference.

Eggs, for example, can trap an incredible amount of air when whisked. Normally, eggs are beaten into a creamed mixture at room temperature. There will be some expansion, but baking powder will be required to make the cake rise sufficiently. If the same eggs are whisked over a bowl of hot water, they will expand significantly more than if they are whisked at room temperature, but both will lighten sponges without any real need for chemical leavening. Similarly, if you separate eggs and whisk them with the sugar, combining them later, they will provide a very light texture to cakes as long as you do not overwork the batter, thereby allowing some of the air to escape.

Baking powder is usually a combination of sodium bicarbonate and an acid agent. Single-action baking powder starts to work as soon as it is moistened and will lose its strength if you delay, hence the need to preheat the oven. Single-action baking powder is no longer widely used, and double-acting baking powder has become standard. Double-acting baking powder works in two ways: it starts acting as soon as it is moistened and then again when subjected to heat. It is slightly more tolerant than single-action baking powder but, nevertheless, it is always a good policy to bake cake batter as soon as it is prepared.

Baking soda does not have much power on its own. It needs an acid agent. In baking powder, this has already been added, but if you use baking soda on its own, you will have to add the required proportion of an ingredient such as cream of tartar, soured milk or buttermilk to create the desired reaction.

Cream of tartar is obtained from fermented grape juice and is not in itself a raising agent, but forms a component of one, as described above, to produce carbon dioxide. It is sometimes used to stabilize whisked egg whites.

Yeast is a living organism that multiplies very rapidly under favorable conditions. Warmth, moisture and sugar feed it, and it converts the sugar into ethanol and carbon dioxide. However, it needs to be handled correctly. Too much sugar can slow down the rising process. If the liquid is too cold, the process will take far longer; while a liquid that is too hot will kill off yeast cells, severely retarding the rising process. This is why recipes always call for milk to be warm or lukewarm. Salt can also kill yeast and should not come into direct contact with the moistened yeast unless the dough is to be kneaded immediately. **Compressed** or **fresh yeast** is sold in small cakes that must be kept refrigerated. It is not always readily available and needs to be very fresh to work properly. Due to its moist nature, it weighs more than dry yeast. It is not interchangeable and its use is not specified for the recipes in this book. **Dry yeast granules** are sold in packets or small boxes. The coarser granules should be allowed to "sponge" first with some of the flour from the recipe, along with the sugar and warm liquid; never add salt at this stage. The yeast that is easiest to use and the

one that gives the most consistent results is **active dry** or **instant yeast**. The granules are extremely fine and the yeast is added to the dry ingredients prior to being moistened and kneaded. This is the type specified in my recipes.

CHOCOLATE AND COCOA

Very few people can resist this most divine of foods, and the cocoa tree is very aptly named *Theobroma cacao*, "food of the gods." Ever since the Spanish conquistador Hernán Cortez drank the bitter beverage at Montezuma's court in 1519, it has held the world in its thrall. Once their initial mistrust and prejudice had subsided, the Spaniards were able to experiment with the beans they took back to Spain, and they eventually found that roasting released more flavor. When they added sugar and vanilla, the taste became much more pleasant to the European palate. It was an exclusive product, available at first only to the rich, but by the eighteenth century chocolate houses had sprung up in many European cities, bringing it within the reach of more people. It was believed to have health-giving properties, an idea to which many physicians subscribed. In 1778, the Frenchman Doret introduced the first chocolate press, and chocolate culture developed steadily from that point. In 1828, Dutchman Coenraad van Houten patented a fabulous invention: a wooden screw press to extrude the cocoa butter. He had discovered that when the fatty matter was removed, a cake remained and this could be ground to powder. This **cocoa powder** was far more palatable than the greasy substance that had previously been drunk. He went on to apply potash to the powder, refining a technique that the Aztecs had used when they added wood ash to their chocolate. This process is referred to as **"Dutching"** and produces **alkalized cocoa**, also known as **European-style cocoa** in some countries outside Europe, particularly the United States. Dutching gives a mellower, smoother taste.

Cocoa trees thrive in a warm, moist climate, and most of the world's supply of cocoa comes from the Caribbean and West Africa. There are three main varieties: Criollo, Trinitario and Forastero. Criollo and Forastero are older varieties while Trinitario is a hybrid. Criollo is the King of Beans. It accounts for a mere 10% of world production and is grown primarily in Mexico, Central America and Venezuela, the region where it originated. An excellent quality of chocolate is also obtained from Trinitario, which constitutes 20% of world production and is grown in Trinidad, Ecuador, Sri Lanka and Indonesia. Forastero is the more common bean and is cultivated mainly in Brazil and West Africa. Much of the chocolate we buy in supermarkets is Forastero or a blend that relies heavily on it. Specialist companies often manufacture the chocolate equivalent of vintage wine, and it is possible to buy chocolate made from a particular type of bean or beans from a specific location. The price tags tell their own story.

After the cocoa beans have been removed from their pods, they are left to ferment and are then dried, reducing their moisture content from about 80% to 8%. On reaching the factory, they are cleaned, winnowed and roasted, then ground to an oily paste. Once the cocoa butter has been extracted, cocoa can be made from the residue. For chocolate, the cocoa butter is not extracted or is only partially extracted, and extra may be added for a smoother texture. The other ingredients (such as milk, sugar and any flavorings) are added and the mixture is stirred continually for a period of time ranging from a few hours to a few days. This process is referred to as "conching": the longer chocolate is conched, the smoother its texture becomes.

Beware of marketing tricks. There are products touted as **chocolate coating** or **compound chocolate** and these are described in flattering terms: "dark Continental style," "luxury" etc. They are often imitations of the real thing, with vegetable oils and fats replacing the cocoa butter. Similarly, the term "baker's chocolate" has no technical meaning and the confusion is made even greater by the fact that this also happens to be an American brand name. **"Couverture"** is a more reliable indicator; this is good-quality chocolate with a generous amount of cocoa butter. It melts easily, both on the stove and on the tongue, and is prized by bakers and chocolatiers alike. There are excellent Belgian and French brands available.

White chocolate is, properly speaking, not real chocolate at all. It contains a high percentage of cocoa butter but no cocoa solids. The composition varies from brand to brand but averages out to around 40% sugar, 25% milk solids and 35% cocoa butter. More than with any other kind of chocolate, you need to be sure of the presence of a great deal of cocoa butter, or it will be next to impossible to melt it for baking.

Milk chocolate usually contains about 10% cocoa mass, 40% sugar, 25% milk solids and 25% cocoa butter. Connoisseurs tend to ignore it due to its sweetness and supposed lack of depth. Again, that depends on the manufacturer. One of my favorite milk chocolates has a cocoa mass content of 40% and is only lightly sweetened. However, it remains more of an eating than a baking product.

Unsweetened chocolate, the home baker's favorite in the United States, is not readily available elsewhere. It has no sugar and is composed of an almost equal proportion of cocoa mass and cocoa butter, giving it a very strong flavor.

Dark chocolate is a **semi-sweet chocolate** made up of at least 40% cocoa mass with about 45% sugar and 15% cocoa butter and is the best chocolate for baking. I favor chocolate with at least 50% cocoa mass. There are many extra bitter varieties and it is a popular misconception that the higher the cocoa mass content is, the better the chocolate will be. That is only a single contributing factor and is more a matter of personal preference than a proportionate reflection of quality. In baking, it may even give a drier result than a chocolate with less cocoa solids but more cocoa butter.

Chocolate needs to be treated with care, especially when melting it. It can scorch and burn when subjected to high temperatures and can seize if it comes into contact with moisture. When chocolate seizes, it loses its malleability and becomes grainy. Both scorched and seized chocolate are unfit to be used. It is something of a paradox that while small amounts of moisture will make chocolate seize (e.g. steam escaping from the bottom pan when it is heated *au bain-marie*), larger amounts of liquids have no ill effect and allow themselves to be incorporated without any trouble as long as the temperatures match.

Both **cocoa** and chocolate are used as flavorings and each gives a different, equally delicious result. Cocoa is easier to use because it doesn't need to be melted; it also produces a stronger chocolate flavor because it is so concentrated. I have never been a proponent of the "two tablespoons per cake" theory: the outcome will be a brownish cake, not a chocolate cake. If a fair amount of the flour is replaced with cocoa, however, it will make a cake with a deeply satisfying chocolate taste.

Unsweetened cocoa is used for baking, and alkalized and non-alkalized cannot be used interchangeably in recipes. In many cases, alkalized cocoa can be substituted for non-alkalized without any trouble. However, non-alkalized cocoa requires a catalyst in the form of an acidic product to perform well, and this is usually catered for in the recipe. My recipes all use alkalized, or European-style, cocoa. When using cocoa in a cake, it is always advisable to mix it with hot water. This helps to release flavor and makes it easy to blend it into the batter. Dry cocoa, even if it has been sifted with the flour, has a tendency to form unappetizing clumps at the bottom of a cake.

DRIED FRUIT

The range of dried fruit seems to increase so rapidly that it is hard to keep track of what is currently available. Just a few years ago, dried cranberries were exotic. They are now mainstream and have been joined by all manner of tropical and temperate dried fruits, including pineapple, papaya, mango, cherries, blueberries and strawberries. However, the more traditional currants and raisins (particularly sultanas/golden raisins) remain the mainstay for baking purposes. As currants are quite tart and raisins generally sweet, the two are often combined in recipes to give a good balance of flavors. Always buy good-quality, fresh dried fruit. This may sound like a contradiction in terms, but it is all too easy to be fooled into buying stale dried fruit. You will recognize the staleness by the hardness of the fruit and a tendency to whiteness around the edges. I always like to rinse raisins and currants in warm water before using them and then pick them over, removing any stems and foreign particles. If you need the fruit for a yeast loaf, it will be sufficient to dry it well with paper towels and use it straight away. For cakes, though, the fruit must be dried very thoroughly or it will sink to the bottom. Washing and drying it the evening before you use it will allow enough time for any residual moisture to evaporate.

COCONUTS

Coconuts are not nearly as bad for us as many lobbyists would have us believe and can even have beneficial effects. For instance, they are high in lauric acid, which has good antibacterial and antiviral qualities and boosts the immune system. Even the oil, which always receives particularly negative attention, is not as bad as it is often described. True, it is high in saturated fats, but these consist of medium-chain fatty acids, which are metabolized far more efficiently than many other kinds, putting less strain on internal organs. Because it is burned so quickly, it also has a neutral effect on cholesterol levels.

Fresh coconuts no longer present the problem they used to and can easily be bought frozen, in various cuts and textures. This shredded or grated frozen coconut is generally far fresher and sweeter-tasting than if you buy a whole coconut and take it home to grate yourself, unless you live in a region that produces them. If you find that the cut is too coarse for the purpose, whiz it in the food processor for a few seconds to make it finer. If you prefer to get a fresh coconut and start from scratch, use a sharp tool such as a screwdriver to pierce the eyes. Drain and discard the water. Give the coconut several sharp taps with a mallet or the back of a cleaver to break it into pieces. Pry the flesh loose from the shell and grate it.

Shredded coconut is a reasonable substitute in most of the recipes, but not all. Always use unsweetened kinds for these recipes. I have given instructions, where appropriate, for reconstituting it slightly so that it does not need to steal too much moisture from the other ingredients in the batter, which can produce a dry result. It should be left to stand for a few minutes before being used. Be warned, however, that its concentrated nature makes shredded coconut far more calorific, weight for weight, than fresh coconut.

Coconut milk has become a convenience product and is sold in cans and in powdered form. Canned coconut milk is generally of a high quality, but read the label to make sure that it is pure – undiluted and free of additives as far as possible. It can be used for its own delicious flavor and can also be substituted for dairy milk when baking for those who are lactose intolerant. There are still a few people who believe that coconut milk is the liquid you hear sloshing around when a coconut is shaken. Coconut milk is actually the liquid extracted from grated coconut flesh, and its milky whiteness does not in any way resemble the transparent liquid enclosed by the flesh. This is **coconut water,** a completely different thing. Those of us who come from the tropics know that the water from mature coconuts is best discarded. It is a far cry from the water of young, green coconuts, whose flesh has yet to set into the characteristic hardness of a mature coconut. If you ever see a West Indian or Asian vendor selling young coconuts, do not pass up the chance to taste one. They will lop off the top and stick a straw into the coconut so that you can drink the sweet, refreshing water, which is high in potassium and other minerals. And when your thirst has been quenched, you can ask them to split the coconut so that you can scrape out the lovely "jelly" from the inside, using a slice of the green outer husk as a disposable spoon.

NUTS

Nuts impart a great deal of flavor to baked goods and also add body when used in larger quantities to replace all or part of the flour. The texture or fineness of the nuts will also affect the texture of the finished product. When purchasing nuts, your taste is the best guide. For this reason, it is advisable to buy them in a shop where you can taste them. Failing that, buy them from a source with a good turnover. Buy them in small quantities, as not all kinds will keep well. The oilier the nut, the more quickly it goes rancid. Most nuts can be bought shelled, unshelled, whole, chopped, sliced or ground. With a few exceptions, I recommend buying shelled whole nuts and preparing them further yourself. Walnuts stay fresher in the shell; sliced almonds are better bought, as it is impossible to slice them properly at home without specialist equipment; blanched almonds, ground to the consistency of powder, are often better produced commercially. A food processor or rotary grater will grind most types of nuts quite well. The food processor is amazing in terms of speed, and if you add a tablespoon or two of the flour from the recipe, this will improve the result because the flour will absorb some of the oil and allow you to keep the motor running for a little longer. Rotary graters give a drier and finer result but take more time. Many bakers advise toasting nuts before using them. I never toast nuts for breads and cakes because they lose some of their natural sweetness, but almonds and hazelnuts can be lightly toasted if they are to be used for garnishing. Put them on a baking sheet in a moderate oven and watch them like a hawk because they change color very quickly once they have warmed up.

ALMOND PASTE AND MARZIPAN

Commercially prepared almond paste can shorten your preparation time considerably and good marzipan is impossible to make at home, so it always needs to be bought. However, there are many inferior products masquerading as almond paste and marzipan, so always check the list of ingredients to make sure that you are getting what you want. Peach and apricot kernels are often used in combination with almonds, and their pungent flavor, a bit like artificial almond essence, is nothing like the real thing. Almond paste is sometimes cut with cheaper nuts and even beans, and wily manufacturers leave just enough almonds in the product to justify the use of the word "almond" on the label.

Marzipan is made by repeatedly crushing almonds with sugar between steel rollers to give a very fine and close texture. Its main use in cakes is as an edible decoration. It can be rolled out to cover a cake, and can be used to make all kinds of figures, such as flowers and animals. Marzipan for molding and sculpting figures often has a high sugar content so that it can retain its shape.

Almond paste is not as fine as marzipan and is used in the United Kingdom and a few other countries as a base topping to separate the cake from any icing that is to follow. In Europe, almond paste can have an even coarser structure. The recipes in this book require a coarse type of almond paste, which will give good results when baked. Marzipan cannot be used as a substitute because it has a completely different structure. You can easily make your own almond paste by mixing blanched ground almonds with an equal amount of granulated sugar, a little lemon zest and enough beaten egg to make a malleable mixture. Put it in an airtight container in the refrigerator for a day or two to allow it to mature before using it.

FLAVORINGS

While sugar, flour, butter and eggs form the backbone and body of cakes, the judicious use of flavorings can contribute greatly to the taste. Natural flavorings are best and, of these, **salt** is perhaps the most necessary. It brings out the flavor of the other ingredients and without it most baked goods would taste quite flat. However, it should be used in small amounts and you should not be able to isolate it in the finished product. This is often one of the chief failings in commercially produced bakery items; the salty taste is so overwhelming that it overshadows the other ingredients.

Spices such as cinnamon and cardamom are traditional baking favorites. **Cinnamon** is the aromatic bark of the *Cinnamomum verum*. Some countries permit the sale of cassia bark (*Cinnamomum cassia*) as cinnamon, but real cinnamon is far superior. It is sold in sticks or in powdered form. Ground cinnamon is easiest to use, especially if you want it to be very fine.

Cardamom is the small green, white or black pod of the *Elettaria cardamomum*, one of the most expensive spices. The green ones are best for baking. The tiny seeds are housed in three cells and when bruised or ground, they release a fantastic aroma that enhances whatever other ingredients they touch.

Ginger (*Zingiber officinale*) is a rhizome that is used extensively in Asian cooking. Ginger that has been candied or preserved in syrup adds a spicy kick to baked goods, and ground ginger is one of the main flavoring components for many spice cakes.

Similarly, a pinch of ground **cloves** (*Syzygium aromaticum*) also adds extra depth to spice cakes, but the flavor is too powerful to be used in large quantities.

Many people like to add **nutmeg** (*Myristica fragrans*) to milk-based drinks and desserts and the lacy outer covering (mace) is a welcome addition to a variety of stews and savory dishes. However, it is underused in baking, which is a great shame because, true to its Latin name, it can add a great deal of fragrance. It is best used freshly grated.

Vanilla beans (pods) and **extract** are among the most essential flavorings employed in baking and desserts. The vanilla bean is the cured green pod of a tropical orchid-like plant and it becomes black as it ferments and oxidizes. *Vanilla planifolia* is most widely cultivated, followed by *Vanilla tahitensis*, and both have specific flavor characteristics. Beans are usually marketed as Tahitian, Madagascar and Mexican, in order of connoisseurs' preference, and price tags correspond. The well-known term "Bourbon" vanilla refers to a variety of *V. planifolia* that grows chiefly in Madagascar, the Comoro islands and Réunion. Split pods reveal thousands of tiny black seeds held together by a resinous substance. These are scraped off and used as an exquisite flavoring second to none. The scraped pods still retain quite a bit of fragrance and can be used to infuse other dishes with residual flavor or to scent sugar as described earlier. Vanilla extract is made from the beans and liquids in the form of water and alcohol. Always read the labels carefully to ensure that you are buying natural extract and not a synthetic imitation. Many brands are extremely expensive, but you generally get what you pay for.

Citrus zest contains a great deal of flavor that is released by grating it or paring it with a special zester. Grating brings out more flavor. Always try to do this over the other ingredients so that you manage to catch as much of the oil as possible. Lemon zest is most widely used, but oranges and limes also provide their own excellent and unique tang. Unwaxed, undyed fruit from an organic source is best because treated fruits may harbor traces of harmful chemicals. Producers sometimes subject the fruits to various treatments to enhance the color and to get rid of any green spots and blemishes, so if you see fruit with the odd small green freckle, choose them above the uniformly colored ones. **Citrus oils** extracted from the rind are pure and concentrated and a few drops will perfume a batter or dough. Most manufacturers advise the use of ¼ teaspoon to replace 1 tablespoon fresh zest. Be careful how you handle these oils, as they are very aggressive and corrosive. They are not always easy to find and, once opened, have a limited shelf life. When diluted, they are sold as **citrus extracts**.

Flower extracts, notably **rose water** and **orange blossom** or **orange flower water**, impart a delicate scent and flavor to baked goods. They are made from rose petals and the flowers of bitter oranges, respectively. Both kinds are usually extracted by water distillation and the pungent oils that rise to the surface (attar of roses and neroli respectively) are used in perfumes rather than food. The fragrant water that remains is used in a variety of dishes, generally sweet, and sometimes in drinks. When you buy them, make sure that they are not the cheap – and awful-tasting – imitations that are made from chemical components. Some of the best rose water comes from Iran, where it has been distilled for centuries. There are good brands of French and Middle Eastern orange flower water available. If you detect even a hint of artificiality, discard it and try to get a better one next time. I have come across suggestions to substitute orange oil or orange liqueur if orange flower water is not available. This will not work; the oil in question comes from the fruit rind and is also used in making liqueurs. It tastes quite different; the oil is fruity and more robust in flavor while the flower water is elusively fragrant and understated.

Liqueurs and other spirits can enhance cake batters as well as fillings. It is never a good idea to buy "cooking" versions because the quality will not be very high. Buying good ones means that you can enjoy them in a glass too. Most of the alcohol will evaporate when the batter is heated, leaving a pleasant aroma.

Garam masala is a blend of roasted and ground sweet and sharp spices and is used to add flavor to Indian dishes. It can be bought from large supermarkets or ethnic groceries all over the world. There are subtle distinctions between subcontinental Indian mixtures and Caribbean ones. Caribbean Indians prefer a darker roast and a sharper combination and usually cook it in the dish from the start, whereas subcontinental Indians tend to use it more as a condiment to be sprinkled on a cooked or almost cooked dish.

EQUIPMENT

OVEN

Electric ovens are generally the most reliable as far as temperatures go. Always preheat the oven to the required temperature unless specifically advised to the contrary. You need to get acquainted with your oven and see how it will work best for you. It is a frustrating fact that all ovens bake differently, even those of the same model from the same manufacturer. Even the best brands can have a special, annoying characteristic. The most common one is a hot spot that will make part of your cake set and brown slightly faster than the rest of it. Another touchy point is the advice given by many manufacturers of convection/fan-assisted ovens to decrease temperature and cooking time by 10% when using recipes compiled for conventional ovens. I find this advice a bit contradictory because 350°F/180°C in a convection oven is surely no hotter than the same temperature in a more traditional model. At the same time, it must be acknowledged that a fan-assisted oven distributes the temperature more evenly in all parts of the oven and the heat is therefore used very effectively. However, this may be more relevant for roast meats with a longer baking time than for bakery items. In my experience, it makes no difference whether I bake a cake in a fan-assisted or conventional oven, but if your oven is very sophisticated, consult the manufacturer or supplier. The best advice I can give is to stick to the temperatures indicated in the recipes and, if you are using a conventional oven, make allowance for a possible slight increase in the baking time.

OVEN RACK

Unless otherwise indicated, position the oven rack just below the center of the oven so that the bread or cake ends up being in the middle of the oven.

BROILER

Some recipes require a broiler. Any good broiler will do as long as it can accommodate the pan in question. The recipes here were written with an electric broiler in mind, so you might need to make adjustments for a gas broiler.

TAWA, GRIDDLE OR HEAVY FRYING PAN

A *tawa* is an Indian griddle used for cooking flatbreads. Subcontinental Indians use a slightly concave type, Turks use a convex kind called a *saç*, and Caribbean diaspora Indians use a flat one. A good griddle or a heavy frying pan is fine for making the flatbreads in this book.

STEAMER

A large two-tiered bamboo steamer is perfect for the steamed recipes. If you have a steamer oven, follow the manufacturer's guidelines and adjust the time to suit. You need to put the food into the oven before it starts to build up steam. Consequently, the overall time will be longer, but the time needed after the steaming temperature has been reached will have to be shortened. A high-pressure steam oven is not suitable.

MIXER

While a mixer is not a necessity, it is extremely handy. It saves you a lot of time and hard work, especially when kneading yeast doughs, creaming butter and sugar, and whisking eggs. My personal preference is for a heavy-duty countertop model and I always buy an extra mixing bowl and whisk. These can come in handy when, for instance, you need to whisk egg whites and yolks separately for the same recipe. A handheld mixer is fine for light jobs, but it will not knead yeast doughs, even though manufacturers supply dough hooks with them. By the same token, not all countertop models are powerful enough to tackle heavy doughs and some may stall.

FOOD PROCESSOR

A food processor is never essential but it is the best and quickest tool for chopping nuts and blending butter into flour for pastry. It will not whisk or whip as well as a mixer, though, and will knead only small quantities of dough at a time.

BAKING PANS

All of the cakes and breads given here can be baked in a few basic baking pans. I always find it useful to have duplicates, especially in the case of loaf pans and round pans for layer cakes. It is just as easy to make two cakes or loaves, and spares can be frozen for a future occasion. Heavy-duty metal pans, preferably non-stick, work best, but do grease them as advised in the recipes. Thin and shiny aluminium pans distort easily and tend to burn whatever they contain, but use them if that's all you have, and keep a close eye on them. The sizes stamped on pans, springform ones in particular, are sometimes a bit of a mystery. An 8-inch pan is often stamped 20 cm and a 9-inch one, 24 cm. The arithmetic is a little inaccurate but it does help to standardize things. If in doubt, measure the pans and if you are forced to deviate, a little larger is better than slightly smaller.

COOLING RACKS

Wire cooling racks are essential. You can buy them in all shapes and sizes and you can never have too many. A few smaller ones are better than a single large one. The safest way to invert a cake onto the cooling rack is to invert the cooling rack over the top of the pan and, pressing the bottom of the pan (with mitt-covered hands) against the rack, swiftly turning both so that the cake slips gently onto the rack. You will need to repeat the procedure with a second rack to turn the cake the right way up.

SILICONE MAT

Silicone mats are resistant to exceedingly high temperatures and are often used by professional cooks and bakers to line baking and roasting pans. However, they are even better out of the oven as they make the ideal non-stick surface for kneading dough and rolling out pastry, minimizing mess. They come in a wide variety of sizes and some even have pre-printed circles that can be used as guides for rolling out pastry.

PASTRY BOARD, MARBLE SLAB AND COUNTERTOP

I find that the silicone mat has made both pastry board and marble slab redundant in my kitchen, but that is my preference. If you have them, do use them, but you will need more dusting flour when you knead bread or roll pastry. An impermeable granite or similar natural stone countertop is also good for pastry but too cold for yeast doughs. Check first to see if it is scratch-resistant. Marble countertops tend to stain quite easily and develop matte patches when they come into contact with acidic substances.

SCALES

Good digital scales are absolutely essential. More than any other culinary discipline, baking depends on accurate weighing. Choose a flat plateau model with a deviation of no more than .07 oz and a reach of 4 lb 8 oz. A tare function, allowing you to return to 0 without removing the bowl, makes it easy to keep on adding ingredients to a bowl without trying to work out the mathematics of it all.

MEASURING JUG (CUP)

A heatproof glass or plastic jug with small increases is best. The liquid for yeast doughs can be warmed in the same vessel in the microwave, saving an extra pan.

MEASURING SPOONS

A teaspoon and a tablespoon are specific volume measurements, not a vague term depending on what kind of silverware is available in your kitchen drawer. A teaspoon is .1 fl oz and a tablespoon is .5 fl oz, and good sets go right down to ⅛ teaspoon. All spoon measurements are level. For dry ingredients such as salt and baking powder, run the straight edge of a knife across the top of the spoon and use only what is left in the spoon.

BOWLS
It is always useful to have a good selection of larger sizes as well as several small ones for weighing out ingredients such as nuts, chocolate and dried fruits beforehand. A double boiler can be improvised using a heatproof bowl that fits snugly over one of your saucepans.

BOWL SCRAPER
A flexible plastic scraper is ideal for removing dough from bowls and for leveling the batter in cake pans.

BENCH SCRAPER
This straight-sided gadget usually has a wooden grip and a clear metal or non-stick blade. It is not essential, but is very handy for portioning pastry and dough and for scraping work surfaces clean.

ROLLING PIN
I use simple wooden ones made from one piece, as well as a few dowels for the filo recipes. The wood seasons itself beautifully with use and develops its own non-stick properties.

SPOONS AND SPATULAS
Wooden spoons are fine for stovetop stirring. For other jobs, I like the so-called "spoonulas" that are made of silicone. The spoonlike indentation makes it easy to scoop out batter as well as to clean the sides of the bowl or mix ingredients together.

PALETTE KNIFE
A long-bladed offset palette knife is easier to use than a flat one, but either will do. This is the ideal tool for spreading chocolate glazes.

LONG RULER
A ruler is essential. A metal or plastic one has the advantage of being washable and therefore more hygienic in the kitchen.

WHISKS

A good selection of whisks is always useful in the kitchen, and a large balloon whisk is the best implement for folding flour into cake batters.

STRAINER (SIEVE)

I use a simple plastic one and find it as effective as any other kind.

FLOUR DREDGER

You can buy sophisticated crank-handled ones that take up lots of room, but a simple stainless steel confectioner's sugar dredger with a very fine mesh makes it easier to sprinkle smaller quantities of flour.

PASTRY BRUSH

Real bristle is best. A narrow one is good for egg washes and a very wide one is useful for spreading melted butter on large sheets of pastry quickly and efficiently.

GRATERS AND ZESTER

A fine grater is best for nutmegs and a zester removes zest neatly from citrus fruits. However, a coarse microplane grater is even better for zest, as long as you stop as soon as you get to the bitter white pith. Rotary graters also grate nuts and cheese very well.

SKEWERS

Thin bamboo skewers or plain metal ones make good testers for doneness. Avoid non-stick kinds because it is often difficult to tell whether the mixture is cooked or has simply failed to stick to the coated surface.

PARCHMENT PAPER

Use good-quality parchment paper for lining pans. You can also buy packages of precut liners for round pans, but it is just as easy to cut one yourself. If you pencil in a line, drawing around the pan, remember that you need the inner measurement, so cut slightly within the circle.

PLASTIC WRAP

Plastic wrap is great for wrapping baked goods for storage, but I also like to use it for rolling out delicate pastry. If you roll the pastry between two sheets of plastic wrap, you will not have to add extra flour. There will be no mess to clean up and no need to fear that the pastry will break on its way to the pan if you use the bottom sheet to transport it.

FLATBREADS

Plain and filled, baked and griddled, rolled, coiled, folded and more…

TIPS FOR MAKING FLATBREADS

The flatbreads in this chapter are made in various ways, using different doughs. Every recipe tells you what you need to know, but these preliminary tips may help speed you on your way.

KNEADING THE DOUGH
The dough can be kneaded by hand, but a mixer fitted with a dough hook or a food processor fitted with a plastic kneading blade will make quicker work of it. A well-kneaded and well-rested dough will give far better results than one that has been put together in a hurry, unless the recipe says otherwise, so always allow enough preparation time. Some of the flatbreads can be made in easy stages. For instance, the filling can be prepared in advance and resting times can often be varied to suit your scheme of work.

WHAT TO COOK ON
The different kinds of griddles are described in the general chapter on Equipment (p. 35). You can choose from the concave Indian subcontinental *tawa* or the flat Caribbean one, or even the convex Turkish *saç*. However, a heavy frying pan or a flat griddle is perfect for making the stovetop flatbreads. Always heat it in its dry state, i.e. without adding oil or butter, unless the recipe advises to the contrary. Once it is very hot, reduce the heat to medium, to prevent the flatbreads from browning too fast. Over-browning will result in a stiffer texture.

CHOICE OF FAT
The recipes for most of the Indian flatbreads offer you the choice of using vegetable oil, ghee or butter. Ghee and butter are richer and more flavorful than oil. If you use oil, make sure that it is a neutral type such as corn, peanut or sunflower. Olive oil is not suitable because its flavor is too pronounced. Never use the product advertised as "vegetable ghee," which is simply another name for concentrated margarine. More information on ghee and other fats can be found in the Ingredients chapter (pp. 19–20).

BRUSH
Use a bristle or good silicone brush. Plastic ones will melt when they come into contact with the hot metal.

TURNING
A large, flat fish slice or metal spatula is useful for turning and pressing the flatbreads as they cook. Narrow or curved ones may cause tearing.

ROLLING OUT

Wooden pastry boards and marble slabs are good surfaces for rolling out the flatbreads, but a silicone mat is even better because you will not need to add too much extra flour. Roll gently but firmly, changing position a few times to ensure an even thickness.

TRANSPORTING THE FLATBREADS

In the case of the thin griddle flatbreads, use the rolling pin to help transport them to the cooking surface. Otherwise, they may stretch or break. Always peel them gently off the rolling surface to prevent stretching. Put the rolling pin just above the center of the flatbread and pick up the top quarter and wrap it loosely around the rolling pin, then gently roll the rolling pin downwards to collect the rest of the flatbread. Always do this loosely, or the dough might stick!

KEEPING THEM WARM

Have a large plate standing by to receive the griddle flatbreads. Place a spoon upside down on the plate and spread a dish towel over this. Each time a flatbread is cooked, wrap the dish towel around it, opening it only to add a fresh one. This will keep them reasonably warm· and the spoon will prevent too much moisture from building up and making the bottom ones soggy. If you live in an area with a large Hispanic population, look out for a tortilla keeper – which also makes an ideal *roti* keeper. It is usually round, with a close-fitting lid and made from thick insulating plastic material. It is cheap and effective. Do, however, line these containers with some paper towels or a napkin to absorb some of the excess moisture.

LEFTOVERS

The three *parathas* (plain, *alu roti* and *dal puri*) can be wrapped and kept until the next day in the refrigerator, or frozen for later. All the other flatbreads are best eaten fresh. Of the three, *alu roti* is the best keeper because the filling keeps it quite soft and pliable, and it is worth the effort to make an extra batch to freeze for another time. Fold the *parathas* into quarters and wrap individually in plastic wrap. Pack them into freezer bags, or keep them in the refrigerator for the next day. To reheat, allow the frozen flatbreads to thaw at room temperature or thaw them very carefully in a microwave oven. Remove the plastic wrap and wrap them in paper towels. Reheat briefly in the microwave, until just warmed through. If you leave them in for too long, they will become tough. They can also be eaten at room temperature.

ACROSS THE BLACK WATER

My ancestors and their fellow voyagers were a motley bunch. Among them were wild Dhangar hill tribals, aloof Brahmins, proud Rajputs, Sepoys who deemed it politic to absent themselves temporarily from the scene, and wives who sought to escape domestic tyranny. Coerced, cajoled or kidnapped, fleeing justice or injustice, persuaded by the tempting tales of silver-tongued recruiters or by the stark reality of poverty, famine and scarcity, they crossed the *Kala Pani*, that endless stretch of unknown Black Water that separates India from the rest of the world.

The long and hazardous voyage ended in Demerara, a British colony that was on the verge of financial ruin because the newly emancipated slaves were unwilling to continue working in the sugar industry. My ancestors, each one of them, were bound by indentureship to a specific plantation. Once the terms of the indenture had expired, they could, in theory, invoke the repatriation clause in their contract and return to India as men and women of substance. But they stayed, all but a handful. By the time they had come to terms with the hollowness of promises made, they had lost all urge to return, and many found a new straw to clutch at: the settlement and colonization schemes that encouraged Indian laborers to commute their passages for land grants. Many did so willingly, realizing that the new colony had more to offer than they could hope for in India. Indeed, an immigration agent in charge at the time observed stereotypically – but nonetheless prophetically – that "the natives of India with their love of land and fondness of agriculture and pastoral pursuits will probably have a greater impact on the future of the colony than all the other races put together." Despair and hopelessness were soon replaced by a vigorous determination to get ahead, and a new offshoot of India took root and started to bloom. In the same time frame, similar developments were taking place in Trinidad, Surinam and, to a lesser extent, Jamaica, and these would eventually enrich all of these Caribbean nations with a wealth of Indian-based culture: music, dance and religion and, above all, food.

The pattern of their diet was set from the start as each person was issued with daily rations. It was basic fare – mainly rice, lentils, cooking oil, *masala*, sugar and salt. Interestingly, the *masala* (the combination of spices needed to make a curry) was given to them ready-mixed. Later, when indentureship was over, the *masala* remained virtually unchanged, still relying heavily on basic local availability. This standardization, coupled with the subsequent use of proprietary brands of "curry powder," has given Guyanese and other Caribbean curries their consistent, though by no means uniform, taste.

Roti and rice are still standard accompaniments to savory dishes, especially in Indo-Caribbean households, and roti is also a form of local fast food, sold with the curry wrapped into it. Roti is a generic Hindi word for "bread," which comes in several forms: thick, leavened sada roti; parathas stuffed with potato or split peas; and the extremely popular and time-consuming layered paratha often referred to as "oil roti."

In recent years, the middle classes may have turned to bread and breakfast cereals, but in the not so distant past, when it was still common for extended families to live together, it was often the task of the newest daughter-in-law to produce the enormous piles of hot, flaky parathas required each morning and evening. To be adept at the kneading, folding and rolling is a matter of pride, as is the skill of turning out perfectly circular rotis. Less skillful practitioners of the art live in dread of the aspersions that may be cast on their efforts, and the blighting comparison of one's roti to the map of Trinidad is a favorite put-down in Guyana. Look at a map of Trinidad to see why!

Of course, many of these expert roti rollers have had lots of practice. The slightest rumor of an event such as a wedding, wake or religiously tinted occasion (all of which seem to require large quantities of roti) produces a squad of volunteers, all armed with roti boards and rolling pins. These affairs are great social equalizers and even those women who no longer roll their own rotis in the comfort of their own homes pride themselves on keeping their hand in. Maids and mistresses roll side by side, tongues and hands moving apace as they entertain each other with an endless, cacophonous flow of gossip, chatter and witticisms, often bursting into snatches of Hindi melodies warranted by the occasion.

After all these preparations, guests are given a fresh lotus leaf and then wait for the train of servers to deposit their delicacies onto this environmentally friendly, disposable plate. The green, leafy scent permeates the food, giving eaters a sense of belonging and a flavorful reminder of their roots.

FLAKY INDIAN FLATBREAD
PARATHA

Caribbean *parathas* have a slightly different texture than Indian subcontinental ones. The layering technique used to make them produces several soft, paper-thin layers. The dough is kneaded, rolled out, brushed with ghee or oil, then coiled and re-rolled. Once it is cooked, the layers are separated.

In Trinidad, cooks give it a good whacking and the finished look, like the shreds of a garment, has earned it the local name of "buss-up shut" (burst-up shirt). In Guyana, we clap the *roti*. The cook removes it from the griddle and tosses it into the air several times, catching it each time with a clapping motion before sending it up again. This is designed to break up the layers and loosen them – and sends volleys of crumbs flying into every nook and cranny of the kitchen. When I taught this technique to a group of ladies in Manila, I also showed them how to do it the mess-free and hand-friendly way: folding the *roti* into a dish towel and banging it with a fist, changing position a few times. All of them spurned this tip. They flung and clapped and showered the entire kitchen with a generous amount of crumbs. And once they had finished their own, they enquired solicitously and hopefully of slower neighbors if they needed any help. The dish towel method just isn't that fun.

This recipe uses all-purpose white flour, Caribbean-style, but you could also use very fine whole-wheat flour (called *atta* in Indian groceries) or varying proportions of the two. I find the whole-wheat version a little on the heavy side, but I often use a mixture of two-thirds white to one-third fine whole-wheat flour with excellent results.

9 oz/1⅔ cups all-purpose flour
   (or 5½ oz/1 cup all-purpose and 3½ oz/
   ⅔ cup very fine whole-wheat flour)
½ tsp sugar
1 tsp baking powder
about 5 fl oz/⅔ cup lukewarm water
2 tsp vegetable oil or ghee
about 3½ fl oz/scant ½ cup vegetable oil, or ghee
   or melted butter
flour for dredging + small bowl of flour
   for dipping

EQUIPMENT:

a tawa (preferably flat), or griddle or heavy frying pan

TIMING:

At least 2 hours for kneading, resting and shaping; and about 20 minutes for rolling and cooking.

MAKES 4

Mix together the flour, sugar, baking powder, water and oil to make a soft and pliable dough. You can do this by hand, or in a mixer fitted with a dough hook. A food processor fitted with a kneading attachment makes really quick work of it.

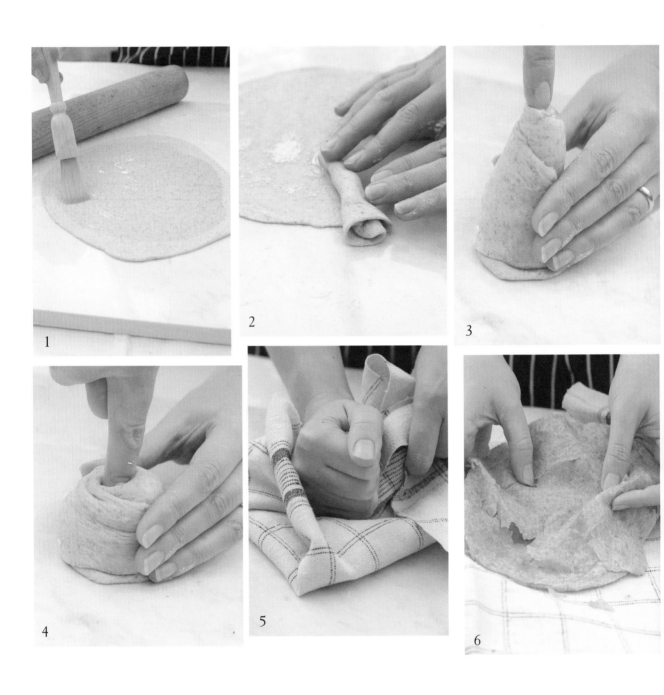

Shape the dough into a ball and put in a bowl. Cover with plastic wrap or a damp cloth and leave to rest for at least 30 minutes.

Knead the dough again lightly and divide into 4 pieces, shaping them into balls. Lightly oil a large plate. Roll out a piece of dough to form a 9-inch circle. Brush the circle with oil (1). Dredge with flour; this is important, or you won't get the layers!

Make a cut in the dough from edge to center and roll up to form a cone (2). Press the cone down through the center to form a bun shape (3 and 4), then put it on the oiled plate and cover with plastic wrap. Shape the remaining pieces of dough in the same way. Leave to rest again for at least 30 minutes.

When you are ready to start cooking the *parathas*, preheat the *tawa* or griddle. Put a second plate near to the stove, then invert a spoon on it and cover with a dish towel – this will keep the *parathas* warm while protecting them from condensation. Keep a second dish towel handy.

Dip a dough bun on both sides in the small bowl of flour and then roll out to a circle a little smaller than the first time; this will give a flakier effect. Slap it onto the *tawa* or griddle. Brush the top with oil. After a minute or so, turn it over and brush the second side with oil. Cook on both sides until small golden flecks appear; overcooking will make them crisp and hard. Transfer to the second dish towel and fold to cover it.

Dip the second piece of dough into the small bowl of flour. Roll out and slap onto the *tawa*. While it is cooking, bash the cooked *paratha* that is in the dish towel with your fist to break up the layers, changing its position a few times during the process (5 and 6). Fold and place on the plate and cover with the tea towel. Check the *paratha* on the *tawa* and continue the process as before.

Eat warm. Serve with a dish that has a rich sauce, such as curry.

POTATO-STUFFED FLATBREADS
ALU ROTI

These potato-stuffed flatbreads belong to the *paratha* family, which includes *parathas* stuffed with grated radish, split peas and even crude sugar. This is one of the more forgiving recipes. The flatbreads stay soft and pliable and also freeze well, individually wrapped, so it is worth the effort to make up a big batch. *Alu roti* are especially popular in Indian communities in the Caribbean, where they are used to accompany gravy-laden curries. But they are also delicious on their own: smeared with hot pickle or chutney, they make a tasty snack. Bear in mind that the filling will have to compete with the dough, so over-season it a little and taste, making any necessary adjustments.

FILLING

14 oz floury potatoes, peeled and cut into chunks
  (peeled weight)

½ tsp ground coriander

¼ tsp ground cumin

⅛ tsp ground chili

1 tbsp oil

salt to taste

DOUGH

9 oz/1⅔ cups all-purpose flour

¾ tsp baking powder

½ tsp sugar

5½ fl oz/generous ⅔ cup lukewarm water

a few tablespoons oil, for cooking

EQUIPMENT:

a tawa (preferably flat), or griddle or heavy frying pan

TIMING:

The filling should be made in advance. Set aside at least 2 hours for kneading, resting and shaping and another 30 minutes for rolling and cooking.

MAKES 6

For the filling, first boil the potatoes, then mash them very well. If you have a ricer, use it. If not, be very thorough – the mash must be totally lump-free. Add the remaining ingredients to

 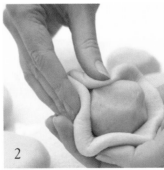 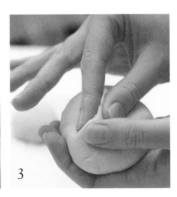

the potato and mix well, then leave to cool. When cool, shape into six balls, cover and set aside.

For the dough, sift the flour and baking powder into a large bowl. Add the sugar and water and knead for a few minutes, or until the dough is very supple. You can do this by hand, or in a mixer fitted with a dough hook. A food processor fitted with a kneading attachment makes really quick work of it. Cover with plastic wrap and set aside to rest for at least 1 hour and up to 3 hours.

Now knead the dough for a minute or two, then divide into 6 pieces. Flatten each piece in your palm. Put a ball of potato in the center (1), then coax the dough around it (2) and pinch the edges to seal (3). Brush the surface with oil. Keep covered on a well-floured surface or an oiled plate, well apart, until you are ready to start rolling them. When the last piece of dough has been filled, you can start making the *rotis*.

Preheat the *tawa* or griddle. Flatten a dough ball with your hand and roll evenly to a 8-inch circle. Try not to let the filling escape, but if a little does, don't despair. This *roti* is quite forgiving. Brush the *tawa* with oil and slap the *roti* onto it. Brush the top with more oil. Turn after a minute or two and brush with a little more oil. The *roti* should balloon. It is cooked when both sides are faintly speckled. Don't let it brown, or it will become hard. Fold the *roti* into a quarter circle on the griddle, then transfer to a plate and wrap it in a dish towel to keep warm while you make the rest.

Eat warm, served with curry. Alternatively, roll up and eat cold as a snack.

FLATBREADS FILLED WITH SPLIT PEAS
DAL PURI

Dal puri is another member of the *paratha* family and this is the *roti* that Caribbean Indians make when they want to lend a festive air to an occasion. The stuffing of yellow split peas must be made in advance, and the boiled peas have to cool before they can be ground to the right consistency, so be sure to budget enough time. Before the advent of the food processor, the peas were boiled very soft and passed through a strainer, which was quite a chore. Nowadays, a few bursts of power with the food processor do the trick, but remember that the filling must be extremely finely ground, or it will tear the dough. Once the filling and the dough have been made, they can be put together a few hours later, ready to be eaten warm. Like the potato-stuffed flatbreads, *dal puri* also make an excellent snack on their own.

This is one of the more challenging flatbreads to make. Practiced cooks can roll the same dough (without bursting) to a thinner and larger disc than described in the recipe. Mrs Lee, the cook at my school (St Rose's High School, Georgetown), was such an expert and her "*puri* and sour" (*dal puri* with a smear of hot green mango sauce) was one of the most popular items on the menu. So light was her hand that I once saw a girl's *dal puri* literally sail off her plate into the air as she rounded the drafty corner of the canteen building, landing on the ground in front of our amazed eyes.

FILLING
4½ oz/scant ⅔ cup dried yellow split peas
½ tsp ground coriander
½ tsp ground cumin
⅛ tsp ground chili (or to taste)
1 tsp ground turmeric
1 tsp garam masala (optional)
scant ½ tsp salt, or to taste
1 tbsp oil

DOUGH
9 oz/1⅔ cups all-purpose flour
¾ tsp baking powder
½ tsp sugar

about 5 fl oz/⅔ cup lukewarm water
2 tsp oil

a few tablespoons oil, for cooking

EQUIPMENT:
a tawa (preferably flat), griddle or heavy frying pan

TIMING:
The filling should be made in advance. Set aside at least 2 hours for kneading, resting and shaping and another 30 minutes for rolling and cooking.

MAKES 6

For the filling, rinse the split peas in a strainer and put them in a pan with about 17 fl oz/generous 2 cups water. Cover the pan and bring to a boil. Give the peas a good stir and lower the heat, then allow to simmer until just cooked; this will take

12–20 minutes, depending on how fresh the peas are. The peas should still be firm, or it will be difficult to grind them. (The water froths a lot, so you may need to leave an opening between the pan and lid to let the steam escape.) Drain and allow to cool.

Put the cooled peas with the spices and salt in a food processor, and then pulse until very fine. Stir in the oil and set aside in a cool place until needed.

For the dough, sift the flour and baking powder into a large bowl. Add the sugar, water and oil and knead for a few minutes to make a soft and supple dough. You can do this by hand, or in a mixer fitted with a dough hook. A food processor fitted with a kneading attachment makes really quick work of it. Shape the dough into a ball and rub some oil lightly over it with your fingers. Cover with plastic wrap and set aside to rest for at least 30 minutes and up to 3 hours.

Re-knead the dough for a minute or two and then divide it into 6 pieces. Flatten each piece on a lightly floured work surface to a diameter of about 5 inches. Press the outer edge to make it thinner than the rest. Brush lightly with oil, leaving about 1 inch free around the circumference. Put the disc of dough in your cupped palm. Spoon one-sixth of the filling into the center, then coax the dough around it and pinch the edges to seal. Brush the surface with oil and put it on an oiled plate. Make the rest in the same way and space them well apart so that they won't stick to each other. When the last piece of dough has been filled, you can start making the *dal puris*.

When you are ready to start cooking the *dal puris*, put a second plate near to the stove. Invert a spoon on it and cover with a dish towel.

Preheat the *tawa* or griddle. Flatten a dough ball with your hand and roll evenly and gently to a 8-inch circle. The oil should keep it from sticking, especially if you use a silicone mat, but dust with flour if necessary. Try not to let the filling escape. Brush the *tawa* with oil and use the rolling pin to help carry the *dal puri* onto it.

Turn after a minute or two and brush with a little oil. Repeat with the other side. The flatbread is cooked when both sides are faintly speckled. Don't let it brown, or it will become hard. Fold the *dal puri* in half on the griddle, then transfer to the plate and wrap it in the tea towel to keep warm while you make the rest.

Eat warm, served with curry. Alternatively, roll up and eat cold as a snack.

SUGAR FLATBREAD
MEETHA ROTI

Meetha roti (literally "sweet bread") is not something everyone can expect to taste. It is usually made by an indulgent grandmother, mother or maid for any children hanging around the kitchen. A small piece of the dough used for making the rest of the *rotis* is reserved, stuffed with sugar, then cooked on the *tawa* until the sugar dissolves. There's a good reason for cooking this one last. It makes a huge mess on the *tawa* because the dough is almost bound to burst, releasing sugar that subsequently caramelizes and burns, making quite a bit of work for the person who has to clean up. If you are undeterred and would like to try it, take a portion of dough (half the regular size) from the basic recipe for any of the *parathas*. Flatten it in your palm and fill the center with about 2 tsp white or brown sugar. Pinch the edges to seal in a ball again and flatten on your work surface. Roll out to the size of a saucer and cook as for a filled *paratha*. The sugar is very hot when it comes off the heat, so wait a few minutes before eating it.

THICK SEASONED FLATBREAD
SADA ROTI

This thick, breadlike *roti* is a great favorite with the older generation in Guyana and it is one of the simplest kinds to make. Many people like it to have a few crisply charred spots on the outside, and the old-fashioned clay fireplaces, which were fed with fresh wood, gave a lovely smoky flavor if the cooked *roti* was shifted slightly off the *tawa* so that the direct heat could catch it. It makes a good accompaniment for grilled meats as well as curries.

9 oz/1⅔ cups all-purpose flour

2½ tsp baking powder

¼ tsp salt

1 tsp sugar

1 tbsp finely chopped onion

1 green or red bird's-eye chili, finely chopped

about 5 fl oz/⅔ cup lukewarm water

1 tbsp oil, ghee or butter, plus about 3 tbsp
    for brushing

EQUIPMENT:
a tawa (preferably flat), or griddle or heavy frying pan

TIMING:
Set aside at least 1 hour for kneading and resting, and about 20 minutes for rolling and cooking.

MAKES 4

Mix together all the ingredients to make a supple dough. You can do this by hand, or in a mixer fitted with a dough hook. A food processor fitted with a kneading attachment makes really quick work of it.

Shape the dough into a ball, then put it in an oiled bowl and cover with plastic wrap. Leave to rest for 30–60 minutes. Re-knead the dough lightly, then divide into 4 pieces. Roll out each piece to a 6-inch circle, dredging with a little flour if necessary.

Preheat the *tawa*. When the pan is hot, turn the heat down. Slap a *roti* onto it and cook until tiny brown spots appear on the bottom. Flip the *roti* over and allow the other side to cook. Brush with oil, ghee or butter on both sides and keep wrapped in a dish towel until ready to eat.

CHICKPEA FLATBREAD
BESAN KI ROTI

Besan means chickpea flour in Hindi, and that is the main flavoring ingredient in these nutty-tasting flatbreads. Many Indian recipes recommend coiling the dough before rolling it, but I find that there is too little to be gained by this step. The stickiness of the chickpea flour prevents effective layering, so I prefer to save time and effort by rolling just once. Instead of making full-sized *rotis*, you could also make tiny ones and serve them as appetizers, topped with spicy tidbits of meat or with roasted or grilled vegetables. Try to get *besan* from an Indian grocer or well-stocked supermarket; Mediterranean chickpea flour is not quite the same.

4½ oz/scant 1 cup chickpea flour (*besan*)

6 oz/scant 1¼ cups all-purpose flour

2 tsp baking powder

½ tsp salt, or to taste

2 tsp garam masala*

small handful cilantro or flat-leaf parsley, finely
  chopped

1 tbsp oil, ghee or butter

about 5 fl oz/ ⅔ cup lukewarm water

about 3 tbsp melted butter, for brushing

EQUIPMENT:

a tawa (preferably flat), or griddle or heavy frying pan

TIMING:

Set aside at least 1 hour for kneading and resting, and about 20 minutes for rolling and cooking.

MAKES 4

Make a supple dough from all the ingredients. You can do this by hand, or in a mixer fitted with a dough hook. A food processor fitted with a kneading attachment makes really quick work of it.

Shape the dough into a ball. Put it in a lightly oiled bowl, then cover with plastic wrap and leave to rest for 30–60 minutes. Re-knead the dough lightly, then divide into 4 pieces. Put one piece on a well-floured surface, such as a silicone mat, and roll out to a circle with a diameter of 7–8 inches, dredging with flour as necessary.

Preheat the *tawa* and once it is hot, reduce the heat to low. Slap a flatbread onto it and let it cook until small bubbles appear on the surface. Flip it over and allow the other side to cook. Brush both sides with melted butter and keep wrapped in a dish towel until ready to eat.

* If you don't have garam masala, use the following mixture:

1 tsp ground coriander

½ tsp ground cumin

¼ tsp ground black pepper

¼ tsp ground allspice

MEAT-FILLED GRIDDLE PASTIES
SAÇ BÖREK

My pocket Turkish dictionary succinctly defines *börek* as "flaky pastry, pie." It is actually an umbrella name for a myriad of savory pastries that form one of Turkey's favorite snacks. Both pastry and filling can vary greatly, and there are endless combinations to be made. Lean bread dough, plain phyllo pastry, phyllo pastry enriched with eggs and even puff pastry are all used to enclose fillings based on cheese or meat, seasoned and shaped in various ways. They are then fried, baked or griddled. *Su börek* (water *börek*) is a remarkable Anatolian variant: sheets of enriched phyllo are precooked, then layered, like lasagna, with a filling of (the ubiquitous) cheese or meat, nuts and dried fruit, which is, finally, baked in the oven.

This recipe uses a fairly plain dough with a meat filling. The pasties make a delicious lunch or supper dish, supplemented by a soup or generous salad. In Turkey, they would be cooked in a *saç*, a griddle shaped like an upturned shallow wok, but they are easy to make at home using a heavy frying pan. Two things are very important here: the meat must be very lean and the tomato must be fleshy and not watery, or you will end up with a soggy, mushy product. Both the filling and the dough can be made several hours in advance and kept in a cool place until you are ready to assemble the pasties. This recipe makes two, and they will fit comfortably together in the frying pan. It is easily doubled to make a second batch.

For a vegetarian suggestion, see page 58.

DOUGH
4½ oz/scant 1 cup white bread flour
¼ tsp salt
2 tsp olive oil
about 5 tbsp lukewarm water

FILLING
3½ oz/scant 1 cup lean ground lamb or beef
1 tbsp very finely chopped onion
generous ¼ tsp salt, or to taste
a few sprigs of parsley, finely chopped
generous grind of pepper
  or sprinkle of chili flakes

1 small tomato, seeded and chopped
butter, for brushing
flour, for dredging

EQUIPMENT:
large heavy frying pan

TIMING:
Set aside about 1½ hours for kneading and resting, and about 30 minutes for assembling and cooking.

MAKES 2

Combine the ingredients for the dough and knead well for several minutes. The dough should be soft but not sticky. This dough can also be kneaded in a food processor fitted with a plastic kneading attachment or a mixer fitted with a dough hook.

Shape the dough into a ball and place it on an oiled plate. Dust with flour and cover with plastic wrap. Set aside until needed, or at least for 1 hour.

Combine the filling ingredients and set aside. If you are going to set it aside for several hours, omit the tomato, and add it just before you are ready to use the filling.

Preheat a large, heavy frying pan.

Divide the dough into 2 pieces and roll one piece out to a circle with a diameter of about 10 inches, or slightly smaller if your frying pan is not that large. Spread half of the filling over half of the circle, leaving about 1 inch free along the edge. Moisten the edge of the dough with a little water and fold to form a semi-circle. Press down the edges to seal. This is important, or the filling will leak out while cooking.

Transfer the pasty to the hot pan and make the other one in the same way. Both will fit in the pan at the same time. After a few minutes, flip over a pasty to check if there are nice golden patches. When both sides are cooked, transfer to plates and brush with butter. Eat warm.

NOTE
For a vegetarian version, use the filling for Cheese and Parsley Buns on p. 253.

YOGURT DOUGH FLATBREAD
BAZLAMA

This Turkish flatbread is traditionally made using a yogurt starter, a bit of which is kept back for subsequent batches. I have added a pinch of yeast to give it a nudge in the right direction and because of this, the starter needs to rest only overnight.

STARTER

2 tbsp all-purpose flour

2 tbsp yogurt

2 tbsp warm water

1 tsp sugar

⅛ tsp active dry yeast

9 oz/1⅔ cups white bread flour

¼ tsp salt

about 4 fl oz/½ cup lukewarm water

about 3 tbsp melted butter, for brushing

EQUIPMENT:

large heavy frying pan

TIMING:

The starter must be made the day before. Set aside at least 1 hour the next day for kneading and resting, and about 15 minutes for rolling and cooking.

MAKES 2

For the starter, mix all the ingredients together in a small bowl and cover with plastic wrap. Leave at room temperature overnight.

Next day, make a soft dough using the starter and all the remaining ingredients. You can do this by hand, or in a mixer fitted with a dough hook. A food processor fitted with a kneading attachment makes really quick work of it.

Shape the dough into a ball. Put this in an oiled bowl, then cover with plastic wrap and leave to rest for 30–60 minutes.

Re-knead the dough lightly and divide into 2 pieces. Put one piece on a well-floured surface, such as a silicone mat, and pat or roll into a 8-inch circle, dredging with flour as necessary.

Preheat the frying pan. Slap a flatbread onto it and let it cook until tiny brown spots appear on the bottom. Flip it over and allow the other side to cook. Brush with melted butter on both sides and keep covered with a dish towel until ready to eat.

MEAT-TOPPED FLATBREADS
ETLİ PIDE

These Turkish flatbreads are quite easy to prepare. They are a kind of meat pizza and make a delicious snack or lunch component. They are generally quite mildly spiced, but a sprinkle of chili flakes, as used here, will liven them up.

DOUGH
4½ oz/scant 1 cup white bread flour

¾ tsp active dry yeast

¼ tsp salt

½ tsp sugar

1 tbsp olive oil

about 5 tbsp lukewarm water

FILLING
5½ oz/generous 1¼ cups lean ground lamb
  or beef

1½ tbsp very finely chopped onion

½ tsp salt, or to taste

a few sprigs of parsley, finely chopped

generous grind of pepper
  or sprinkle of chili flakes

1 large tomato, seeded and chopped

TIMING:
This is a yeast dough, so it will need to rise. Set aside about 2½ hours for the whole process, including baking for 15–20 minutes.

MAKES 2

Combine the ingredients for the dough and knead well for several minutes. The dough should be soft but not sticky. This dough can also be kneaded in a food processor fitted with a plastic kneading attachment or a mixer fitted with a dough hook.

Shape the dough into a ball and put it in a bowl. Cover with plastic wrap or a dish towel wrung out in hot water and leave in a warm, draft-free place until doubled in volume.

Combine the filling ingredients, except the tomato, and set aside. Add the tomato just before you are ready to use the filling.

Punch down the risen dough and knead briefly, then divide into 2 portions.

Roll out one portion to a 9-inch circle and spread half of the filling on it, leaving about 1 inch free around the edge. Fold about ½ inch of the dough edge inwards and then fold it again, so you get a double thickness that forms a raised ridge. Pinch two opposing sides together to form a point, so that the flatbread is shaped like a boat, and place it on a baking sheet. Repeat with the second portion of dough and filling.

Leave to rest for about 15 minutes. Preheat the oven to 400°F/200°C.

Bake the flatbreads for 15–20 minutes, or until crisp and golden brown around the edges.

YEAST BREADS, CAKES & ROLLS

Pampering your dough for fantastic flavor

WORKING WITH YEAST DOUGHS

There is magic in yeast. I have baked scores of breads and rolls, but even now I still get a thrill to see it convert ordinary flour and liquids into something beautiful and tasty. Yeast is a living organism and, as such, responds well to a bit of pampering. However, it is easily satisfied and will reward the slightest effort well.

BUDGETING YOUR TIME

Yeast doughs are easy to make, and the process of kneading and shaping is a relaxing one. However, they require two fairly long resting periods in addition to the initial kneading and subsequent shaping. Large panned loaves are shaped very quickly, but freeform versions such as Festive Dutch Spiced Loaf (*Duivekater*) and Aniseed Braid take a little more time. The smaller items vary and the Majorcan and Filipino coiled rolls (*Ensaimadas* and *Enseymadas*) will take longer than, say, Tennis Rolls or Chestnut Buns. It is always a good idea to read through the recipe first to see exactly what is involved, and set aside enough time to do it. There is a pleasant side benefit: the resting times will allow you to catch up with a multitude of other tasks while waiting.

TOO LITTLE OR TOO MUCH YEAST

You can never really use too little yeast; it will simply take longer for it to work sufficiently to lift the dough. Many bakers even feel that a longer rising time improves the flavor and keeping qualities of bread. It is very easy – and quite pointless – to use too much yeast. The dough will billow out beautifully but uncontrollably, producing an unpredictable texture and a strong, yeasty flavor.

ACTIVE DRY YEAST

These recipes all specify active dry or instant yeast, which is very fine and easily incorporated into the other dry ingredients. Fresh yeast and coarse-grained dried yeast need to be sponged first before adding them to the dry ingredients and are not interchangeable with active dry yeast here. Active dry yeast can also be sponged.

SPONGING

Sponging means mixing the yeast with enough warm liquid and a little flour and sugar to give it a head start before adding it to the other ingredients. This is useful in cases where the dough is enriched with a generous amount of sugar, butter and eggs, as the combination can prove too rich and the yeast has to put up too much of a fight to grow properly. Never add salt to the sponge as it will retard the growth of the yeast cells, which defeats the purpose. Yeast thrives in a warm, damp atmosphere and it will come to life and start feeding on the sugars in the sponge. When the cells become active and grow, large bubbles will appear on the surface of the sponge – it is then ready to be used.

TEMPERATURE OF LIQUIDS

The recipes say "warmed" milk or water. If the liquid is too cool or cold, it will take a very long time for the yeast to start to work. On the other hand, if the liquid is too hot, cells will be killed and the yeast will be effectively deactivated. The perfect temperature is somewhere between lukewarm to body temperature: 77–98.6°F/25–37°C. Don't worry; there's no need to mess about with thermometers. The easiest way to check is to plunge a finger into the liquid – it should feel warm without causing any discomfort. That's all there is to it. If anything at all, err on the cooler side.

WHY "ABOUT"?

Recipes often say "about … fl oz." The reason for this is partly explained in Ingredients, under Flour (pp. 17–19). No two flours are the same. Even the same variety of wheat planted under different climatic conditions can vary, and this affects the way the flour absorbs liquids, which is why these recipes do not offer a clearly defined amount. Bread flour comes from hard wheat and has greater powers of absorption than other kinds of flour, such as all-purpose flour, which will have a tendency to turn sticky with the same proportion of liquid. It is always best to add all of the liquid to the dry ingredients before you start to knead, but use the two following tips if you run into minor difficulties. If you find that the dough is too firm and needs more liquid, knead it in 1 teaspoon at a time until you get the desired consistency. You can add an extra 1–2 tablespoons of flour if the dough is too sticky to handle, but adding too much will change the texture, particularly of richer breads.

OVERKNEADING AND UNDERKNEADING

Bread flour has a high gluten content and this will provide elasticity. However, it will not do that on its own and must be kneaded well to encourage the gluten to develop and stretch, forming a web to trap carbon dioxide and make the dough rise. If you underknead, there will be less development and the dough will not rise evenly to its full potential. There is such a thing as overkneading, but this rarely happens. In fact, it is almost impossible to overknead by hand, as you will feel the texture and stop – besides, you will be tired long before that stage is reached. However, it could happen if you leave the dough unattended in the mixer for a long time. The dough breaks down after the gluten has been overworked and turns into a sticky unusable mass that cannot support itself when baked.

MIXER OR HAND?

A heavy-duty mixer fitted with a dough hook makes light work of kneading: the dough is ready when it leaves the sides of the bowl and forms a smooth ball. However, doughs usually respond well to the warmth generated by your hands and

most will allow themselves to be easily manipulated. Very soft doughs and stickier types, such as rye-based doughs, are best kneaded in a mixer, but can also be kneaded by hand. They will just require a little more patience – and a large bowl because they will stick to most other potential work surfaces. A flexible plastic scraper will help to bring the dough together at regular intervals and make it easier to handle. Even in the case of firmer doughs, it is easier, when kneading by hand, to mix the ingredients together in a bowl and moisten them into a lumpy dough before turning the whole thing out onto a work surface to continue. When kneading, use the heel of your hand to press the dough and stretch it, folding it back on itself and changing position several times. Kneading times vary, so pay attention to the texture described in the recipe. In general, the dough should be smooth and supple and free of lumps.

WORK SURFACE

Cold surfaces like marble and granite are unsuitable for kneading yeast doughs as they will "shock" the warm dough and reduce the temperature too much. A wooden worktop or large pastry board makes a good surface. Failing that, use a thick silicone mat to insulate the dough against the cold. A large silicone mat also happens to be my favorite kneading, rolling and shaping aid. This has the great advantage of being virtually non-stick, eliminating the need to add too much extra flour. In fact, it usually needs no extra flour at all unless the dough is extremely sticky. It also makes cleaning up less of a chore because you simply carry the mat to the sink and rinse it, with minimal mess. This simple piece of equipment makes a baker's life even more enjoyable.

RISING AND PROVING

In general, yeast doughs need to rise twice. Some professional bakers may even give their special breads extra rises. Rising conditions the dough, and you will notice that even hard-to-handle doughs improve in texture and suppleness after the first rise. It is absolutely essential that rising takes place in a draft-free place. Warmth is desirable but less important in this case, as the dough will also rise in a cooler environment (even the refrigerator), simply taking longer to do so. Keep the dough away from direct heat, or it will over-ferment. The covered bowl or baking pan can be placed near a warm (but not too hot) radiator, in an airing cupboard or on a rack in a warming drawer at an extremely low setting. Failing that, leave it on the worktop at room temperature and be patient. The second rise or proof takes place after the bread has been shaped and put in a suitable pan and, as the yeast is well and truly active by this time, it is faster than the initial one. If the bread is not covered properly, a skin will form on its surface. A sheet of oiled plastic wrap will prevent this from happening. If the surface of the bread has been dusted with flour, however, do not oil the plastic wrap; the flour will keep it from sticking. Always cover the dough loosely because it will need room to expand.

PUNCHING DOWN AND SHAPING

Punching down means deflating the dough. You press it down and re-knead it lightly to redistribute the gases. In so doing, you give the yeast new feeding grounds and possibilities for expansion. This will improve the texture of the finished loaf. Loaves are generally shaped by creating a flat sheet that is rolled up into a "sausage" and put into the baking pan. A rolling pin is not really necessary; you can easily flatten the dough to the required shape and size with your hands. Once you have rolled the dough into a "sausage" shape, pinch the seam to seal and place the "sausage" in the pan with the seam at the bottom.

SLASHING

Some loaves are slashed, and this is not always purely a decorative measure. Pretty though the cuts may be, their main purpose is to allow controlled expansion. Use a very sharp knife so that you do not tear the dough.

OVEN TEMPERATURES

Baking temperatures for yeast breads are usually quite high compared with those for cakes. This blast of heat gives the loaf an extra impulse to rise a little more and then set rapidly into what will be its finished shape. The extra rising in the oven is referred to as "oven spring." The main goal is to kill the yeast as quickly as possible as soon as it has reached its peak. If the temperature is too low to start with, the dough will keep on rising for too long and will over-rise. The loaf will look untidy and the texture will be uneven. Richer doughs are baked at slightly lower temperatures so that the sugar and eggs cannot make the crust darken too quickly and burn. However, they set more quickly, due to the eggs. If you notice that your loaf is browning too much on one side, turn it around to give the lighter side a chance to catch up. The temperatures advised here should not make your loaves burn, but if you find that they are darkening too quickly after the first half of the baking time, reduce the temperature slightly (by about 10%) or cover the top loosely with a piece of aluminum foil.

COOLING AND KEEPING

Cooling on a wire rack allows excess moisture to evaporate, leaving the crust crisper. However, this period of crustiness is quite short because bread begins to go stale as soon as it leaves the oven. The internal moisture will have redistributed itself within a few hours, and even crisp crusts will soften. Many breads are good eaten slightly warm from the oven. If you want to wrap them to keep or freeze, always allow them to cool completely. Well wrapped in suitable material, they will freeze beautifully, so it is worthwhile to make two loaves instead of one or a full batch of rolls, even if your household is small.

SIMPLE BROWN BREAD

It hardly costs any extra time to make two loaves instead of one, and the second loaf can be frozen for later. I sometimes add chopped walnuts to one loaf, but you can also try pumpkin and sunflower seeds. The recipe is easily halved if you prefer to make a single loaf.

9 oz/1⅔ cups white bread flour

1 lb 2 oz/generous 3 cups whole-wheat flour

2¼ tsp active dry yeast

3 tbsp brown sugar

1½ tsp salt

1¾ oz/scant ½ stick butter, melted and cooled slightly

about 16 fl oz/scant 2 cups milk, warmed

2¼ oz/½ cup chopped walnuts per loaf
   or the same weight of sunflower and/or
   pumpkin seeds (optional)

EQUIPMENT:

2 x 1 lb loaf pans, greased

MAKES 2 LOAVES

Put all the ingredients except the walnuts and seeds in a large bowl and mix to moisten the dry ingredients. Use a heavy-duty mixer fitted with a dough hook to knead thoroughly until smooth and supple. The dough should be medium-soft. Alternatively, turn out onto a floured surface or a non-stick silicone mat and knead until smooth and supple. Bring together in a ball and return to the bowl. Cover the bowl with plastic wrap or a damp dish towel and set aside in a warm, draft-free place until doubled in size.

Punch down the dough and knead lightly until smooth again. Divide into 2 portions. Add the walnuts or seeds, if using. Roll or flatten each piece out to a rectangle that is as wide as your pan is long, to a thickness of about ½ inch.

Roll up the dough, starting at a short side, then pinch the seam to seal. Place it seam-side down in the pan and shape the other loaf in the same way. Cover both loaves loosely with lightly oiled plastic wrap and leave in a warm, draft-free place until almost doubled in size.

Preheat the oven to 400°F/200°C.

Bake the loaves for about 30 minutes. To test, remove the loaves from the pan. Tap sharply on the top and bottom; they should sound hollow. Cool on a wire rack.

The loaves will keep for a few days if well wrapped and can also be frozen as soon as they have cooled.

JAMAICAN HARD DOUGH BREAD

Jamaican immigrants abroad often pine for this simple and familiar taste of home. Hard dough bread is traditionally a baker's product and is made using a starter of a firm sponge dough that has been allowed to ripen overnight. As both the sponge and new dough are very stiff, they are passed several times through a dough brake with rollers designed to press them into each other. Bakers who cannot justify the expenditure and extra time involved prefer to use a straight dough, as in this recipe. It is a fairly plain bread, made from a few basic ingredients, and it is suitable for those who are lactose intolerant, because it is mixed with water instead of milk. Its crumb is characteristically dense and slightly chewy, with a sweetish taste. Leftovers make very good toast, especially eaten warm with butter.

1 lb 10 oz/5 cups white bread flour

2¼ tsp active dry yeast

4 tbsp sugar

1 tbsp molasses

about 12¾ fl oz/generous 1½ cups lukewarm
   water

1½ tsp salt

1¾ oz vegetable shortening

EQUIPMENT:

2 x 1 lb loaf pans, greased

MAKES 2 LOAVES

Put all the ingredients in a large bowl. Mix well to moisten the dry ingredients and knead well until smooth and elastic. This is a very firm dough, so if you use a mixer, make sure it is a heavy-duty one that won't stall. Alternatively, turn out onto a floured surface or a non-stick silicone mat and knead until smooth and supple. Bring together in a ball and return to the bowl. Cover the bowl with plastic wrap or a damp dish towel and set aside in a warm, draft-free place until it is only about one-and-a-half times its original size. Do not allow it to double in volume.

Punch down the dough and knead lightly until smooth again. Divide into 2 portions and roll or flatten each piece out to a rectangle that is as wide as your pan is long, and with a thickness of about ½ inch.

Roll up the dough, starting at a short side, and pinch the seam to seal. Place it seam-side down in the pan and shape the other loaf in the same way. Cover both loaves loosely with lightly oiled plastic wrap and leave in a warm, draft-free place until the loaves are once again one-and-a-half times their original size.

Preheat the oven to 400°F/200°C.

Bake the loaves for about 30 minutes. To test, remove the loaves from the pan. Tap sharply on the top and bottom; they should sound hollow. Cool on a wire rack.

The loaves will keep for a few days if well wrapped and can also be frozen as soon as they have cooled.

FREEFORM RYE LOAVES

German bakers are the undisputed masters of rye-based breads and produce them in their pure form or in varying combinations with wheat. These range from simple loaves baked in modern commercial ovens to the absolutely delicious naturally leavened ones baked to perfection on the stone floor of wood-stoked ovens. The latter generally have a thick crust and instead of becoming stale, they seem to improve after a day or two when all the flavors have mellowed.

The following recipe is simplicity itself and produces a tasty loaf, with a slightly closer texture than pure wheaten bread. It does, though, contain a fair amount of wheat, which gives it more elasticity and makes it easier to handle. Its character will alter slightly, depending on the type of liquid used, and adding 1 tsp of caraway seeds will give it a twist. The buttermilk version is particularly delicious with cold cuts and keeps well. I always think of it as a cheat's sourdough bread: it has the tanginess, without all the extra effort of nurturing starters and the like.

The dough can be shaped into freeform rectangular loaves or simple round ones. These are crusty when you remove them from the oven, but the crust will soften and become slightly chewy afterwards.

15 oz/scant 3 cups white bread flour

11½ oz/2 cups fine rye flour

2 tsp active dry yeast

2 tsp brown sugar

1½ tsp salt

about 17 fl oz/generous 2 cups buttermilk, milk or water, warmed

1 tsp caraway seeds (optional)

MAKES 2 LOAVES

Put all the ingredients in a large bowl and mix well to moisten the dry ingredients. Use a heavy-duty mixer fitted with a dough hook to knead thoroughly until smooth and supple. It will be a fairly firm dough. Alternatively, turn out onto a floured surface or a non-stick silicone mat and knead until smooth and supple. The rye flour makes the dough a bit sticky and squelchy to start with, but the texture will improve as you continue kneading. Bring together in a ball and return to the bowl. Cover the bowl with plastic wrap or a damp dish towel and set aside in a warm, draft-free place until doubled in size.

Grease a baking sheet.

Punch down the dough and knead lightly until smooth again. Divide into 2 equally sized portions.

For rectangular loaves, roll or flatten each piece out to a rectangle about 9½ x 8 inches and with a thickness of about ½ inch. Roll up the dough, starting at a short side for a squat loaf, or a long side for a slim one, and pinch the seam to seal. Place it seam-side down on the sheet and shape the other loaf in the same way.

For round loaves, shape each piece into a ball and flatten them slightly with your hand to a diameter of about 6 inches.

Cover both loaves loosely with lightly oiled plastic wrap and leave in a warm, draft-free place until almost doubled in size.

Preheat the oven to 400°F/200°C.

Make 6 or 7 parallel diagonal slashes on the top of each loaf and bake for about 30 minutes. To test, remove the loaves from the pan. Tap sharply on the top and bottom; they should sound hollow. Cool on a wire rack.

The loaves will keep for a few days if well wrapped and can also be frozen as soon as they have cooled.

ANISEED BRAID

On the plantation at Skeldon, most families usually ate homemade breads and cakes, but my hopes were always raised when I saw the baker's delivery boy from the neighboring village, the carrier on his bicycle filled with breads such as this simple but delicious aniseed braid. While researching the history of Dutch baking, I was delighted to find that there is a similar loaf in the southern province of Zeeland. The chief difference between this loaf and the one of my childhood is that it usually contains some nutmeg and a hint of mace and it is baked in a pan. Nowadays, I often bake a hybrid version with the optional mace and nutmeg. Well wrapped, this will keep for a few days and also makes good toast.

Serve this sliced, with butter and a slice or two of mature cheese.

2 tsp whole aniseed (anise), bruised

1 lb 2 oz/3⅓ cups white bread flour

scant 2 tsp active dry yeast

3 tbsp sugar

1 tsp salt

about 9 fl oz/1 cup milk, warmed

1¼ oz/scant ½ stick butter, melted and cooled

1 egg, lightly beaten

¼ tsp freshly grated nutmeg and a pinch of ground mace (optional)

MAKES 1 LOAF

To bruise the aniseed, simply put the seeds in a mortar and bang them with a pestle.

Put the flour, yeast, sugar, salt, aniseed and spices (if using) in a large bowl. Add the milk, butter and egg and mix with a spoon or spatula until the dry ingredients are well moistened.

If you are kneading by hand, turn out onto a floured surface or a silicone mat and knead until elastic. Alternatively, use a heavy-duty mixer fitted with a dough hook and knead until elastic. This dough needs to be a little stiffer than for a panned loaf because it must hold its shape during baking. Shape into a ball and place in a large bowl. Cover with plastic wrap or a dish towel wrung out in hot water, and leave in a warm, draft-free place until doubled in bulk.

Grease a baking sheet.

Punch down the risen dough and knead lightly until once more smooth and elastic. Divide the dough into 3 equal portions. Shape each portion into a rope about 20 inches long, making the middle of the rope a little thicker and the ends tapering. Pinch the tips of the three ropes together at the top to seal and braid the strands a little loosely, pinching the bottom ends to seal. Place diagonally on the baking sheet. Cover loosely with lightly oiled plastic wrap and leave in a warm, draft-free place until doubled in bulk. This step is very important because if the loaf has not been allowed to expand fully, it will burst in the oven.

Meanwhile, preheat the oven to 400°F/200°C.

Bake for 30–35 minutes, or until brown. To test, remove the loaf from the pan. Tap sharply on the top and bottom; it should sound hollow. Cool on a wire rack.

COCONUT ROLL
SALARA

Salara is a yeast cake made from white bread dough, spiraled with a filling of sweetened coconut. It is a very homely kind of cake, sold by many bakeries, and it used to be made by housewives in Guyana and some parts of the Caribbean when the weekly batch of bread was being baked. The filling is made from freshly grated coconut, which is usually colored a vibrant red to contrast sharply with the enclosing dough. I prefer a more subdued pink tint, but you can omit it altogether if you prefer, though the loaf will then lose some of its visual appeal. Frozen grated coconut is widely available in Asian shops and larger mainstream supermarkets, but if you cannot find it, fine shredded (dry, unsweetened) coconut makes a reasonable alternative.

Well wrapped, *salara* will keep for a day or two and may also be frozen for up to three months. I always find it to be at its best straight from the cooling rack!

DOUGH

1 lb 2 oz/3⅓ cups white bread flour

2 tsp active dry yeast

3 tbsp sugar

¾ tsp salt

2¼ oz/generous ½ stick butter, melted and
   cooled slightly

1 egg, beaten

about 8 fl oz/scant 1 cup milk, warmed

FILLING

12 oz finely grated fresh coconut, thawed to room
   temperature if frozen, or 10½ oz/
   3 cups fine shredded (dry, unsweetened)
   coconut, mixed with 6 tbsp warm water

3½ oz/½ cup granulated sugar

red food coloring (optional)

MAKES 2 LOAVES

Put the ingredients for the dough in a large bowl and mix to moisten the dry ingredients. Use a heavy-duty mixer fitted with a dough hook to knead thoroughly until smooth and supple. This is a medium-soft dough. Alternatively, turn out onto a floured surface or a non-stick silicone mat and knead until smooth and supple. Bring together in a ball and return to the bowl. Cover the bowl with plastic wrap or a damp dish towel, and set aside in a warm, draft-free place until doubled in size.

In the meantime, mix the filling ingredients together in a bowl and set aside.

Grease two baking sheets.

Punch down the dough and knead until smooth again. Divide into two portions and roll each piece out to a rectangle about 14 x 10 inches.

Spread half of the filling on each rectangle, leaving ½ inch free along the two long sides and 2½ inches free along the short sides. Starting at a short side, fold the free 2½ inches of the dough inwards so that it overlaps, and keep on folding it over loosely so that you get a flat

Swiss roll (jelly roll). Rolling it too tightly will make it burst as it bakes. Moisten the end slightly and pinch to seal. Make sure that the seam is under the roll, or the roll itself will open out while baking. Press the two ends to seal. Place on a baking sheet and cover loosely with lightly oiled plastic wrap. Shape the other loaf in the same way, then place on the second baking sheet.

If your oven cannot take both sheets at the same time, leave one in a slightly cooler place so that it takes longer to proof. Leave until almost doubled in size.

Preheat the oven to 400°F/200°C.

Bake for 30–35 minutes, or until golden brown. Cool on a rack and cut into thick slices to serve.

Some advice: bite through all the layers at the same time – and don't turn the slice around so that the cut sides face up and down, or you will lose a lot of filling.

WALNUT ROLL POTICA

Potica is a yeast cake that is very popular in Eastern European countries. It is often made at home, with fillings varying from nuts to poppy seed and Turkish delight. This walnut version is usually made in autumn, when the walnut harvest is brought in. I hardly need mention that the quality of the walnuts is extremely important, especially in recipes for which they form a major component. Even a slight rancid taste will spoil the cake, so choose your nuts wisely. I love eating my version of it for breakfast, accompanied by a cup of milky coffee.

DOUGH

7 oz/1⅓ cups white bread flour

1 tsp active dry yeast

3 tbsp granulated sugar

¼ tsp salt

2 oz/½ stick butter, melted and cooled

about 3¼ fl oz/scant ½ cup milk, warmed

1 egg yolk

FILLING

4½ oz/generous 1 cup walnuts

1¾ oz/¼ cup superfine sugar

¼ tsp ground cinnamon (optional)

4 tbsp warm milk

1 egg white

MAKES 1 LOAF

This dough is quite soft, but the texture will improve after the first rising and it will be easier to handle. The easiest thing to do is to use a mixer with a dough hook. Mix all the ingredients together in a large bowl and knead until the dough becomes smooth and leaves the sides of the bowl. If you are going to do this manually, it is a good idea to start with a wooden spoon and switch to your hands when the dough becomes more manageable. Knead for about 10 minutes, or until the dough becomes smooth. Shape the kneaded dough into a ball and return to the bowl. Cover with plastic wrap or a damp dish towel, and leave in a warm place until doubled in size.

For the filling, pulse the walnuts, superfine sugar and cinnamon in a food processor until fine. Pour in the warm milk and egg white with the motor still running and pulse until homogenous. Set aside until you need it.

Punch down the dough and knead for about 5 minutes, or until it is smooth and supple. Grease a baking sheet.

On a well-floured surface, roll the dough out to a rectangle about 14 x 10 inches. Spread the filling evenly on this, leaving about ¾ inch clear on all sides. Moisten this clear area with a little water, then roll up the dough from one short side. Do not roll it too tightly, or it will burst as it rises. However, try to make it more or less cylindrical in shape, because this is a soft dough and has a tendency to spread. Place the roll diagonally on the baking sheet. Cover with lightly oiled plastic wrap and leave in a warm place until almost doubled in size.

Preheat the oven to 350°F/180°C.

Bake for 35–40 minutes, or until light brown. Transfer carefully to a wire rack to cool.

Serve in slices. The *potica* will keep, well wrapped at cool room temperature, for about three days. It also freezes well. If you are not eating it freshly baked, you might like to heat each portion for a few seconds in the microwave. This helps bring out the flavors.

VARIATION

For a chocolate version, add 1 tbsp cocoa and 1 tbsp extra milk to the filling ingredients. Be warned, though, that this does tend to push the walnuts into the background.

COCONUT MILK BREAD

This white loaf is kept moist and subtly flavorful with coconut milk instead of water or dairy milk. The butter can be replaced with vegetable shortening or another similar product to make it suitable for people who are lactose intolerant.

1 lb 10 oz/5 cups white bread flour

2¼ tsp active dry yeast

3 tbsp sugar

1½ tsp salt

3½ oz/generous ¾ stick butter, melted and
  cooled slightly

12 fl oz/1½ cups lukewarm coconut milk

EQUIPMENT:

2 x 1 lb loaf pans, greased

MAKES 2 LOAVES

Put all the ingredients in a large bowl and mix to moisten the dry ingredients. Use a heavy-duty mixer fitted with a dough hook to knead thoroughly until smooth and supple. This is a medium-soft dough. Alternatively, turn out onto a floured surface or a non-stick silicone mat and knead until smooth and supple. Bring together in a ball and return to the bowl. Cover the bowl with plastic wrap or a damp dish towel, and set aside in a warm, draft-free place until doubled in size.

Punch down the dough and knead lightly until smooth again. Divide into 2 portions and roll or flatten each piece out to a rectangle that is as wide as your pan is long, with a thickness of about ½ inch.

Roll up the dough, starting at a short side, and pinch the seam to seal. Place it seam-side down in the pan and shape the other loaf in the same way. Cover both loaves loosely with lightly oiled plastic wrap and leave in a warm, draft-free place until almost doubled in size.

Preheat the oven to 400°F/200°C.

Bake in the oven for about 30 minutes. To test, remove the loaves from the pans. Tap sharply on the top and bottom; they should sound hollow. Cool on a wire rack.

The loaves will keep for a day or two if well wrapped and can also be frozen.

LARDY CAKE FOR TODAY'S BAKER

Lardy Cake is a traditional British yeast cake dating from around the second half of the nineteenth century. It has fallen from grace in recent years, regarded as a health hazard: it has been variously described as a "dietary nightmare," "artery clogger" and "lethal fattener." The writer Elizabeth David even suggested that every Lardy Cake should carry a health warning. I suspect that many of its detractors would not hesitate to pour cream sauce over a huge steak on a regular basis, yet they begrudge the bit of butter that goes into an excellent cake. Perhaps they simply don't like cakes. Of course, the name may be partly responsible for the image: the word "lard" conjures up decidedly more negative images than butter, and some recipes used it with abandon. My version uses just enough butter for flavor and texture, and I am even inclined to stick a label on it saying "Healthy Choice," especially if you treat it as a cake to be eaten and savored instead of a bread to fill the stomach.

Lardy Cakes were traditionally harvest cakes. In small rural communities where sugar, spices and dried fruit were luxuries, they were made for special occasions. When a pig was slaughtered, every part was carefully used. The offal would be eaten fresh, hams and bacon laid away, and fat rendered to lard. Sprigs of rosemary might be added to some of the lard, especially if it was to be used for spreading on bread. Most, however, was put away in its pure form for cooking purposes during the coming months, and a pig's bladder made an excellent receptacle. Due to the unaccustomed abundance, a Lardy Cake or something similar was almost certain to be made. It was made from plain bread dough but with sugar, spices and, perhaps, dried fruit. The Oxfordshire Lardy, for instance, does not contain dried fruit; the Wiltshire Lardy has only currants; and the Gloucestershire Lardy has both currants and raisins.

The dough is folded and rolled out much like puff pastry. Before being put into the oven, a cross-hatched pattern can be cut into the top. This touch is decorative but also practical because it was traditional to break the cake, not cut it. The cake turns out beautifully veined with the delicious filling, and crisp and sticky from sugar that has escaped and caramelized, adding to its rugged charm.

DOUGH

13 oz/2½ cups white bread flour

1½ tsp active dry yeast

1 tbsp sugar

¾ tsp salt

1¼ oz/scant ⅜ stick butter, melted and cooled

about 7 fl oz/¾ cup milk, warmed

FILLING

3½ oz/⅞ stick butter, softened

2¾ oz/⅓ cup soft dark brown sugar

½ tsp ground cinnamon

¼ tsp freshly grated nutmeg

1¾–2¾ oz/⅓–½ cup currants or raisins, or a
    mixture (optional)

beaten egg, to glaze

EQUIPMENT: *9-inch round springform pan*

Put all the ingredients in a large bowl and mix to moisten the dry ingredients. Use a heavy-duty mixer fitted with a dough hook to knead thoroughly until smooth and supple. Alternatively, turn out onto a floured surface or a non-stick silicone mat and knead until smooth and supple. Bring together in a ball and return to the bowl. Cover the bowl with plastic wrap or a damp dish towel, and set aside in a warm, draft-free place until doubled in size.

For the filling, beat all the ingredients together until creamy. Set aside.

Punch down the risen dough and re-knead it briefly. On a lightly floured surface, roll it out to a rectangle about 20 x 10 inches. Spread the filling evenly on two-thirds of the dough sheet, leaving one outer third empty and about 1½ inches clear on all other sides (1). If using, sprinkle the dried fruit over this and press down to embed. Fold the empty third over the middle third and the remaining third over this (2 and 3). Pinch all the edges well to seal the filling in (4). Cover with a sheet of plastic wrap and leave to rest for about 5 minutes to make it more manageable.

Give the dough parcel a quarter turn (90°) and roll it into a rectangle about 12 x 6 inches. Fold this into thirds again and leave to rest for 5 minutes. Repeat this procedure three more times, turning the dough by a quarter turn and rolling and folding. If you find that you are losing too much filling, omit the final turn.

I must warn you that this can be very messy work because the filling tends to ooze out in weak spots. Just patch it up as well as you can and continue to work. All these oozing bits will caramelize nicely as the cake bakes. Equally, though, you don't want to lose too much of the filling, as the lamination will be less effective. After the final rolling and folding, grease the pan and put the dough packet into it, then flatten with your hands so that it fits as snugly as you can get it. Cover the pan with plastic wrap and leave it in a warm place until almost doubled in size.

Meanwhile, preheat the oven to 350°F/180°C.

Brush the dough with beaten egg, then lightly score a cross-hatched pattern onto the surface (if wished). Don't cut too deeply, or too much filling will be able to escape. Place the baking pan on a baking sheet (to catch leaks) and bake for 25–30 minutes, or until brown. Remove from the oven, but leave in the pan for about 5 minutes. Then carefully release the clip and turn the cake upside down on a wire rack. Remove the bottom of the pan, which will probably still be attached to it, and leave to cool further.

Eat lukewarm or cold, cut into wedges or slices.

FESTIVE DUTCH SPICED LOAF
DUIVEKATER

In former days, Dutch bakers rewarded loyal customers with a rich fruit loaf at Easter and another at Christmas. In the province of North Holland, particularly in the Zaandam area, the Christmas gift often took the shape of a *Duivekater*, a delicately spiced and beautifully decorated shinbone-shaped bread. It was also customary in wealthier households to present domestic servants with a *Duivekater* at the end of the year, along with their wages and a new pair of clogs.

The bread is now a specialty item, made by a handful of bakers in North Holland, where a considerable amount of bickering goes on as to who sells the genuine article – and who doesn't. Quite a futile pastime, if you ask me, as the *Duivekater* goes back such a long way that it is impossible to define "genuine."

The name is derived from *Duive(l)* and *kater*, literally "Devil's tomcat." Its original use was as a midwinter offering to pagan gods and natural forces, to induce them to keep the year's crop safe from harm. The bread was probably buried in the appropriate field and may have replaced an animal or even human sacrifice, hence the evocative shape. Over the centuries, it became a more stylized affair with great visual appeal.

Jan Steen (1626–1679), best known for his generally merry depictions of Dutch life, incorporated *Duivekaters* into a few of his paintings, most notably in a large canvas of St Nicholas' Eve and a smaller one of the Leiden baker, Arend Oostwaert, and his wife. In the painting of St Nicholas' Eve, a large diamond-shaped loaf is propped up against a table in the foreground. The loaf displayed by the baker and his wife among the selection of their wares is an elongated one with the typical shinbone-shaped knobs at either end (see right). Both loaves are decorated with intricate cuts, which subsequently came to be known as "Jan Steen cuts" and were copied by the more artistically minded bakers.

You don't need to be a great artist to turn out a beautiful loaf, though. A few simple strokes with a sharp knife, scored onto the glazed surface of the bread, will produce an eye-catching result after baking. If you are hesitant about trying the freeform shape, the dough can also be baked in a suitable loaf pan and cuts can be made on the surface. In that case, make a slightly softer dough by adding a little extra milk. This is delicious eaten fresh, but connoisseurs advise leaving the well-wrapped loaf for a few days to allow the flavor to develop before slicing it thinly and serving with butter.

Right: *The Leiden Baker Arend Oostwaert and His Wife Catharina Keyserswaert*, Jan Havicksz Steen, 1658. The baker's wife holds up a large rusk, while pretzels and a variety of rolls and loaves frame the beautiful *Duivekater* propped against the wall.

1 lb 2 oz/3⅓ cups white bread flour

scant 2 tsp active dry yeast

3½ oz/½ cup granulated sugar

¾ tsp salt

zest of ½ lemon

¼ tsp freshly grated nutmeg

½ tsp ground cardamom

about 7 fl oz/generous ¾ cup milk, warmed

2¾ oz/⅔ stick butter, melted and cooled slightly

1 egg, lightly beaten

extra beaten egg for glazing

Put the flour, yeast, sugar, salt, lemon zest and spices in a large bowl. Add the milk, butter and beaten egg, and mix with a spoon or spatula until the dry ingredients are well moistened. If you are kneading by hand, turn out onto a floured surface or a silicone mat and knead until elastic. Alternatively, use a heavy-duty mixer fitted with a dough hook and knead until elastic. This dough needs to be a little stiffer than for a panned loaf because it must hold its shape during baking. Shape into a ball and place in a large bowl. Cover with plastic wrap or a dish towel wrung out in hot water, and leave in a warm, draft-free place until doubled in bulk.

Grease a baking sheet.

Punch down the risen dough and transfer to a lightly floured surface. Knead until once more smooth and elastic. Roll out to an elongated oval shape, about 10 inches long. Make a cut at the top, about 4 inches long. Make a similar cut at the bottom. Place on the baking sheet. Twirl the cut pieces between your fingers to lengthen them a little. Coil them inwards into a spiral. You will have two spirals at the top and two at the bottom. Cover loosely with lightly oiled plastic wrap and leave in a warm, draft-free place until almost doubled in bulk.

Preheat the oven to 350°F/180°C.

Brush well with beaten egg and use a very sharp knife to score a decorative pattern into the top. A series of shallow semi-circles goes well with the shape. Start in the middle, making cuts the shape of a parenthesis – ( ) – and then make four or five parallel cuts on either side.

Bake for 30–35 minutes. The loaf should be a rich golden brown with the scored pattern much lighter. To test, tap the loaf sharply on the top and bottom; it should sound hollow. Cool on a wire rack.

CRADLE SHAKING

Dutch fruit breads vary from region to region but share the characteristic of being well filled with fruit. The fruit is housed in a variety of doughs, ranging from whole-wheat to rye and white flour, with varying combinations of these. They are stocked all week and, in addition, many bakers make a white fruit loaf filled with almond paste for the weekend crowd.

In the region of Twente, in the east of Holland, there is a very special loaf called a *Krentenwegge*, which can be more than 40 inches long. Modern bakers sell it pre-packaged, a fixed number of slices or weight to a pack, and it is eaten as part of a bread-based meal or served with coffee. In Twente it is invariably served to the numerous guests who come to visit a newborn baby, replacing the "*beschuit met muisjes*" (rusks with sugar-coated aniseed that look like minute mice) that are common in the rest of the country. Its symbolic use as a *Kraamschudderswegge* stretches back over several centuries. *Kraamschudden* is an expression for visiting a newborn baby, and literally means "cradle shaking." An old and hospitable custom dictated that, in this area of often grinding poverty, neighbors clubbed together to buy the loaf that would be served to visitors. It cost them very little per time and they were secure in the knowledge that the favor would be returned whenever necessary. (This solidarity lies behind the expressions "Dutch treat" and "going Dutch," both of which have sadly now become derogatory.) The size of the loaf varied, of course, depending on how much money had been collected.

Nowadays huge pans may be used, but early loaves were baked on a sheet or on the oven floor, with the dough held in place by wooden planks and bricks, allowing the baker to regulate the size at will. The planks served as insulation and the loaf was baked slowly to succulent perfection and served slathered with butter. Those who were better off or happened to belong to an association of some kind might be presented with more than one loaf, and givers vied to outdo each other in terms of size and presentation. Old photographs show loaves being fetched ceremonially on long ladders decorated with garlands of flowers, underlining their great length, and a brass band was sometimes invited to accompany the bearers, especially if the recipient was someone of good social standing.

FRUIT LOAF

This well-filled fruit loaf stays moist for a few days and is a good breakfast bread. A forgotten piece in the corner of the bread bin, discovered after a few days, makes nice toast. If you double the recipe, the second loaf can be frozen for another time.

12 oz/2⅓ cups white bread flour

1¾ tsp active dry yeast

2 tsp sugar

¾ tsp salt

½ tsp ground cardamom or zest of ½ lemon

2 oz/½ stick butter, melted and cooled slightly

1 egg, beaten

about 5 fl oz/⅔ cup milk, warmed

3½ oz/⅔ cup currants

2 oz/⅓ cup sultanas (golden raisins)

2 tbsp dried cranberries

1 tbsp candied orange peel

EQUIPMENT:

1 lb loaf pan, greased

MAKES 1 LOAF

Place all the ingredients except the fruit in a large bowl. Mix to moisten the dry ingredients and knead thoroughly until smooth and supple. This may be done either by hand or using a mixer fitted with a dough hook, to make a soft dough. Bring the dough together in a ball, then cover the bowl with plastic wrap or a damp dish towel, and set aside in a warm, draft-free place until doubled in size.

Meanwhile, rinse the currants and sultanas in hot water. Drain the fruit, then pat dry with paper towels and leave in a warm place with the cranberries and orange peel until needed.

Punch down the risen dough and transfer to a lightly floured surface. Knead the fruit thoroughly into the dough. Roll or flatten the dough into a rectangle that is as wide as your pan is long, and about ½ inch thick. Roll up the dough, starting at a short side, and pinch the seam to seal.

Grease the pan. Place the dough roll seam-side down in the pan and remove any loose fruit from the surface, or it will burn while baking. Cover the loaf loosely with lightly oiled plastic wrap and leave in a warm, draft-free place until almost doubled in size.

Preheat the oven to 400°F/200°C.

Bake in the oven for about 30 minutes. To test, remove the loaf from the pan. Tap sharply on the top and bottom; it should sound hollow. Cool on a wire rack.

RYE FRUIT LOAF

Rye flour makes moist and satisfying fruit loaves, and this kind of bread is often made in the eastern Netherlands, in the area bordering on Germany. A similar mixture is baked into squat, round loaves for the annual horse market held in Zuidlaren on the third Tuesday in October. This is one of the oldest markets of its type in Europe and has been held since the thirteenth century. Few visitors leave without purchasing one or more of the loaves after they have tasted the lavishly buttered sample slices. This recipe is for freeform loaves that are easy to shape. They will keep well for a few days.

13 oz/2½ cups white bread flour

9 oz/1½ cups fine rye flour

2¾ tsp active dry yeast

1½ tbsp sugar

1 tsp salt

2 oz/½ stick butter, melted and cooled

1 egg, lightly beaten

11 fl oz/generous 1¼ cups milk, warmed

5½ oz/1 cup currants

5½ oz/generous ¾ cup sultanas (golden raisins)

2¾ oz/½ cup walnuts, coarsely chopped

2 tbsp candied orange peel

MAKES 2 SMALL LOAVES

Place all the ingredients except the fruit and nuts in a large bowl. Mix to moisten the dry ingredients and knead thoroughly until smooth and supple. This may be done either by hand or using a mixer fitted with a dough hook. Rye flour is very slippery and will squelch between your fingers, but persevere: it improves with kneading. Bring the dough together in a ball and return to the bowl. Cover with plastic wrap or a damp dish towel, and set aside in a warm, draft-free place until doubled in size.

Meanwhile, rinse the currants and sultanas in hot water. Drain the fruit, then pat dry with paper towels and leave in a warm place with the walnuts and orange peel until needed.

Punch down the risen dough and transfer to a lightly floured surface. Knead the fruit and nuts thoroughly into the dough. Divide the dough in half and roll or flatten each piece into a rectangle about 9½ x 8 inches and about ½ inch thick. Roll up the dough, starting at a short side, and pinch the seam to seal.

Grease a baking sheet. Place the loaves side by side, seam-side down on the sheet, and remove any loose fruit from the surface or it will burn while baking. Cover loosely with lightly oiled plastic wrap and leave in a warm, draft-free place until almost doubled in size.

Preheat the oven to 400°F/200°C.

Make 6 or 7 parallel diagonal slashes in the top of each loaf and bake for about 30 minutes. To test, remove the loaves from the pan. Tap sharply on the top and bottom; they should sound hollow. Cool on a wire rack.

The loaves will keep for a few days if well wrapped and can also be frozen as soon as they have cooled.

SESAME-COATED RINGS
SİMİT

The *simit* is one of the most ubiquitous street foods in Turkey, and whatever the time of day, people love to nibble or munch on the cheap but delicious sesame-coated rings. There is a vendor at practically every street corner, and boys on bicycles fitted with glass cases in front turn up regularly at open-air markets to ply their trade. Vendors collect their wares from specialist bakeries and return several times a day to replenish their stock.

There are two basic types: the chewy one that is similar to the bagel, and the softer and richer milk *simit*. The former is poached in a *pekmez* (pomegranate molasses) solution before being baked, and this gives it a dark and shiny crust and firm texture. The recipe below is for milk *simit*. Both kinds are generously coated with sesame seeds, and *mahleb* is often added to the dough for special occasions, giving the streets a festive aroma. *Mahleb* is a greatly prized flavoring in Turkey and Greece and comes from the tiny seeds of an indigenous black cherry (*Prunus mahaleb*). Its perfume has often been compared with almonds, but that sells it too short. It is far more complex, with hints of musk, citrus, vanilla and other heady fragrances – in short, a spice box in a seed. It is sold as powder or in kernel form and is not easy to obtain outside the region. If you get the opportunity, do try it, and if you have the choice, go for the kernels, which you can pound to a powder yourself; the ready-ground powder loses its freshness more quickly. A scant ½ tsp will give the dough below a hauntingly delicious flavor.

Note that this recipe creates mere babies compared with the ones you'll find on the streets. But commercial bakers have cavernous ovens and long peels while most of us have to make do with domestic ovens and standard-sized baking sheets. Eat on the day of baking or freeze as soon as they have cooled.

9 oz/1⅔ cups white bread flour

½ tsp salt

1 tsp active dry yeast

1 tbsp sugar

1 egg, beaten

1¼ oz/generous ¼ stick butter, melted

about 3¼ fl oz/scant ½ cup milk

1 egg, beaten, for dipping

4–6 tbsp sesame seeds

½ tsp *mahleb* (optional)

MAKES 6 RINGS

Combine the flour, salt, yeast and sugar in a large bowl. Add the beaten egg, butter and milk and mix with a spatula to moisten the dry ingredients. Use a heavy-duty mixer fitted with a dough hook to knead thoroughly until smooth and supple. Alternatively, turn out onto a floured surface or a non-stick silicone mat and knead until smooth and supple. Bring together in a ball and return to the bowl. Cover the bowl with plastic wrap or a damp dish towel and set aside in a warm, draft-free place until doubled in size.

Punch down the dough and knead briefly until once again elastic. Divide into 6 pieces. Shape each piece into a rope about 16 inches long; the longer the rope, the more elegant the finished *simit*. Shape each piece into a ring, with an overlap of about 1¼ inches. Pass your hand through the ring and roll the two ends, which are now overlapping, back and forth under your fingers to join them and seal the ring neatly and securely. Grease a baking sheet, then place each ring on the sheet.

Put the beaten egg into one dish and the sesame seeds into a second. Take one ring and dip it thoroughly into the egg. Then turn it around several times in the sesame seeds to coat well on both sides. Replace on the baking sheet. Space the rings neatly on the sheet. Cover loosely with plastic wrap and leave in a warm, draft-free place until puffy but not quite doubled in bulk.

Meanwhile, preheat the oven to 425°F/225°C.

Bake the rings for 12–15 minutes, or until golden brown. Cool on a wire rack.

Above: Street stall in Konya (Turkey) selling *simit* and other rolls.

TENNIS ROLLS

It's a mystery how these sweetish lemon-flavored Guyanese favorites came by their name, as they have absolutely no connection with the game. Professional bakers add minute quantities of lemon oil to the dough, but this is not widely available to home bakers. If you do find it, be very careful how you handle it, as it is very aggressive. A kind baker once offered me a few spoonfuls from her stock, but as soon as she poured it into a Styrofoam container, the container dissolved in front of our eyes. Lemon extract, or the freshly grated zest of an organic lemon, make excellent substitutes and the latter option is what I normally use.

This dough is very soft and a bit sticky and is best kneaded in an electric mixer fitted with a dough hook. If you are forced to knead it by hand, do so in the bowl to avoid having to add flour when it sticks to the work surface. The good news, however, is that the texture improves considerably after the first rising so that the rolls can be shaped without problem. Fresh from the oven, they have a soft brioche-like texture, but the flavor mellows properly by the next day. Eat them split and buttered, with optional cheese. They can also be wrapped and frozen as soon as they are cool.

1 lb 4 oz/3⅔ cups white bread flour

2 tsp active dry yeast

2¾ oz/generous ⅓ cup granulated sugar

1 tsp salt

¼ tsp lemon oil, or 1½ tsp lemon extract,
  or zest of 1 lemon, preferably organic

2¾ oz/scant ¾ stick butter, melted and cooled
  slightly

1 egg + 1 yolk, beaten

about 9 fl oz/1 cup milk, warmed

MAKES 12 ROLLS

Put the flour, yeast, sugar and salt in a large bowl. If using fresh lemon zest, grate it over the flour. Add the remaining ingredients, including the lemon oil or extract (if using), then mix to moisten the dry ingredients. Knead thoroughly. This may be done either by hand, in the bowl, or using a mixer with a dough hook. This is a very soft dough that stays slightly sticky to the touch, so the mixer is the better option. Scrape the dough together in a ball. Cover the bowl with plastic wrap or a damp dish towel and set aside in a warm, draft-free place until doubled in size.

Punch down the risen dough and transfer to a silicone mat or a very lightly floured surface. Divide the dough into 12 equal pieces and shape each piece into a neat ball. Arrange them on a greased baking sheet. Cover loosely with lightly oiled plastic wrap and leave in a warm, draft-free place until almost doubled in size.

Meanwhile, preheat the oven to 400°F/200°C.

Bake for 12–15 minutes, or until light brown. Remove from the baking sheet and transfer to a wire rack to cool.

SWEET CURD CHEESE ROUNDS
VATROUSHKI

Vatroushki are sweet curd cheese buns of Russian origin, usually made with a yeast dough. They are similar to the Central European *Kolatshen* in shape, but *vatroushki* are commonly made with cheese, whereas most *Kolatshen* are filled with jam or fruit purées. This recipe uses quark and makes light, guilt-free buns, but if you cannot find it in the shops, use another smooth curd cheese. Cream cheese can also be used for a richer if slightly less authentic article. They are best eaten fresh but may also be frozen.

DOUGH

12 oz/2⅓ cups white bread flour

1½ tsp active dry yeast

2 tsp sugar

½ tsp salt

2 oz/½ stick butter, melted and cooled slightly

1 egg, beaten

5 oz/⅔ cup milk, lukewarm

FILLING

9 oz/1 cup quark or other smooth curd cheese

3½ oz/½ cup granulated sugar

2 tbsp flour

1 egg, well beaten

1 tsp vanilla extract or a pinch of lemon zest (optional)

1 egg, beaten, for glazing (optional)

MAKES 8 ROUNDS

Place all the ingredients for the dough in a large bowl and mix to moisten the dry ingredients. Use a heavy-duty mixer fitted with a dough hook to knead thoroughly until smooth and supple. Alternatively, turn out onto a floured surface or a non-stick silicone mat and knead until smooth and supple. Bring together in a ball and return to the bowl. Cover the bowl with plastic wrap or a damp dish towel and set aside in a warm, draft-free place until doubled in size.

Meanwhile, mix all the filling ingredients together until well combined. Chill until needed.

Punch down the dough and re-knead lightly. Divide the dough into 8 pieces. Roll each piece into a ball between your palms. Grease a baking sheet, and place each ball on it, then flatten to a diameter of about 3½ inches and dust with flour. Press the bottom of a large tumbler or jam jar into the center of the dough to make as deep an indentation as possible. You will need to do this a few times in order to make a fairly large well. The outer edge of the dough should not be more than ¾ inch wide. Leave to rest for about 15 minutes. This step is very important. If the center has puffed up a lot, press it down gently again.

Spoon in the filling, trying not to let any drip over the sides. Leave for 10–15 minutes. Meanwhile, preheat the oven to 350°F/180°C.

If desired, carefully brush the dough edges with beaten egg. This gives an attractive sheen but is not absolutely necessary.

Bake for about 20 minutes. Transfer to a wire rack to cool.

COILED SWEET ROLLS
ENSAIMADAS MALLORQUINAS

Saim is the Majorcan word for lard, so you could say that these coiled yeast cakes are Majorcan lardy cakes. I prefer to substitute butter for a variety of reasons, including flavor and allergic reactions, but if you are a fan of lard you could always do it the authentic way. *Ensaimadas* are sometimes made as one large cake, and some bakers sell them beautifully packaged in special boxes. The rolls are more common and are an ideal breakfast item. They are delicious when freshly baked but will also keep for a day or two. If you want to freeze a few, wrap them individually in plastic wrap before putting them into a storage container. They can be thawed in the microwave. In fact, even if you are not using them from frozen, reheating them for a few seconds in the microwave helps to loosen the layers and brings out the buttery flavor.

10½ oz/2 cups all-purpose flour

1 tsp active dry yeast

1¾ oz/¼ cup granulated sugar

scant ½ tsp salt

1 oz/¼ stick butter, melted

2 eggs, lightly beaten

about 5 tbsp milk, lukewarm

2 oz/½ stick butter, softened, or 4 tbsp lard

confectioner's sugar, for dusting

MAKES 6 ROLLS

Put the flour, yeast, sugar and salt in a large bowl. Add the melted butter, eggs and milk. Mix well with a spatula to moisten the dry ingredients. Use a heavy-duty mixer fitted with a dough hook to knead thoroughly until smooth and supple. Alternatively, turn out onto a floured surface or a non-stick silicone mat and knead until smooth and supple. Bring together in a ball and return to the bowl. Cover with plastic wrap or a damp dish towel and set aside in a warm, draft-free place until doubled in size.

Punch down the dough and knead again for about 3 minutes. Divide the dough into 6 portions and cover them loosely with plastic wrap. Lightly flour your work surface; a silicone mat works very well here. Take one portion and roll it out to a shape like the sole of a shoe or an elongated oval measuring roughly 12 x 4 inches.

Brush the dough with the softened butter, taking care not to go over the edges. From a long side, roll the dough up to form a cylinder and pinch all along the seam to seal. Roll this cylinder back and forth across your work surface, under your outstretched fingers, to neaten it and lengthen it to about 14 inches. Coil it into a loose spiral and tuck the end underneath. Grease a baking sheet, then put the spiral on it. Shape the other 5 pieces of dough.

Cover with lightly oiled plastic wrap and leave in a warm place until almost doubled in size. Meanwhile, preheat the oven to 400°F/200°C.

Bake the rolls for about 10 minutes. Cool on a wire rack and dust with confectioner's sugar.

FILIPINO SWEET AND CHEESY COILS
ENSEYMADAS

This is an adaptation of a Filipino heirloom recipe. It was given to me by my friend Pia from Manila, who is a generous source of goodies and recipes. This is her grandmother's recipe, and as she gave it to me she conjured up a picture of Spanish galleons coming into port in full sail with all kinds of European delicacies in their holds, including the red-waxed heads of well-aged Edam cheese, called *queso de bola* (ball cheese) locally. It was easy to imagine throngs of Filipinos on the wharves, eagerly awaiting the cheese so that they could dash off home and whip up a batch of these delicious buns.

The origin is undoubtedly Spanish: a descendant of the Majorcan *ensaimadas*. The Majorcan version is made from thinly stretched dough, generously coated with lard (the eponymous *saim*) and then coiled. This is the version the Filipinos originally learned to make, but when proper refrigeration became available the elite classes started making their *enseymadas* with butter instead of lard and the dough became richer and richer. However, there are still some pockets of traditional lard-based *enseymadas* remaining in places such as Bulacan. The combination of salty and sweet is much loved in the Philippines, and cheese is used in a number of sweet dishes. And as if the buns were not already rich and calorific, they are usually served with more butter, sugar and cheese on top. Although the classic *enseymada* always has cheese, I have also tasted a delicious variant filled with mashed *ube* (purple yam), another popular Filipino staple.

Like the Majorcan version, they are best eaten fresh but will also freeze well. Freeze and reheat in the same way.

13 oz/2½ cups all-purpose flour

2¾ oz/generous ⅓ cup granulated sugar

scant 1¾ tsp active dry yeast

4 fl oz/½ cup milk, warmed

3½ fl oz/scant ½ cup water, warmed

3 egg yolks

¼ tsp salt

3½ oz/⅞ stick butter, softened

1¾ oz/scant ½ stick butter, melted

4½ oz well-aged Edam or Gouda cheese, finely
   grated

OPTIONAL INGREDIENTS

melted butter

grated cheese

superfine sugar

EQUIPMENT:

8 x 4-inch pans, greased *

MAKES 8 BUNS

This is a very rich dough, so it's best to make a sponge first to help the yeast on its way before adding the butter and yolks.

Put 2¾ oz/½ cup flour together with the sugar and yeast in a large bowl. Stir the milk and water into the ingredients in the bowl. Cover the bowl with plastic wrap or a damp dish towel and leave in a warm, draft-free place until bubbles appear on the surface.

Now whisk in the egg yolks. Add the salt and remaining flour a little at a time and beat well with a wooden spoon or spatula. When all of the flour has been absorbed, add the softened butter. The dough will be very soft. An electric mixer fitted with a dough hook makes short work of it. Alternatively, you can continue beating it with a wooden spoon for about 5 minutes if you don't fancy getting your hands messy, or use one hand to work it really well in the bowl. When it's smooth, scrape all the dough together into the center of the bowl, then cover with plastic wrap and leave in a warm, draft-free place until doubled in size.

Punch down the dough and beat it for a minute or so, then turn it out onto a well-floured surface. Divide into 8 pieces and cover them loosely with plastic wrap. Roll each piece of dough out to a shape like the sole of a shoe or an elongated oval about 9½ in x 5½ inches, dusting with flour as necessary. A silicone mat is a blessing here.

Brush each piece of dough with melted butter and sprinkle with one-eighth of the grated cheese (½ oz). From a long side, roll the dough up to form a cylinder and pinch all along the seam to seal. Shape into a coil and place in the pan, seam-side down. If using individual pans, arrange them on a baking sheet and cover with lightly greased plastic wrap. Leave in a warm, draft-free place until almost doubled in bulk.

Meanwhile, preheat the oven to 400°F/200°C.

Bake for 15–20 minutes, or until golden brown. Cool on a wire rack.

If you like, brush with more melted butter and sprinkle with grated cheese and superfine sugar before serving.

* I use small individual pans, which are 1¼ inches high with a diameter of 4 inches. You could use muffin or brioche pans, but don't overfill them. The shaped buns should occupy half of the space in the pans, so portion your dough accordingly. This amount will fit in a 12-cavity muffin pan with fairly large cavities – the kind called a "Texas muffin pan." Divide the dough correspondingly and bake for 12–15 minutes. If you want to try these *enseymadas* but lack a suitable pan, bake the original 8 buns on a sheet lined with parchment paper and shorten the baking time to 10–15 minutes so that they do not dry out.

CHEESY RINGS
PAN DE QUESO

I discovered these rings that look like elegant bagels in a Colombian bakery in New Jersey, and since then have never been able to drive by without stopping. They make a great snack and are best eaten fresh, but can also be frozen for later.

9 oz/1⅔ cups all-purpose flour

¼ tsp salt

¾ tsp active dry yeast

2 tbsp granulated sugar

1 egg, beaten (reserve 1 tbsp)

1 oz/¼ stick butter, melted

about 3½ fl oz/scant ½ cup milk

2¾ oz mature (sharp) dry cheese (such as Parmesan, Edam or Grana Padano), very finely grated

MAKES 12 RINGS

Combine the flour, salt, yeast and sugar in a large bowl. Add the beaten egg, butter and milk, then mix with a spatula to moisten the dry ingredients. Use a heavy-duty mixer fitted with a dough hook to knead thoroughly until smooth and supple. Alternatively, turn out onto a floured surface or a non-stick silicone mat and knead until smooth and supple. Bring together in a ball and return to the bowl. Cover the bowl with plastic wrap or a damp dish towel and set aside in a warm, draft-free place until doubled in size.

Punch down the dough and knead in the grated cheese. Divide into 12 pieces. Shape each piece into a rope about 10–12 inches long, then shape into a ring with an overlap of about 1¼ inches. Pass your hand through the ring and roll the overlapping part with your fingers to seal it neatly and securely. Place the rings on 2 greased baking sheets, spacing them well apart. Cover loosely with plastic wrap and leave in a warm, draft-free place for about 20 minutes.

Meanwhile, preheat the oven to 400°F/200°C.

Bake for 8–12 minutes, or until golden brown. Cool on a wire rack.

Eat on the day of baking, or freeze as soon as they are cool.

CHOCOLATE AND HAZELNUT BUNS

These chunky and chocolaty buns make a pleasant change from the perennial cinnamon buns and are delicious with coffee or as a breakfast roll. They are not too sweet, which allows the chocolate flavor to come to the front.

DOUGH

12 oz/2⅓ cups white bread flour

1½ tsp active dry yeast

2 tsp sugar

½ tsp salt

2 oz/½ stick butter, melted and cooled

1 egg, beaten

about 5 fl oz/⅔ cup milk, lukewarm

FILLING

3½ oz/⅔ cup hazelnuts

2¾ oz/generous ⅓ cup granulated sugar

1 oz/scant ¼ cup cocoa

1¾ oz/½ stick butter, very well softened

EQUIPMENT:

8-inch square pan

MAKES 9 BUNS

Place all the ingredients for the dough in a large bowl and mix to moisten the dry ingredients. Use a heavy-duty mixer fitted with a dough hook to knead thoroughly until smooth and supple. Alternatively, turn out onto a floured surface or a non-stick silicone mat and knead until smooth and supple. Bring together in a ball and return to the bowl. Cover the bowl with plastic wrap or a damp dish towel and set aside in a warm, draft-free place until doubled in size.

For the filling, pulse all the ingredients except the butter in a food processor until the nuts are very finely chopped. Set aside until needed.

Punch down the dough and knead briefly until it is smooth. On a lightly floured surface, roll it out to a rectangle about 16 x 12 inches. Use a pastry brush or your fingers to spread the butter over the dough, leaving about ¾ inch clear on all sides. Sprinkle the filling evenly over this. It is a generous amount, but the butter will eventually absorb it. Roll up from one long end. Trim the roll so that it measures 14 inches and discard the end pieces. Cut the resulting log at intervals of 1½ inches, so that you end up with 9 pieces.

Grease and line a 8-inch square baking pan, then arrange the dough pieces in three rows of three. Cover loosely with plastic wrap and leave it in a warm place until almost doubled in size. The buns will now be pressing cozily against each other; this slight over-crowding gives nice soft sides.

Meanwhile, preheat the oven to 350°F/180°C.

Bake in the oven for 25 minutes, or until golden brown. Leave in the pan for about 5 minutes before turning out in its entirety onto a wire rack. Break the buns off as needed. That way, the sides stay softer for longer.

SWEET BROWN SUGAR PRETZELS OR COILS
HAAGSE/ZEEUWSE BOLUSSEN

These Dutch buns have a delicious toffee flavor and come in two basic shapes. Coiled, they are called *Zeeuwse Bolussen* (*Bolussen* from Zeeland, a province in the south of Holland); the *pretzel*, or figure-of-eight, version is called *Haagse Bolussen* (*Bolussen* from The Hague). A few bakers enrich the dough with dried fruit, but I find that less is more in this case, the fruit just adds sweetness without delivering flavor.

The word "*bolus*" is not Dutch in origin and was borrowed with the buns. There are two probable explanations for its appearance in the Dutch vocabulary and culinary repertoire. A similar roll may have been issued as rations to the Spanish soldiers stationed in the Low Countries during the Eighty Years War (1566–1648) and the word bears a striking similarity to the Spanish word for bun or bread roll: *bollo*. Another possible means of entry is also indirectly Spanish. Many Sephardic Jews sought refuge in Amsterdam when the pressure of the Inquisition became too much to bear, and they are thought to have introduced the coiled version of the roll. A variant made with preserved ginger is still the specialty of the few remaining kosher-style bakeries in Amsterdam.

When the rolls are removed from the oven, the sugar coating still has a bite to it. If you put the rolls in a plastic bag for a few hours, the sugar will soften to a very desirable state of stickiness.

DOUGH
1 lb 2 oz/3⅓ cups white bread flour
2½ tsp active dry yeast
2 tbsp granulated sugar
1 tsp salt
4½ oz/generous 1 stick butter, melted
1 egg, lightly beaten
about 7 fl oz/¾ cup milk, lukewarm

SUGAR COATING
7 oz/1 cup, solidly packed soft light or dark
    brown sugar
2 tsp ground cinnamon

MAKES 15 ROLLS

Put the flour, yeast, sugar and salt in a large bowl. Add the melted butter, egg and milk, and mix well with a spatula to moisten the dry ingredients. Use a heavy-duty mixer fitted with a dough hook to knead thoroughly until smooth and supple. Alternatively, turn out onto a floured surface or a non-stick silicone mat and knead until smooth and supple. Bring together in a ball and return to the bowl. Cover the bowl with plastic wrap or a damp dish towel and set aside in a warm, draft-free place until doubled in size.

Mix the sugar with the cinnamon and scatter it onto a large extra baking sheet or a clean, washable tray. Set aside until needed.

Punch down the dough and knead for a few minutes until it is smooth again. Divide the dough into 15 equal portions and cover them loosely with plastic wrap. Lightly flour your work surface; a silicone mat works very well here. Take one portion of dough and roll it out to make a rope about 13½ inches long. Put it in the pan or tray with the sugar and turn a few times to coat. Leave it to rest there as you make 14 more ropes in the same way. Turn the ropes in the tray from time to time and leave them there to "sweat" in the sugar.

When you have made all of the ropes, you can start shaping them. For coils, coil each rope into a loose spiral and tuck the end underneath. Place on a baking sheet lined with parchment paper. For pretzels, fold the rope as if you were making a capital letter B and tuck the two end pieces under the straight left side so that they overlap each other slightly to make a small triangle where the middle bar of the B should be.

Scatter any remaining sugar over the rolls. Cover loosely with plastic wrap and leave in a warm, draft-free place until almost doubled in size.

Meanwhile, preheat the oven to 400°F/200°C.

Bake for 12–15 minutes, or until fully cooked through; don't let them dry out unnecessarily.

Remove immediately from the parchment paper and cool on a wire rack.

Eat fresh, or allow the sugar to soften a little as described above. If you want to freeze a few, wrap them individually in plastic wrap before putting them into a freezer bag or storage container. They can be thawed in the microwave.

CHESTNUT BUNS

Canned chestnut purée is an excellent stock item for a baker's pantry. You can use it European-style, pressed through a ricer or coarse shaker, as a garnish for ice cream and cakes; or, as in this Chinese-inspired recipe, as a sweet filling for buns.

DOUGH

9 oz/1⅔ cups white bread flour

¾ tsp active dry yeast

2 tbsp granulated sugar

½ tsp salt

about 6 fl oz/¾ cup milk, warmed

1 oz/¼ stick butter, melted and cooled slightly

FILLING

7 oz unsweetened chestnut purée
  (about ½ can)*

2¼ oz/⅓ cup superfine sugar

about 1 tbsp milk

beaten egg, for glazing

MAKES 8 BUNS

For the dough, put the flour, yeast, sugar and salt into a large bowl. Add the warm milk and butter and mix well with a spatula to moisten the dry ingredients. Use a heavy-duty mixer fitted with a dough hook to knead thoroughly until smooth and supple. Alternatively, turn out onto a floured surface or a non-stick silicone mat and knead until smooth and supple. Bring together in a ball and return to the bowl. Cover the bowl with plastic wrap or a damp dish towel and set aside in a warm, draft-free place until doubled in size.

For the filling, put the chestnut purée and superfine sugar in a bowl. Add the milk and mix well to a smooth, malleable paste. Add a little more milk if necessary. Divide into 8 portions, then cover and set aside.

Punch down the dough and knead again briefly. Divide into 8 pieces. Take one piece of dough and flatten it with your hands to a rough circle with a diameter of about 4 inches. Alternatively, use a rolling pin, but hands are easier and quicker.

Put a portion of chestnut purée in the center and coax the dough around the filling to encase it. Pinch the edges to seal well. Arrange on a greased baking sheet. Cover loosely with oiled plastic wrap and leave until almost doubled again.

Meanwhile, preheat the oven to 400°F/200°C.

Brush the dough with beaten egg and bake for 15–20 minutes. Cool on wire racks.

* If you can only get sweetened chestnut purée, use 9½ oz – the combined weight of the sugar and the unsweetened purée.

FRUIT BUNS

The dough for Fruit Loaf (see p. 90) can also be baked as buns that can be eaten fresh with butter and cheese or frozen for later. Make up the dough as described in the recipe for Fruit Loaf and follow the shaping and baking instructions given below.

MAKES 12 BUNS

Divide the dough into 12 equal pieces. Dust the pieces and your hands with flour and shape each piece into a ball, trying to get the fruit as well embedded as you can and covered with a layer of dough. Loose fruit on the surface will burn. Space well apart on a greased baking sheet and flatten each roll very slightly with the palm of your hand. Cover loosely with lightly oiled plastic wrap and leave in a warm, draft-free place until almost doubled in size.

Meanwhile, preheat the oven to 400°F/200°C.

Bake the buns for 15–20 minutes, or until browned but not dry. Remove from the baking sheet and transfer to a wire rack to cool.

CAKES &
CAKE-MAKING

CAKES AND CAKE-MAKING

A good cake seldom fails to delight, and it is truly extraordinary how many variations can be made from the same basic ingredients. Changing the proportions of ingredients will, of course, have an effect on the finished article, but it will affect the taste most of all. The mixing method is one of the most important factors to determine texture. Creaming, whisking, beating and rubbing in all produce different results. It is not difficult to produce an excellent cake, as long as you follow the instructions given in the recipe and use the right techniques. The following tips will help you get the best results from the recipes.

OVEN TEMPERATURES

The oven should always be preheated to the required temperature, ready to accommodate the batter as soon as it has been put together. Most cake batters are best baked at moderate temperatures, and this applies particularly to those leavened with baking powder. A lower temperature allows the batter to expand gradually and more evenly. By contrast, a blast of heat has the effect of making the outer part of the cake set very rapidly, leaving the inner part struggling to catch up. This may result in doming (where the sides of a cake remain far lower than the middle) as well as cracks. Cakes that rely on whisked eggs to lighten them and to determine their structure can be baked at higher temperatures, since most of the expansion has already taken place before the cake is put into the oven.

GREASING AND FLOURING

Even non-stick pans benefit from greasing and flouring. This allows a finished cake to slip neatly and gently onto a cooling rack, without leaving any fragments stuck to awkward parts of the pan. I use butter for greasing and keep little leftover bits in the refrigerator for this purpose. A small cube of cold butter is easily rubbed back and forth along the inside of a pan to coat it. Always pay special attention to the creases.
To flour a pan, sprinkle about 1 tbsp flour into it and shake the pan around so that the flour sticks to the butter and coats it. Hold the pan over the sink and turn it onto its side. Make a circular movement with the pan, while tapping lightly to encourage the flour to move where you want it to. Once the pan is well coated, turn it upside down and tap the base sharply a few times, allowing any excess flour to fall into the sink.

LINING PANS

Sometimes greasing and flouring are not enough. Cakes with a high percentage of chocolate, for instance, or those made with molasses can prove to be just that little bit stickier and may cling too much to the sides of the pan. Pieces of fruit in a cake will have the same tendency and once they are firmly stuck, they will remain there and the cake may break when you try to remove it. Lining the pan with parchment paper is the best solution in these cases. Round pans are very easy to line. Simply rest the pan on a piece of parchment paper and draw around the base with a pencil. Cut slightly inside this line, especially for springform pans, and you will have a base-liner that fits perfectly. If the side also needs to be lined, you just need to cut a separate strip of the right length (the pan circumference) and height.

A base-liner for a rectangular pan is cut in the same way. To fully line a rectangular pan, place the pan on the baking paper and cut it so that it will be as wide as the bottom width of the pan + the height of two sides, and as long as the bottom length + the height of two sides. In other words, if the bottom of the pan is 8 x 4 inches, and the sides are 3 inches high, you will need to cut a sheet of paper 14 x 10 inches. Rest the pan in the center of the sheet and cut from each point of the paper to each point of the pan. This works better than cutting away the unused pieces, as there will be less chance of leakage once the paper is in the pan. If the sides of the pan slope, remember to measure the slope, which will be slightly more than the straight height from base to top.

SIFTING

Even if your flour is nice and loose, sift it. Sifting the specified ingredients together mixes them and also introduces some air, making it easier to fold the flour into the rest of the mixture.

SOFTENING BUTTER

Butter should be soft if it is to be creamed with sugar. Leaving the butter at room temperature for a few hours usually works, especially if you live in a warm climate. A microwave is my favorite shortcut. Cut the cold butter into cubes and put them on a plate. Put the plate in the microwave and give it short bursts of power a few times, rather than a longer stretch in one go. I never give it more than 20 seconds at a time. Be very careful and check it after each burst, prodding a cube with your finger to see if it is soft enough. The center of the cubes may melt before the outside disintegrates, and too much heat will make the butter explode in the microwave. Remember that you need to soften the butter, not melt it.

CREAMING BUTTER AND SUGAR

"Light and fluffy" and "lightened in color" are indications of how the mixture should look compared to its original state. When the butter and sugar are creamed properly, they form a homogenous mixture and the texture lightens along with the color, increasing the volume slightly.

EGGS

Always have your eggs at room temperature for baking. Cold eggs will make the creamed mixture curdle, and this will affect the texture of the cake. If you have to use eggs straight from the refrigerator, put them in a large bowl about 10 minutes beforehand and fill it with hot (not boiling) water to allow the temperature of the eggs to rise. The recipes almost always call for the eggs to be lightly beaten before adding them to the other ingredients. This loosens them up nicely and allows them to be easily incorporated.

WHISKING EGGS

Some of the recipes require eggs and sugar to be whisked until the mixture falls off the whisk in a thick ribbon rather than a thin stream. This means that the volume will have increased considerably, the color will have become paler and the mixture will be thick enough to fall off the whisk in a wider band (the ribbon) and not simply run off the whisk as a fluid. Always switch off electric mixers before raising the whisk!

FOLDING IN FLOUR

Flour should be gently folded into the rest of the mixture. If you do this too heavy-handedly, you will toughen the structure unnecessarily. A balloon or other large whisk is the best tool for this job. However, do not whisk. Use the whisk as you would a spoon and make gentle circular movements or figures of eight. Stop as soon as you reach the desired consistency.

LEVELING THE BATTER IN THE PAN

Most cake batters need to be leveled, unless they happen to be so fluid that they will flow into all the corners of their own accord. A few strokes with the straight side of a plastic scraper will level batter in a pan very effectively.

CHECKING FOR DONENESS

Baking times are always approximate, as ovens vary. It is always a good idea to start checking for doneness a few minutes before the time stated in the recipe. Once you have done that a few times, you will be able to make any necessary allowances for future baking sessions. Use wooden skewers or an uncoated metal one. Non-stick skewers are not reliable for this purpose: if they come out clean, it might mean that the batter has simply failed to stick because the non-stick skewer is living up to its name.

INVERTING AND RE-INVERTING

Not all cakes need necessarily be re-inverted so that the top faces upwards again. The bottom is an ideal flat surface for glazing, particularly for square cakes. In

Europe, loaf cakes and many sponge-type cakes are seldom re-inverted; they are usually served upside down for a neater presentation. It is a personal choice.

HOW TO INVERT A CAKE

If you turn a cake pan upside down to invert the cake onto a cooling rack, it will start to fall as soon as you tilt the pan. Sturdy cakes may hold their own, but light-textured ones will not be up to it. The best way to do this is to have two wire cooling racks ready, or a wire rack and a plate large enough to fit the cake. Take one cooling rack (or the plate) and position it upside down over the pan. Grip the edges of the rack (or plate) and cake pan securely with oven mitts and quickly invert the pan. Remove the pan, position the second rack over the bottom of the cake, grip both racks firmly but gently (or hold the plate down) and re-invert so that the bottom of the cake now rests on the second rack. If you have used a springform pan, release the clip and remove the outer ring before taking the steps described above.

COOLING AND KEEPING CAKES

Some cakes are excellent served slightly warm, but on the whole, they need to cool on a wire rack, or condensation will spoil the texture. If you plan to keep the cake, wrap it well as soon as it is cool and store it in a cool place or freeze suitable ones for later. Plastic wrap provides an excellent protective layer. Even if cakes are to be stored in pans or put into freezer bags or boxes, the extra wrapping will prevent them from drying out too quickly. Portions destined for the freezer can be wrapped individually, making it easy to remove one at a time without exposing the rest.

FRUIT CAKES

RICH CARIBBEAN FRUIT CAKE
BLACK CAKE

Black Cake is a rich and rum-laden fruit cake, without which no celebration in the Caribbean would be complete. It is not jet black as its name suggests, but the dried fruit and the generous proportion of "burnt sugar" generally used to color it make it dark. I use molasses because I have learned from experience that burnt sugar usually leads to burned pots, and it can give a very unpleasant taste if not done properly.

How this rich fruit cake came into being is anybody's guess. My pet theory is that some long-gone colonial cook, in a fit of either rebellion or adventurousness, used the mince pie filling to make a cake. The whole manner of preparation points to this and it also bears a striking resemblance to the Scottish Black Bun. Black Cake is definitely not a cake to be made on the spur of the moment, unless you always have a supply of Black Cake Fruit at hand. The dried fruit must be finely chopped and steeped in rum and left for at least 1 week to mature. One month is even better and it can be kept for more than a year if properly stored.

In Guyana in the 1970s, a ban was imposed on most imported items, ostensibly to promote self-sufficiency while admirably concealing a lack of foreign exchange. Imported foodstuffs were the first to go and the recipe for Black Cake took a new twist. Local fruits like star fruit and papaya were preserved and used to replace the unobtainable currants and raisins. This process is particularly tedious, involving several sun dryings and boilings in thick syrup, but it made a never-to-be-forgotten cake. One of my aunts was an acknowledged expert and her cakes traveled the world. Each cake had its own personality, as the fruit was prepared at home, and the local fruit imparted an underlying tartness that contrasted very favorably with the richness. In recent years, the ban has been lifted and most people have gone back to using imported dried fruit. This makes a truly excellent cake but, regrettably, the tang of the Black Cake of the 1970s and 1980s has perhaps gone forever.

As with most fruit cakes, the flavor of this cake improves after a week or two. It will keep for at least 2 months in an airtight container in a cool place. If you want to ice the cake with Royal icing for a special occasion, first cover it with marzipan at least ½ inch thick to avoid discoloration.

5½ oz/scant 1½ sticks butter, softened

5½ oz/¾ cup soft dark brown sugar

2 tbsp molasses

4 eggs, lightly beaten

1 jar Black Cake Fruit (see opposite)

5½ oz/1 cup all-purpose flour

1 tsp mixed spice (or ½ tsp cinnamon;
   ¼ tsp cardamom; ¼ tsp nutmeg)

¼ tsp salt

3½ fl oz/scant ½ cup ruby port, warmed

EQUIPMENT: *8-inch springform pan, at least 3 inches high*

Preheat the oven to 325°F/160°C. Grease the pan and line the bottom and sides with a double thickness of parchment paper.

Beat the softened butter until smooth. Add the sugar and molasses, then cream until light and fluffy. Add the beaten egg in three batches, scraping down the sides of the bowl after each addition and beating well. Add the fruit and mix well.

Sift the flour, mixed spice and salt together and fold into the mixture, then transfer the mixture to the prepared pan.

Bake in the oven for about 2 hours. After 1 hour, reduce the heat to 275°F/140°C and cover the top with a folded sheet of parchment paper.

Checking for doneness is tricky with Black Cake because the fruit keeps the cake a bit sticky. You have to look very carefully to see whether it is uncooked batter or just fruit adhering to the skewer.

As soon as you remove the baked cake from the oven, prick with a skewer in numerous places. Pour the warmed port evenly over the top. Leave to cool in the pan.

Store in a non-corrosive container. Do not freeze.

BLACK CAKE FRUIT

9 oz/generous ⅓ cup raisins

9 oz/1⅔ cups currants

9 oz/1⅓ cups sultanas (golden raisins)

9 oz candied orange peel

3½ oz/½ cup candied cherries
   or 3½ oz/scant ⅔ cup dried cranberries

3½ oz/generous ½ cup candied citron

9 oz/generous 1 cup pitted prunes

22 fl oz/scant 2¾ cups dark Caribbean rum

MAKES 3 JARS

For the Black Cake Fruit, wash and thoroughly dry the raisins, currants, sultanas and prunes. I always do this the evening before grinding and spread them out well on paper towels.

Use a meat grinder fitted with a coarse disc to grind the dried and candied fruit. A food processor will also work, but pulse in bursts, or the texture will be too mushy.

Mix the minced fruit with the rum and spoon into three 17-fl oz/2-cup spring-clip sterilizing jars or similar vessels. Store in a cool dry place for up to 1 year.

PINEAPPLE TART
ANANASTAART

This recipe is based on a homely cake from Surinam, and is actually a cross between a cake and a tart. It uses pineapple jam (see p. 235) and has a deliciously tropical flavor. It is best served fresh, perhaps with a little crème fraîche or whipped cream on the side. It may also be frozen, but the citrus taste will become quite dominant.

PASTRY

5½ oz/1 cup all-purpose flour

¼ tsp salt

1 tbsp confectioner's sugar

2¾ oz/scant ¼ stick butter, chilled, cubed

1 egg yolk

2–3 tbsp cold water

CAKE LAYER

5½ oz/1 cup all-purpose flour

¼ tsp baking powder

¼ tsp salt

3 eggs, plus 1 egg white

grated zest of ½ lime or ¼ lemon

5½ oz/¾ cup superfine sugar

2¾ oz/scant ¼ stick butter, melted and cooled
   slightly

about 9 oz/¾ cup pineapple jam (p. 235)

EQUIPMENT:

9-inch springform pan

For the pastry, sift the flour, salt and confectioner's sugar into a large bowl. Rub in the butter until the mixture resembles fine breadcrumbs. Alternatively, pulse in a food processor up to this stage and transfer to a bowl.

Mix the egg yolk with 2 tbsp water, then add to the flour mixture and bring it together with your fingertips to make a smooth pastry. Add extra water if necessary. Shape into a ball, then wrap it in plastic wrap and let it rest in a cool place for about 30 minutes.

Roll the pastry between two sheets of plastic wrap to an 11-inch circle. Grease the pan, then line with the pastry, pressing the edges against the side.

For the cake, sift the flour with the baking powder and salt and set aside.

Meanwhile, preheat the oven to 350°F/180°C.

Use an electric mixer to whisk the eggs and extra egg white, superfine sugar and lime or lemon zest until thick and pale. Gently fold in the flour mixture in two batches, using a balloon whisk. Add the melted butter with the second batch of flour and mix just until there are no more streaks of flour or butter apparent in the batter.

Spread the pineapple jam evenly over the pastry and top with the cake batter.

Level the top and bake for 35–40 minutes, or until the cake is golden brown. When you press the top with a fingertip, the indentation you create should slowly regain its original shape. Leave to cool in the pan for about 5 minutes, then release the clip and transfer the tart to a wire rack to cool.

BANANA CAKE

Several years ago, the only difference between the bananas available in Western countries was the exporter's sticker. That has all changed now and it is easy to buy different varieties in several shapes and sizes. However, bananas are poor travelers, especially in the tropical heat with no proper temperature-controlled transportation. As a result, some kinds tend to be bound to a particular region. My grandparents often had a huge bunch of "long bananas" hanging in a dark store room, and these would be broken off as they ripened. They were called long, but this is relative: they were the longest bananas grown in Guyana and were slim and elegant but only about half the size of the bananas available in Western supermarkets. They were considered better than their plumper and shorter bright yellow cousins, probably because they were less common. My other grandmother had a thick red-skinned variety in her kitchen garden and, as far as I can remember, she used them only for cooking. They were not plantains – which are cooking bananas with a higher starch content and less sugar, and eaten both green and ripe – but she thought they were better for cooking than eating raw. My own favorite are the "sweet figs," tiny yellow bananas no bigger than your little finger, with a marvelous flavor. They used to be brought out by boat from the province of Essequibo and have never been very widely available, even in Guyana.

It always surprises me to see people peeling and eating bananas that still have a greenish tinge to the skin. These lack the flavor of a fully ripe banana and I have remarked on this on several occasions, only to be told – paradoxically in my opinion – that they become too sweet if left longer. However you usually like yours, leave them to ripen well for this recipe; they will have much more flavor. This cake is lighter in texture than the following recipe, Banana Loaf (see opposite). It is at its lightest on the day of baking, but it will keep for a few days in a cool place and can also be frozen.

10½ oz ripe bananas (about 2 large)

juice of ½ lime or ¼ lemon

9 oz/1⅔ cups all-purpose flour

2 tsp baking powder

½ tsp baking soda

¼ tsp salt

¼ tsp freshly grated nutmeg

6 oz/scant 1¼ sticks butter, well softened

7 oz/1 cup superfine sugar

3 eggs

1 tsp vanilla extract

EQUIPMENT:

8-inch square pan

Peel and slice the bananas and mash them with the lime or lemon juice on a plate. Set aside.

Preheat the oven to 325°F/160°C. Grease the pan, then line the base with parchment paper and dust with flour.

Sift the flour with the baking powder, baking soda, salt and nutmeg in a bowl.

Cream the butter and sugar together until light and creamy. Beat the eggs lightly with the vanilla, then add to the mixture, a little at a time, beating well after each addition. Mix the bananas into the creamed mixture and add the dry ingredients in three batches, using a balloon whisk to blend it in gently.

Transfer the batter to the prepared pan and bake for 35–40 minutes, or until a skewer inserted into the center of the cake comes out clean.

Invert the cake onto a wire rack, remove the parchment paper and leave to cool.

BANANA LOAF

This banana loaf, with chocolate and walnuts, makes a delicious afternoon treat. It will keep for a few days in a cool place and can also be frozen in separately wrapped portions for lunchbox treats. There will be a lot of batter in the pan compared with other cakes, but don't be alarmed – it won't spill over.

7 oz very ripe bananas (about 2 medium)

2 tsp lime or lemon juice

7 oz/1⅓ cups all-purpose flour

2 tsp baking powder

¼ tsp salt

¼ tsp freshly grated nutmeg

4½ oz/generous 1 stick butter, softened

4½ oz/generous ½ cup (solidly packed) soft dark
  brown sugar

1 egg

1 tsp vanilla extract

1 oz/¼ cup walnuts, chopped

2 oz dark chocolate, chopped into small pieces

EQUIPMENT:

1-lb loaf pan

Peel and slice the bananas and mash them with the lime or lemon juice on a plate. Set aside.

Preheat the oven to 325°F/160°C. Grease the pan and line with parchment paper.

Sift the flour, baking powder, salt and nutmeg in a bowl.

Cream the butter and sugar together until lightened in color and smooth in texture. Lightly beat the egg and vanilla extract together, then add to the mixture and beat well. Mix the bananas into the creamed mixture and add the flour mixture in three batches, using a balloon whisk to blend it in gently.

Fold in the walnuts and chocolate with the last batch of flour.

Transfer the batter to the prepared pan and bake for about 1 hour, or until a skewer inserted into the center of the loaf comes out clean. Leave to cool in the pan for about 5 minutes, then invert onto a wire rack. Remove the parchment paper and leave to cool completely.

LAYERED "DRUNKEN" APPLE CAKE
KUCHEN BORRACHO

Chile is home to a fairly large community of German settlers and their descendants. This Chilean cake, whose Germanic origin is reflected in its name, is out of the ordinary. When it is cut, you see three layers of cake enclosing two bands of creamy apple mixture, which can be gooey or custard-like in places, depending on how the batter and fruit have been distributed. It makes a wonderful pudding served while still warm from the oven and is equally delicious when it cools and sets. This cake will keep at cool room temperature for up to 4 days.

FILLING

1 lb 7 oz tart apples, prepared weight (about 5 medium-sized apples)

2¾ oz/generous ⅓ cup granulated sugar

3½ fl oz/½ cup heavy cream

CAKE

10½ oz/2 cups all-purpose flour

2½ tsp baking powder

¼ tsp salt

5½ oz/scant 1½ sticks butter, softened

8 oz/generous 1 cup granulated sugar

3 eggs, lightly beaten

5 tbsp rum

5 tbsp water

EQUIPMENT:

9-inch springform pan, at least 2¾ inches high

Peel and core the apples. Cut each apple into 8 parts and slice thinly. Put the sliced apples in a bowl and mix in the sugar and cream. Set aside until needed.

For the cake, sift the flour with the baking powder and salt and set aside.

Preheat the oven to 325°F/160°C. Grease the pan and dust with flour.

Beat the butter and sugar until smooth and creamy. Add the beaten egg in four batches, scraping down the sides of the bowl and beating well after each addition. Fold in the flour in four batches, adding the rum and water with the third batch. Gently fold in the last batch of flour and stop mixing as soon as it is incorporated.

You will need to divide the batter into three lots. Unless you have a very accurate eye and are very good at averaging these things, weigh them, because the layering depends on an even distribution of batter and fruit. Weigh two batches of batter, each 11½ oz, into two bowls.

Transfer the batter left in the mixing bowl to the prepared pan. Level the top. Spread one batch of apple mixture evenly on top of this, leaving about ½ inch free around the edge. Add another batch of cake batter and level it. Spread the second batch of apple mixture evenly on top of this, and top with the third and final batch of batter. It will be quite a full pan, but the batter will not spill out while baking.

Level the top and bake for 1½ hours, or until a skewer inserted into the center of the cake comes out clean. Leave to cool in the pan for 15–20 minutes, then release the clip and transfer the cake to a wire rack to cool completely.

DUTCH APPLE TART
APPELTAART

This kind of apple tart is probably the most popular baked item in the Netherlands and is made at home or bought from the baker or supermarket. It is difficult to define it in one word because it is not a pie, nor a tart, nor quite a cake, but a bit of all three. A literal translation is no help either, as the Dutch word neatly covers all the possibilities. The pastry is sweetened and leavened, and the apples should be firm and tart to hold their shape and contrast with the pastry. In the Netherlands, the *Goudrenet* (Golden Reinette) is often used. *Appeltaart* is usually enjoyed with coffee, but it also makes a good dessert served at room temperature or slightly warm with sweetened whipped cream.

PASTRY

10½ oz/2 cups all-purpose flour

1 tbsp baking powder

¼ tsp salt

7 oz/1¾ sticks butter, chilled and cubed

5½ oz/¾ cup superfine sugar

1 egg, well beaten with 1 tbsp water

zest of ½ lemon

FILLING

4 large tart apples

juice of ½ lemon

2¾ oz/generous ⅓ cup granulated sugar

1¾ oz/scant ⅓ cup raisins

1¾ oz/⅓ cup currants

1½ tsp ground cinnamon

2 tbsp cornstarch

EQUIPMENT:

9-inch springform pan

For the pastry, mix the flour, baking powder and salt in a large bowl. Rub in the butter until the mixture resembles coarse breadcrumbs, then mix in the sugar. You can use a food processor up to this point.

Reserve 1 tbsp of the beaten egg. Add the rest of the egg with the lemon zest to the mixture and knead lightly with the fingertips to bring the pastry together in a ball. Cover the bowl with plastic wrap and set aside at cool room temperature.

Peel, quarter and core the apples. Slice them just under ½ inch thick and mix well with the remaining ingredients.

Preheat the oven to 350°F/180°C. Grease the pan and dust with flour.

Shape two-thirds of the pastry into a disc and flatten it out into the pan with the heel of your hand so that the bottom is fairly evenly covered and the sides come up to about 1¼ inches. Use the rest of the pastry to make about 12 ropes, to fit across the top of the tart. If they break, simply press the pastry back together and continue. This pastry responds well to rough treatment.

Stir the apple mixture well, then use it to fill the pastry case. Use the ropes to make a lattice pattern on top of the apples. Brush the ropes with the reserved egg and bake in the oven for 20 minutes. Reduce the heat to 325°F/160°C and bake for a further 40–50 minutes. Leave to cool in the pan for about 10 minutes.

Use a flexible spatula to loosen the sides from the pan, then release the clip and transfer the tart to a wire rack to cool. To avoid breakage, it is best to leave the tart on the springform base.

FRESH CHERRY CAKE

In Central Europe, fresh cherries are often used in cakes. The cherries are not pitted and are simply scattered over the top of the cake. This has triple benefits. The first is that there is no extra work involved in removing the pits; the second is that the pits add a slight almond undertone to the flavor; and the third is that they don't sink to the bottom nearly as far or as fast as bottled or even freshly pitted cherries, so there is quite a good distribution in the finished cake. The only small drawback is the pits left in your mouth. Discreet use of a table napkin should do the trick.

8 oz/1½ cups all-purpose flour

¼ tsp salt

1½ tsp baking powder

7 oz/1¾ sticks butter, softened

7 oz/1 cup superfine sugar

4 eggs, lightly beaten

1½ tbsp Kirsch

10–12 oz fresh cherries, with pits left in

EQUIPMENT:

9-inch springform pan

Preheat the oven to 350°F/180°C. Grease the pan and line the base with parchment paper, then dust with flour.

Sift the flour with the salt and baking powder and set aside.

Beat the butter until smooth. Add the sugar, then cream until light and fluffy. Add the eggs in three batches, beating well and scraping down the sides of the bowl after each addition. Add the Kirsch with the last batch of egg. Fold in the flour in three batches.

Transfer the batter to the prepared pan and scatter the cherries on top. Bake the cake for 45–50 minutes, or until a skewer inserted into the center of the cake comes out clean. Leave to cool in the pan for about 5 minutes, then loosen the edges and carefully turn out onto a wire cooling rack to cool completely.

Pictured on p. 119.

SPICE CAKES

MULTILAYERED SPICE CAKE
KUE LAPIS OR SPEKKOEK

Kue Lapis is a product of Indonesia's Dutch colonial heritage. It is a spice cake that is grilled in layers, spiced mixture alternating with plain to form a striped pattern in the cut cake. In the Netherlands, where Indonesian food enjoys much the same status that Indian food does in Britain, and for much the same reason, it is popularly referred to as *spekkoek*, or "bacon cake," because the stripes give the impression of very streaky bacon (see picture on p. 131). Recipes of various types have appeared in standard Dutch cook books and one of the most remarkable versions I have ever seen is from an 1899 book written by the principal of the Hague Cookery School, in which she stipulates a whole nutmeg and 65 cloves for a cake twice the size of the one below. Nowadays in the Netherlands, most people prefer to buy a slice at a time from an Indonesian food outlet or grocer, where it is usually sold by weight. This has less to do with frugality than richness: a little goes a long way.

This kind of layered cake is also made industrially in Indonesia and sold in small prepackaged blocks. Flavors vary from spices to jackfruit, screwpine (pandan) and more. Ever curious, I decided to sample a few. It was a huge disappointment, as there was little difference in flavor between them and I was left with a very chemical aftertaste. I wasn't surprised to read on the package that the cakes could be kept for at least another year! No doubt there are better brands, but I have yet to find them. You're better off buying a piece from an Indonesian food store, but of course, best off if you make it yourself. It is quite easy to make, although you have to remain on the spot while broiling. Before you know it, you'll be finished, especially if, like me, you take a childlike pleasure in watching the cake grow before your eyes.

This cake has a modest eight layers and the spiced layers contrast deliciously with the baked egg custard-like taste of the plain layer, a combination of flavors that led a friend to remark cryptically that it tasted of her childhood. And the cake does seem to appeal to children, even when they have looked past the intriguing stripes. When they were very young, my children came up with their own serving preference: they liked vanilla-flavored custard poured over it.

Serve this in small slices. The cake keeps for more than a week, well wrapped, in a cool place.

Do give yourself enough time: the layering alone can take up to 45 minutes, after the batter has been prepared.

You will need a broiler for this recipe.

9 oz/2¼ sticks butter, softened

7 oz/1 cup superfine sugar
   (in two portions of 3½ oz/½ cup)

5 eggs, separated

1 tsp vanilla extract

4½ oz/scant 1 cup all-purpose flour

¼ tsp salt

1 tsp ground cinnamon

½ tsp ground cardamom

⅛ tsp ground cloves

⅛ tsp freshly grated nutmeg

1¾ oz/scant ½ stick melted butter,
   for brushing

EQUIPMENT:

8-inch round pan

Beat the butter until smooth. Add 3½ oz/½ cup superfine sugar and cream until light and fluffy. Add the egg yolks and vanilla extract and beat well to incorporate.

Sift the flour with the salt and set aside.

In a scrupulously clean bowl, using a clean whisk or beater, whisk the egg whites until foaming. Pour the remaining superfine sugar in a slow but steady stream onto the whites while still whisking. Continue whisking until stiff peaks hold their shape. Add a generous spoonful of the whites to the creamed mixture and mix well. Gently fold in the rest of the egg whites in three batches, alternating with the flour. Do not overmix.

Transfer half of the mixture to another bowl. Carefully fold the spices into the contents of one bowl. Spread a quarter of the contents of one bowl over the bottom of the greased baking pan and level it off with a plastic scraper.

Place the pan under a hot broiler and broil until the top is puffy and the batter cooked through. The first layer always seems to take a little longer, perhaps about 5 minutes, depending on how close it is to the heat source. Remove the pan from the broiler, then brush with butter and add another layer.

Each subsequent layer will take about 3 minutes – they will be puffed up and golden brown and should be cooked through. You should have a total of eight layers. Always be sure to spread the batter evenly and to wipe any spills off the side of the pan. Spills tend to burn and drop into the batter, spoiling the appearance and taste of the finished cake. When you have broiled all of the layers, carefully loosen the edges and turn onto a wire cooling rack.

Pictured on p. 131.

FRAGRANCE

One day, my parents announced that we were going away on holiday. To us Guyanese children in those days, "away" meant abroad, so this was very exciting news. When I asked where we were going, I was told that we would be island-hopping in the West Indies. My seven-year-old mind grappled with these facts and they soon coalesced into a somewhat hazy image of a blue-green sea dotted with several bits of land, with us jumping from one to the other whenever we felt like moving on. A bit like that game I played with my friends, only we jumped across a wide ditch filled with muddy water into which we occasionally tumbled, emerging covered from head to toe with slime and the odd tadpole, forcing us to reluctantly slink off home to face parental retribution. Common sense soon prevailed and I realized that going away involved planes, airports and hotels, all great novelties to my sister and me. It was to be my only trip to Grenada, but my first impression has remained securely tucked into a tiny crevice of my mind. As we left the chilly aircraft cabin and descended the short flight of steps onto the tarmac, I was enveloped in a blanket of warm and fragrant air. Though I didn't know it at the time, the exotic yet comfortingly familiar perfume was nutmeg wafting from the surrounding groves and storage sheds nearby. The air smelled so delicious, it felt like you could open your mouth and eat it, and ever since then Grenada and nutmegs have become synonymous to me.

NUTMEG CAKE WITH RUM SYRUP

Nutmeg (*Myristica fragrans*) lives up to the promise of its name in being one of the most fragrant of spices. The English word comes to us by way of the old French *nois muguede*, in its turn derived from the Vulgar Latin *nuce muscata*, an unmistakable reference to its musky perfume.

The nutmeg tree is native to the Banda Islands, a group of islands in the eastern part of the Malay archipelago. These 10 small volcanic islands now form part of the Indonesian province of Maluku (Moluccas). Nutmegs were used in ancient Persia and had reached Constantinople by at least the ninth century AD. Journeying further westwards, the precious spice spread to Europe by the twelfth century, and cautiously began to infiltrate local cuisines. Only in the sixteenth century, when the Portuguese reached the Moluccas and established a trade route round the Cape of Good Hope, did the spice begin to reach Europe in significant quantities.

The Portuguese monopoly was broken a century later by the Dutch, who seized control and anxiously sought to retain it by destroying existent plantations on other neighboring islands, and allowing cultivation only under their highly vigilant eye. The strategy worked well for more than 150 years until the French managed to sneak a few plants to Mauritius in 1770 and subsequently started their own production. During their brief occupation of the Moluccas from 1796 to 1802, the British began to plant nutmeg trees in their colonies as far away as the West Indies, and the nutmeg reached Grenada in the 1860s. As in the Moluccas, the trees were planted near the sea in volcanic soil and the tropical climate was similar. Nutmegs soon grew as well there as in their place of origin, and today Grenada is a noteworthy producer of high-quality nutmegs.

The hard brown nut is actually the seed of a golden-colored fleshy fruit that is a thing of beauty in itself, especially when cut open to reveal the seed wrapped in a lacy red covering. This red lace turns orange as it dries and becomes mace, prized as an aromatic in its own right. Some of the Asian countries that cultivate nutmegs also find good use for the outer fruit. In Sri Lanka, jam is made from it; and in some parts of Indonesia, it is candied by mixing it with palm sugar and drying it in the sun. A similar sweet appears to have been known in Europe in the past; it was sold by apothecaries in Elizabethan times as a tasty tidbit with great nutritional value.

Many cuisines use nutmeg as the perfect flavoring for milk-based desserts and drinks. In Europe it is also used in savory cooking and you will find it in a variety of vegetables as well as mashed potatoes and meatballs. It is greatly under-used in Western cakes, forming at the most a component for spice cake mixtures.

This cake is my slightly more sophisticated take on a childhood favorite. It can be served as it is or, even better, with a rum syrup, and the flavor improves after a day or so. This is easy and quick if made without syrup. The syruped loaf should be left for a day before cutting.

6 oz/scant 1¼ cups all-purpose flour

1½ tsp baking powder

⅛ tsp salt

¼ nutmeg, freshly grated (about 1 loose tsp)

4½ oz/generous 1 stick butter, softened

4½ oz/generous ½ cup (solidly packed) soft light
  brown sugar

2 eggs

1 tsp vanilla extract

4 tbsp milk

4 tbsp prepared sugar syrup (see p. 273),
  mixed with 2 tbsp rum

EQUIPMENT: *1-lb loaf pan*

Preheat the oven to 325°F/160°C. Grease the pan, line the base and dust with flour.

Sift the flour with the baking powder, salt and nutmeg and set aside.

Beat the butter until smooth. Add the sugar and beat until light and fluffy.

Whisk the eggs loosely in a small bowl and add the vanilla extract. Add the egg to the butter mixture in two batches, beating well and scraping down the sides of the bowl after each addition. Use a whisk as you would a spoon to fold in the flour mixture in three batches, alternating with the milk.

Transfer to the prepared pan and bake for 40–45 minutes, or until a skewer inserted into the center of the cake comes out clean.

Remove the pan from the oven and pierce it all the way down to the bottom in several places with the skewer. Slowly pour the rum syrup over the surface of the cake. Let it cool for about 5 minutes in the pan, then transfer it, right side up, to a wire rack to cool completely.

When the cake has cooled completely, wrap it well in plastic wrap and keep it for a day before cutting it, to allow the flavors to mature.

AZOREAN SPICE CAKE
BOLL DE MEL

The coming of the Portuguese to Guyana added another thread to the colony's checkered fabric. They came as indentured laborers, like the Indians and Chinese, and were brought from Madeira and the Azores to help fill the labor void created in the sugar industry by emancipation.

This spice cake is a Guyanese–Portuguese Christmas specialty and the recipe was given to me by a friend of my mother's, whose family bakes it for special occasions. It is the kind of cake that defies categorization and usually starts discussions as to whether it really is a cake or more of a sweet. One thing, however, is certain. It is the essence of the Guyanese spirit – generous, the ingredients being put together in what can only be described as happy proportions.

The cake is very easy to make, even for the novice baker. The only thing to watch out for is the three-day resting time for the dough. If you have read the method and are anxious to check every day to see the dough gently bubbling away like a sourdough, don't hold your breath. Nothing happens. The method owes more to the Guyanese penchant for leaving things to "set" rather than to any coherent principle. Having said that, the extra maturation time does give a lovely mellowness to the cake. This recipe will make two cakes and is ideal for serving to large groups of guests or for giving away. It is very easily halved for small households. The cakes are even better if left to mature for a few days and will keep for a few weeks if stored in a cold place to prevent the butter from turning rancid.

1 lb 5 oz/4 cups all-purpose flour

10½ oz/1½ cups (solidly packed) soft brown sugar

½ oz active dry yeast

2 tsp ground cinnamon

½ tsp ground cloves

½ tsp finely ground black pepper

½ tsp ground ginger

1½ tsp baking soda

1 lb 2 oz/scant 4½ sticks butter, melted and cooled slightly

7 oz/generous ½ cup molasses, warmed

3½ oz/scant ⅓ cup honey, warmed

7 oz/1⅓ cups blanched almonds, chopped

14 oz/4 cups walnuts, chopped

2¾ oz/scant ½ cup mixed candied peel

EQUIPMENT:

2 x 9-inch round pans

MAKES 2 CAKES

In a large bowl, mix together the flour, sugar, yeast, spices and baking soda. Add the butter, molasses and honey. Knead the dough until everything is well mixed. Cover the bowl with a dish towel and leave at cool room temperature for 2–3 days.

Preheat the oven to 350°F/180°C.

Grease the pans and line with parchment paper.

Knead the nuts and candied peel into the dough. Divide into two pieces and flatten each piece into a baking pan. Smooth the tops, moistening your hand with a little water if necessary.

Bake in the preheated oven for 25–35 minutes, or until the mixture is cooked through. Remove from the oven and leave to cool to lukewarm in the pans, then transfer carefully to a wire rack.

Once the cakes have cooled completely, wrap well in plastic wrap to store, or keep in an airtight container.

SPICE "CRUSTS"
AMSTERDAMSE KORSTJES

A German price table dated 1393 shows that a pound of ginger had the same value as a sheep and a pound of saffron the value of a horse; a cow could be bought for the equivalent of two pounds of mace and a single pound of nutmeg changed hands for the price of seven fat oxen. After the Dutch East India Company was founded in 1602, the Dutch grasped the spice trade and firmly held on to it for almost two centuries. With shiploads of spices coming in at regular intervals, local cuisine soon came to rely on these once costly flavorings and the tradition of spice cakes was greatly reinforced. Though they no longer commanded the prices they had in the Middle Ages, spices were still not cheap. The generic name for spice cakes is *peperkoek*, or pepper cake, and this spice was once so highly valued that the Dutch language retains the expression *peperduur*: as expensive as pepper.

There are countless kinds of spice cakes in the Netherlands, from the large and airy loaves called *ontbijtkoek* (breakfast cake) to small chewy slabs, with a variety of textures and flavoring combinations in between. Aniseed is the chief spice in *Oudewijvenkoek*, or Old Wives' Cake, while *Groninger Koek*, or Groningen Cake, is studded with pieces of candied citron. *Deventer Koek*, from the town of Deventer, is flavored with bitter orange; it was exported to Scandinavia and the Baltic countries as early as the seventeenth century. Sugar nibs are used in some cakes while others have delicious pockets of melted candy sugar. Large spice cakes are a baker's product, made in batches in huge, specially insulated pans and pried or cut apart afterwards. The doughs are very stiff and must be thoroughly kneaded for a good result. Home bakers content themselves with loaves such as the Gingerbread Loaf in this section.

Some smaller items, such as these Spice "Crusts" that originated in Amsterdam, are easier to knead and quite simple to make at home. These individual, deliciously chewy spice cakes are so wholesome that they could almost be classed as health food, and they make a very virtuous snack for adults and children alike. They will keep for at least 10 days in an airtight container.

These are simple to make, but bear in mind that the traditional two-stage preparation and post-baking ripening time will take two days.

FIRST STAGE (DAY 1)
9 oz/1½ cups fine rye flour
1¼ tsp ground cinnamon
¾ tsp ground ginger
¾ tsp ground cardamom
¼ tsp ground cloves
5½ oz/scant ½ cup honey
5 tbsp water

SECOND STAGE (DAY 2)
3½ oz/½ cup (solidly packed) soft dark brown sugar
1 tsp baking soda
3½ oz/scant ⅓ cup honey

MAKES 12

Mix the rye flour with the spices in a bowl and set aside.

Put the honey and water in a saucepan over medium heat and stir until it is completely liquid. Cool, then pour it over the flour. Blend with two plastic scrapers, then knead to a dough. It will be hard-going, but persevere. Shape into a ball, then cover with plastic wrap and set aside at cool room temperature for 24 hours.

Next day, mix the sugar with the baking soda and knead thoroughly into the ripened dough. Knead the honey into the dough.

Preheat the oven to 400°F/200°C. Line 2 baking sheets with parchment paper.

Turn the dough onto a surface dusted with wheat flour and shape into a "sausage." Cut this into 12 equal pieces.

Take one piece at a time and cut it in half. Roll each of the halves into a neat cigar about 4 inches long and place the pairs side by side on the lined baking sheet, leaving ½ inch space between them. When the first sheet is full, use the second sheet. Leave at least 3 inches between the assembled pairs, as they will spread quite a bit while baking.

Bake one sheet for about 10 minutes. They will be very soft. Pull the paper off the sheet onto a cooling rack and slip the second sheet into the oven.

Allow the crusts to cool on the paper for about 5 minutes before carefully peeling it away.

Store the cooled crusts in an airtight container for 24 hours before eating.

GINGERBREAD LOAF

The moist cake-like gingerbread that we enjoy today is a descendant of the old honey and spice cakes that were usually made in flat and solid slabs. Spice cakes are believed to have slowly made their way westwards with the returning Crusaders. They may even have been used as nourishing traveling rations, just as the honey cake known as *mikong* was carried by Genghis Khan's invading hordes. Even today, Dutch soldiers are routinely issued with spice cake because it keeps well and forms an excellent source of energy.

The original flat type of gingerbread was often given as a gift in medieval times, particularly at tournaments. The background was symbolically decorated with box leaves to form a *fleur-de-lys*, with gilded cloves used to mimic nails. The costly ingredients kept these spice cakes as the preserve of the wealthy for several centuries, but as time went by they also began to be used as fairings – gifts given at fair time. Gradually, the flat slabs evolved into a thicker but lighter cake, and early versions were often made with breadcrumbs instead of flour. Molasses from the overseas possessions eventually superseded the honey in some cases, and the introduction of commercial raising agents made it possible to achieve a consistently light product. By the Victorian period, cake gingerbread had replaced its ancestors in the British Isles, but in Europe, the older kinds are still made alongside airier versions. German *lebkuchen* and Dutch *taai-taai*, for example, are chewy, while Dutch *speculaas* can be made in varying textures, from crisp biscuits to softer slabs.

The following cake gingerbread uses buttermilk in the old Dutch style. In bygone times, when butter was freshly churned on a regular basis on Dutch farms, buttermilk remained as a by-product. It was sometimes given to the animals but more often than not, it was used in breads, pancakes and spice loaves like this one. Buttermilk is now available in cartons in supermarkets and enjoys a dizzy spell of popularity in the warmer months as a healthy thirst quencher. If you cannot get buttermilk, use sour milk or mix 5 fl oz skim milk with ¼ teaspoon cream of tartar and use the required amount as a substitute.

Gingerbread benefits from a short maturation period, so keep the whole loaf well wrapped in plastic wrap for a day before cutting it.

This is quick and easy, but needs to ripen for a day before cutting.

SPICE MIXTURE *

1 tsp cinnamon

½ tsp ginger

¼ tsp cardamom

¼ tsp cloves

¼ tsp ground nutmeg

¼ tsp mace

6 oz/generous 1 cup all-purpose flour

¾ tsp baking powder

¾ tsp baking soda

¼ tsp salt

1¾ oz/scant ½ stick butter

4½ oz/generous ½ cup (solidly packed) soft dark
    brown sugar

2¾ oz/scant ¼ cup molasses

1 egg, beaten

3½ fl oz/scant ½ cup buttermilk

EQUIPMENT:

1-lb loaf pan

Sift the flour with the baking powder, baking soda, salt and spice mixture in a large mixing bowl and set aside.

Preheat the oven to 325°F/160°C. Line the pan with parchment paper.

Put the butter, sugar and molasses in a heavy-based saucepan and heat gently, stirring to dissolve the sugar, then combine everything thoroughly. Let it cool slightly, then stir it into the flour mixture along with the egg and buttermilk. Stir vigorously to combine and get rid of any white streaks. This can also be done with a mixer fitted with a whisk.

When the mixture is smooth, transfer it to the pan and level the top. Bake for 40–45 minutes, or until a skewer inserted into the center of the gingerbread comes out clean.

Remove from the oven and leave to cool for about 5 minutes in the pan. Transfer to a wire rack, then remove the paper and leave to cool completely.

When the cake has cooled completely, wrap it well in plastic wrap and keep it for a day before cutting it, to allow the flavors to mature.

* This mixture can be varied as desired or, if one of the minor components is unavailable, simply add a little more of the first three to compensate the shortfall.

SINTERKLAAS AND SPECULAAS

The word *speculaas* is most probably derived from *speculum* or *speculator*. *Speculum* means "mirror" and the spice cookie is a mirror image of the mold. *Speculator* means "he who sees all," a reference to the omniscience of St Nicholas. A third, not very credible, explanation is that it was first baked as a gamble or speculation by a baker with some spirit of adventure.

Although prepackaged *speculaas* cookies can be bought in the Netherlands all year round, they are really a seasonal item eaten in prodigious quantities in the months leading up to the feast of St Nicholas (6 December). This feast, commemorating his death in AD 324 rather than his birth, has been celebrated in the Netherlands since the twelfth century. Both saint and feast day are called *Sinterklaas* and it is easy to see how the commercial invention of Santa Claus rests on this base, both linguistically and conceptually. St Nicholas is the patron saint of, among others, sailors and young girls on the lookout for a sweetheart, but nobody loves him more than Dutch children. His "official" arrival at the end of November by steamship from Spain, where he now resides, is televised and broadcast nationwide. Once they have arrived, St Nicholas and his helpers start to visit homes and primary schools all over the country to deposit largesse anonymously in expectantly placed shoes. St Nicholas Eve is also called *Pakjesavond* in the Netherlands: Parcel Night. On the anxiously awaited evening itself, a jute sack bursting with parcels is often put in the charge of an obliging neighbor who bangs on the doors and rattles at the window panes after he leaves the sack on the doorstep.

For the occasions when St Nicholas himself must put in an appearance, he can be rented, but a tall and slim local man is usually asked to do the honors. He dons the red robe with lacy white surplice and crowns his snowy locks with the miter that underlines his official role as Bishop of Myra (now Demre) in Turkey, where he was born. Once the flowing white beard has been secured on his face, he is free to grasp his crozier and the Big Book in which the names and conduct of all Dutch children are recorded. He is assisted by a merry band of helpers, each called *Zwarte Piet* (literally "Black Peter") and clad in brightly colored doublet and hose with a floppy velvet hat perched on top of a curly black wig. Mischief radiating from their artificially darkened faces, they do handstands and turn cartwheels at any opportunity and delight young and old with their crazy and generally silly behavior, which often meets with gentle public upbraiding from their master. Eagerly outstretched hands, large and small, struggle to catch the small spice cookies (*pepernoten*) and sweets that the *Pieten* grab by the handful from capacious sacks and fling around with wild abandon.

The role demarcation combined with the skin color of the *Pieten* has caused offense, especially in the former Dutch colonies. In Surinam, for example, the custom was abolished on Independence in 1975 and then reinstated in 1992. No offense is meant and all kinds of politically correct explanations are available for those who need them: the color is caused by climbing up and down soot-ridden chimneys to deliver gifts or the "fact" that the first helper was a devil who was saved from Hellfire by St Nicholas, but not before his skin was badly burned – and more of the same.

SPICE CAKE STUFFED WITH ALMOND PASTE
GEVULDE SPECULAAS

From the end of October, a pleasantly sweet and spicy aroma assails you as you walk past bakeries anywhere in the Netherlands, and supermarkets with their own ovens pop in a few batches of *speculaas* at the start of the day so that the whole shop is temptingly perfumed by the time the first customers walk in. *Speculaas* come in various forms. The best known are what tourists often refer to as "windmill cookies." This crisp type is made by pressing the dough into wooden molds carved in various ways. Souvenir shops sell simplistic replicas, but the original ones were very detailed and often carved by the baker himself in the quieter months or by itinerant carvers who lovingly and skillfully turned lumps of wood into evocative portrayals of social history. All phases of human life were depicted, from St Nicholas to courting couples and babies' cradles as well as trees of life, animals, trades, tools, instruments, boats and the ever popular windmills. But beauty had its price. In order to bring out the details in the baked product, a very firm and dry dough had to be used, nothing like the buttery articles eaten today. Extra-special ones were gilded or decorated with colored frosting.

Nowadays, *speculaas* come in all sizes, shapes and textures: crisp, soft, thick, thin, filled and unfilled. For the filled versions, bakers appear to vie with each other as to how much almond paste can be stuffed into how little pastry, sometimes forgetting to strike a happy balance between the two. This recipe is for a filled cake-like *speculaas*. It remains a sweet and rich treat, so serve it in small squares or wedges. The flavor will be even better if you leave it well wrapped for a day or so.

SPICE MIXTURE *

1½ tsp cinnamon

½ tsp cardamom

¼ tsp ginger

¼ tsp aniseed

¼ tsp cloves

⅛ tsp nutmeg

⅛ tsp mace

9 oz/1⅔ cup all-purpose flour

½ tsp baking powder

¼ tsp salt

7 oz/1 cup soft dark brown sugar

6 oz/1½ sticks butter, chilled and cubed

1 egg, well beaten

10½ oz coarse almond paste

about ½– ¾ beaten egg – reserve the rest for glazing

EQUIPMENT: *9-inch round pan*

Sift the flour with the spice mixture, baking powder, salt and sugar into a roomy bowl. Rub in the butter thoroughly so that the mixture looks like breadcrumbs. A food processor makes short work of this job. If using one, pulse all of the dry ingredients, then add the butter. Continue to pulse until it looks like breadcrumbs and transfer to a bowl.

Add the beaten egg and knead well for a minute or two. Shape into a ball, then wrap in plastic wrap and chill for about 1 hour. It can be chilled longer or even overnight, but will then need enough time at room temperature so that it can be rolled out without breaking.

Preheat the oven to 340°F/170°C. Grease the pan.

Mix the coarse almond paste with enough beaten egg to make a fairly soft, spreadable consistency. Divide the dough into two unequal pieces: one piece about one-third of the total; and the second piece, two-thirds. Shape into balls, then flatten slightly into discs.

Spread a sheet of plastic wrap on the work surface and place the larger piece of dough on it. Cover with a second piece of plastic wrap, stretched tautly so that there are no folds or creases over the dough. Roll this disc out between the plastic wrap to a 11-inch circle and use it to line the pan, pressing the edges against the side of the pan so that they don't fall inwards.

Spread the almond paste mixture evenly over the dough and fold in the dough edges so that they rest on the almond paste. Reuse the plastic wrap to roll the second piece of dough out in the same way to a 8½-inch circle. It should be slightly smaller than the diameter of the pan. Trim the edges so that the circle is fairly neat. Moisten the edges of the dough already in the pan with your finger dipped in water and top with the smaller circle. Press the edges gently to seal. Brush with beaten egg and prick with a fork in several places.

Bake for 30–35 minutes. Leave to cool in the pan, then transfer carefully to a serving plate.

* This mixture can be varied as desired or if one of the minor components is unavailable. Simply add a little more of the first three to compensate the shortfall.

JEWISH NEW YEAR HONEY CAKE
HONIK LEKACH

Honey cakes are used by many people to break their fast on Rosh Hashanah, Jewish New Year, which falls in the Western calendar in September or October. There are many symbolic touches to Rosh Hashanah food. The normally braided *challah* loaf that is customarily broken on Friday evening is made round or coiled for Rosh Hashanah, to represent eternity and symbolize the circle of life. On this holiday, people eat pieces of *challah* or slices of apple dipped in honey, and few Jewish households will be without a honey cake of some kind. Eating honey represents the wish for a sweet and good New Year.

Honik Lekach exists in many compositions and textures. The one I have given here is feather-light since it puffs up during baking and, more importantly, stays that way when it is removed from the oven.

As the cake contains no dairy products, it is considered *pareve*, or neutral, and can be eaten with or straight after both meat and dairy meals. To keep it neutral, use a non-dairy fat to grease the pan. Although it is meant to be served cold, it is also very good eaten warm with a scoop of ice cream or lightly whipped cream – and will then be categorized as dairy.

Well wrapped, this cake will keep for a few days at cool room temperature. It can also be frozen.

This is quick to make and can be eaten straight after baking.

6 oz/generous 1 cup all-purpose flour

½ tsp baking powder

½ tsp baking soda

2–3 tsp ground cinnamon

¼ tsp salt

4 eggs, separated

4½ oz/generous ½ cup superfine sugar

2 tbsp neutral-tasting oil

2 tbsp brandy or rum

zest and juice of ½ lemon or 1 small lime

7 oz/generous ½ cup honey

EQUIPMENT:

9-inch springform pan

Sift the flour with the baking powder, baking soda, cinnamon and salt, and set aside.

In a scrupulously clean bowl, whisk the egg whites until foaming. Add 1¾ oz/¼ cup sugar, whisking all the time, and continue to whisk until stiff peaks form.

In another bowl, beat the egg yolks with the remaining sugar, oil, brandy or rum, lemon or lime juice and zest. When everything is well incorporated, add the honey and beat until homogenous. The idea here is to mix everything well; there will be minimal increase in volume.

Preheat the oven to 325°F/160°C. Grease the pan, then line the base with parchment paper and dust with flour.

Add the flour mixture to the honey mixture and whisk briefly until smooth. Using a balloon whisk as you would a spoon, fold in the egg whites, working the mixture just until there are no more white streaks to be seen.

Transfer to the prepared pan and bake for 45–50 minutes, or until a skewer inserted into the center of the cake comes out clean. Remove from the oven, then carefully loosen the sides of the cake from the pan and release the clip. Turn onto a wire rack to cool.

CHOCOLATE CAKES

TRADITIONAL SACHERTORTE

For years I could never pass a chocolate cake in a bakery window without stopping to gaze at it – and often buy it, especially if it had the magic word *Sacher* written in chocolate script on top. So it was quite obvious that I would eventually end up in Vienna. I dragged my husband off for a weekend of *Sacher*-tasting, earnestly assuring him that we would do all the cultural things too, like Schonbrunn Palace, the Opera, the Prater, Jugendstil house fronts and more. Needless to say, once I got started on my round of bakeries, most of the rest of the tourist itinerary was abandoned.

My expectations soared with each step. I was expecting the ultimate *Sacher* to conform to my personal idea of a wonderful chocolate cake: rich, satisfying and chocolatey without being overly sweet. The great *Sachertorte* dispute is common knowledge. Both the Hotel Sacher and Konditorei Dehmel claim its creation and took each other to court to try and gain exclusive legal rights to the name. Their cakes are certainly not identical, and although I enjoyed both, neither was what I had expected – or hoped – it would be. The composition was similar: two layers of chocolate cake sandwiched with apricot jam and covered with chocolate glaze. The Hotel Sacher's may have been guaranteed authentic by a chocolate seal but it was lighter in texture than Dehmel's (so for me at least, less satisfyingly chocolatey), and Dehmel was so generous with the sweet chocolate glaze that I couldn't finish it. And while Dehmel's gilt and baroque-type interior was packed with neatly hatted and suited Viennese matrons and their appendages, the sparer Hotel Sacher swarmed with camera-toting tourists, snapping away happily at their *Sachertorte* in various stages of demolition. Almost every other bakery I visited had its own *Sacher*-type cake too and many proudly advertised worldwide shipping. Plainly put, *Sacher* is big business in Vienna.

I often use two sandwich pans for this cake, instead of one springform pan, which is the classic way. The advantage is that the cakes bake more quickly (in approximately 30 minutes) and are, to my mind, moister and more tender. The slight disadvantage is that, unless your pans have absolutely straight sides, you get a cake that is not quite as neat as the one baked in a single pan. The choice is yours. If you decide to use the sandwich pans, be sure to check that both will fit in your oven at the same time. This is a straightforward cake to make if you use the alternative chocolate glaze. The "original" boiled frosting takes more time. Both glaze and icing need time to set.

CAKE

7 oz dark chocolate, chopped

2 tbsp rum

5½ oz/1 cup all-purpose flour

½ tsp baking powder

¼ tsp salt

6 eggs, separated

7 oz/1 cup granulated sugar

5½ oz/generous 1¼ sticks butter, softened

3½ oz/scant ⅓ cup strained apricot jam,
  warmed slightly

"ORIGINAL" BOILED CHOCOLATE FROSTING

9 oz/1¼ cups superfine sugar

3½ oz/3½ squares dark chocolate, finely chopped

¼ cup cocoa

8 tbsp water

ALTERNATIVE CHOCOLATE GLAZE

9 oz dark chocolate, chopped

4 fl oz/½ cup cream, light or heavy

EQUIPMENT:

9-inch springform pan

Put the chocolate for the cake in the top part of a double boiler. If you don't have a double boiler, choose a heatproof bowl that fits snugly on top of a saucepan. Put enough water in the bottom of the double boiler/saucepan so that the pan or bowl holding the chocolate will be just clear of the water. Bring the water to a boil, then turn the heat low and put the pan/bowl with the chocolate on top of this. Leave to melt, stirring from time to time. Remove from the heat and stir in the rum. Set aside.

Sift the flour, baking powder and salt together and set aside. Use an electric mixer to whisk the egg whites until foaming. Add 2¾ oz/generous ⅓ cup sugar in a steady stream while still whisking and continue to whisk until stiff peaks hold their shape. Transfer this mixture to another bowl. Rinse and dry the bowl and whisk so that they can be used again.

Cream the butter and the remaining sugar until light and fluffy. Add the egg yolks and whisk until well incorporated. Mix in the melted chocolate.

Use a handheld whisk to fold a third of the egg whites into this mixture. Fold in the flour mixture gradually and gently, followed by the rest of the egg whites. Stop working the batter as soon as the white streaks disappear.

Preheat the oven to 325°F/160°C.

Grease the springform pan, then line the base with parchment paper and dust with flour. Transfer the mixture to the pan and level the top, then bake for about 1 hour, or until a skewer inserted into the center of the cake comes out clean. Loosen the sides with a flexible spatula and release the clip. Invert onto a wire rack, then remove the parchment paper and leave to cool.

For the boiled frosting, put all the ingredients into a heavy-based saucepan and bring slowly to a boil, stirring gently. Boil over moderate heat until a sugar thermometer registers 230°F/110°C. Pour immediately into a large heatproof bowl and beat vigorously until thick and glossy. It is now ready to be used.

For the alternative chocolate glaze, put the chocolate and cream in a heavy-based saucepan over low heat. Stir gently to melt the chocolate. If you stir too vigorously, air bubbles will appear in the glaze. As soon as the mixture is homogenous, remove it from the heat and set aside to cool slightly and thicken. A spoonful dipped up and allowed to fall should do so in large blobs rather than a thin stream.

Cut the cooled cake in half horizontally. Keep it inverted so that the bottom will still be on top. This makes it easier to glaze and gives a neater finish. Sandwich the two halves with the apricot jam. Brush the surface of the cake free of crumbs. Pour the glaze onto the center of the cake and use swift, sweeping strokes to smooth it over the surface and sides. A garnish is optional. Leave to set in a cool place away from strong smells.

To cut the cake, hold a knife under very hot water for a few seconds, then dry it quickly and use it to cut wedges. Hold the knife under hot water and dry it after each cut. That way, the warm knife melts the chocolate and easily slips through the glaze, leaving no ragged edges.

TYROLEANS IN ALUMINUM FOIL GALOSHES

One day, when I was about 12, my friend Ingrid and I thought up a brilliant new hobby: we would adopt a far-off country and learn all about its language, culture and so on. Ingrid immediately opted for Italy and I chose Austria, which I had recently visited with my parents on one of those whirlwind continental tours popular at the time. The picturesque snow-capped peaks (my first sight of snow) and the chalets dripping with vibrantly colored geraniums had made a deep impression, far more so than the rival attractions of neighboring countries. Our first step was to go to Georgetown and search the stores to see what props we could find. Our luck was in; we discovered that the book section at Bookers department store had several phrase books, including Italian and German ones.

We set to work gleaning what nuggets we could from them and soon started regaling each other with choice morsels of factual knowledge and random sentences pronounced in our own inimitable way. The first German sentence I ever learned was very useful: *Muss ich mich bei der Polizei melden?* (Do I have to report to the police?). The craze lasted until my next birthday, culminating in a birthday cake like no other seen before – or since.

When our cook asked what kind of birthday cake I wanted, I had an instant brainwave. I would have the Austrian flag. A large slab of chocolate cake was baked and frosted with one white and two red horizontal bands, every bit as vivid as those remembered geraniums. Further inspiration struck and I ran to get the pair of Tyrolean dolls from my bedroom shelf where they resided with Indian (North American and Eastern), Thai, British and Spanish neighbors, alongside Marie Antoinette and a Beefeater guard thrown in for good measure. These happily smiling flaxen-haired dolls were given sturdy aluminum foil galoshes to complement their *dirndl* and *lederhosen* and were firmly implanted into the center of the cake to beam at all comers. I don't suppose I need tell you that my guests were in turn perplexed, amazed and taken aback before they managed to compose their expressions and string together a few words of politely insincere admiration.

CHOCOLATE SLICES

This is the cake I came up with after my *Sacher*-eating experiences in Vienna. It stands or falls with the quality of the chocolate, and every chocolate has its own unique flavor characteristics. I generally use Belgian Callebaut, a standard ingredient in my kitchen. We like it best with the chocolate slightly softened, so I usually pop the portions into the microwave oven for a few (very few!) seconds.

These slices are quick and simple to make, and can be assembled and served as soon as the cake is cool enough to handle.

9 oz dark chocolate, chopped

6¾ oz/1⅝ sticks butter, cut into cubes

3 tbsp rum or brandy

6¾ oz/scant 1 cup granulated sugar

5 eggs

4½ oz/scant 1 cup all-purpose flour (see note overleaf)

1 tsp baking powder

¼ tsp salt

about 5 oz/generous ⅓ cup strained apricot jam, warmed

lightly sweetened whipped cream, for serving

EQUIPMENT:

Swiss roll (jelly roll) pan,
  15 x 10 x 1 inch

Put the chocolate and butter in the top part of a double boiler. If you don't have a double boiler, choose a heatproof bowl that fits snugly on top of a saucepan. Put enough water in the bottom of the double boiler/saucepan so that the pan or bowl holding the chocolate will be just clear of the water. Bring the water to a boil, then turn the heat low and put the pan/bowl with the chocolate and butter on top of this. Leave to melt, stirring from time to time. Remove from the heat and stir in the rum. Set aside.

Grease the Swiss roll pan, then line with parchment paper.

Meanwhile, preheat the oven to 325°F/160°C.

Use an electric mixer to whisk the sugar and eggs together until the mixture is pale yellow and so thick that it falls off the whisk in a thick ribbon rather than a stream.

Sift the flour, baking powder and salt together.

Fold the chocolate mixture into the eggs, then fold in the flour carefully. Don't overwork the mixture. Stop as soon as there are no more pale streaks left. Transfer the mixture to the prepared pan and level the top with a spatula. Hold the pan about 6 inches above the work surface and then let it drop so that it falls with a gentle thud – right side up, of course! If you are reluctant to do this, don't bother with this step, but your cake will have a slightly spongier, more open texture. The slight impact allows some of the larger air bubbles to burst.

Bake in the oven for about 20 minutes. A skewer stuck into the center should come out fairly clean or with a few crumbs, but the cake should be just cooked and not allowed to dry out.

Leave to cool in the pan for about 5 minutes, then loosen the edges with a small spatula. Turn out very carefully onto a cooling rack. Be gentle – it's fragile. The best way is to invert a rack over the cake and then quickly re-invert the cake and the rack together so that the cake is now on the rack. Remove the parchment paper and leave to cool.

When cool, cut into 3 equal rectangles. Put one layer on a serving plate or board and spread with half of the apricot jam. Sandwich the rest of the cake in the same way. You might like to slip a large piece of cardboard or a thin sheet of metal like a loose pan base under each rectangle as you move each layer; they break easily.

Serve fresh, at room temperature with a dollop of lightly sweetened whipped cream on the side. You can keep it for a day or two, well wrapped, in the refrigerator, but bring to room temperature before serving.

NOTE

This cake is easily adapted to suit a gluten-free diet. Simply substitute very finely ground nuts such as almonds or hazelnuts for the flour and use a gluten-free baking powder. It will be denser than the flour version – but delicious!

DELUXE CHOCOLATE CRANBERRY CAKE

Although it uses a different method, this cake is like an extra-special brownie.
This is simple and fairly quick if the flavoring ingredients are chopped in advance.

5½ oz/1 cup all-purpose flour

1½ tsp baking powder

¼ tsp salt

4½ oz/1⅛ sticks butter, softened

4½ oz/generous ½ cup superfine sugar

2 eggs, lightly beaten with

1 tsp vanilla extract

1¼ oz/generous ¼ cup cocoa, dissolved in 3½ fl
   oz/scant ½ cup boiling water

1¼ oz/⅓ cup dried cranberries, finely chopped

1¼ oz/½ cup walnuts, finely chopped

1¼ oz dark chocolate, chopped into small pieces*

GLAZE

4½ oz/4½ squares dark chocolate, chopped

1¾ fl oz/scant ¼ cup milk

EQUIPMENT: *8-inch square pan*

Preheat the oven to 340°F/170°C. Grease the pan, and line with parchment paper.

Sift the flour with the baking powder and salt and set aside. Beat the butter and sugar until smooth and creamy. Add the beaten egg in two batches, scraping down the sides of the bowl and beating well after each addition. Fold in the flour in two batches, then add the cocoa paste and mix gently to blend. Add the cranberries, walnuts and chocolate and stop mixing as soon as they are incorporated.

Transfer the mixture to the prepared pan and level the top. Bake for 25–30 minutes, or until just done. A skewer inserted into the center of the cake should come out clean; if it still comes out with some mixture after 25 minutes, be sure to check that this really is batter and not just melted chocolate. Leave to cool in the pan for 5 minutes, then transfer the cake to a wire rack to cool completely.

For the glaze, put the chocolate and milk in a heavy-based saucepan over very low heat. Stir gently until the chocolate has melted completely. Remove from the heat and set aside for about 10 minutes, or until the mixture has thickened slightly.

Pour the glaze over the center of the cooled cake and use a spatula to spread it over the surface of the cake. Work with swift strokes for a smoother surface (it will start to set as you work) and don't try to get rid of every blemish – it is a homemade cake, after all! When the glaze has set completely, hold a knife under very hot water for a few seconds, dry it quickly and use it to cut the cake into portions. Hold the knife under hot water and dry it after each cut. That way, the warm knife melts the chocolate and easily slips through the glaze, leaving no ragged edges.

* I use Belgian Callebaut couverture chocolate that comes as small chocolate chips. If you can get good-quality chocolate chips, use them. If not, cut up a bar of good-quality dark chocolate.

CHOCOLATE TRUFFLE CAKE
RIGÓ JANCSI

Rigó Jancsi, or Johnny Thrush in English, was a Hungarian gypsy who created a major scandal at the end of the nineteenth century. As a violinist in a Parisian restaurant, he caught and held the eye of Clara Ward, a wealthy American beauty married to a Belgian prince. She subsequently deserted her husband and children to roam Europe with her handsome gypsy. Straitened circumstances and public ridicule appear to have taken their toll, and the liaison ended a few years later, Clara going on to marry twice more. This rich chocolate marvel, said to have been created by a tender-hearted pastry chef at the height of their romance, survived the break-up and continues to be popular in Hungary. My recipe uses a filling of chocolate and cream, but some Hungarians prefer to use a gelatine-based cocoa mousse.

Two thick pieces of cake are needed to enclose the chocolate filling, hence the pan specified. If you do not have a suitable pan, bake it on a small sheet with sides or a Swiss roll (jelly roll) pan, adjusting the baking time. You will need correspondingly more filling and glaze to cover the larger surface area created.

This is not a simple cake. The ganache filling is best chilled overnight. And you need to allow time for the filling to set before applying the glaze; the glaze will also need to set.

GANACHE FILLING

6 oz dark chocolate, chopped into small pieces

9 fl oz/1 cup whipping cream

CAKE

1 oz/¼ cup cocoa

3½ fl oz/scant ½ cup boiling water

5½ oz/1 cup all-purpose flour

½ tsp baking powder

¼ tsp salt

6 oz/scant 1 cup superfine sugar

3 eggs

2¾ oz/generous ½ stick butter, melted

GLAZE

7 oz dark chocolate, chopped into small pieces

5 fl oz/⅔ cup cream

EQUIPMENT:

12½ x 8½-inch cake pan

Start preparing the filling first. The ganache whips better if chilled for a few hours and may even be chilled overnight. Put the chocolate and cream in a heavy-based saucepan and place over low heat. Stir gently until all of the chocolate is completely melted. The mixture will look like chocolate milk. Remove from the heat and leave to cool, then chill, for at least 1 hour but preferably more.

For the cake, combine the cocoa and boiling water in a small bowl and stir well to remove any lumps. Sift the flour, baking powder and salt together in another bowl and set aside.

Grease the pan, then line the base with parchment paper and dust with flour. Preheat the oven to 350°F/180°C.

Put the sugar and eggs in a large bowl and whisk until thick and pale. Use a balloon whisk to mix in the cocoa, then gently fold in the flour mixture in two batches, alternating with the melted butter. Stop mixing as soon as the pockets of flour have disappeared and all the butter has been incorporated.

Transfer the mixture to the prepared pan, then level the top and bake for 20–25 minutes, or until a skewer inserted into the center of the cake comes out clean. Invert onto a wire rack and carefully peel off the parchment paper. Leave to cool completely, then cut into two equal pieces. If necessary, trim the tops to make them flat.

When you are ready to assemble the cake, make the glaze. Put the chocolate and cream in a heavy-based saucepan and stir gently to melt the chocolate. If you stir too vigorously, you will introduce air into the mixture, and this will result in bubbles in the glaze. Set aside.

Whisk the ganache filling. Transfer the filling mixture to a bowl and whisk until soft peaks hold their shape when you lift the whisk. If you whisk it too much beyond this point, it will become grainy and lose its sheen; it may even separate. Use this filling to sandwich the two pieces of cake and chill briefly so that the filling sets a little before glazing.

The glaze is ready to use when a spoonful dipped up and allowed to fall does so in large blobs rather than a thin stream. Pour the glaze onto the center of the cake and use swift, sweeping strokes to smooth it over the surface. Leave to set in a cool place away from strong smells.

When the glaze has set completely, hold a knife under very hot water for a few seconds, then dry it quickly and use it to trim the edges neatly and to cut the cake into small squares. Hold the knife under hot water and dry it after each cut. That way, the warm knife melts the chocolate and easily slips through the glaze, leaving no ragged edges.

Pictured on p. 153.

SPECKLED CHOCOLATE CAKE

Almonds, chocolate and a hint of cinnamon form a popular flavor combination in Central Europe, and this cake is as perfect for an afternoon snack as it is for dessert. Use a dark chocolate that has at least 50% cocoa solids to give a nice contrast with the sweeter background flavors. Serve with an optional dollop of lightly sweetened whipped cream garnished with a pinch of ground cinnamon.

This recipe is very straightforward and quick, especially if the chocolate is grated in advance.

7 oz/1⅓ cups blanched almonds, finely ground

3½ oz/⅔ cup all-purpose flour

¼ tsp salt

¼–½ tsp ground cinnamon

5½ oz extra bitter or dark chocolate, coarsely grated

3 eggs

8 oz/generous 1 cup superfine sugar

4½ oz/1⅛ sticks butter, melted and cooled slightly

lightly sweetened whipped cream

extra ground cinnamon

EQUIPMENT:

9-inch springform pan

Grease the pan, then line the base with parchment paper and dust with flour. Preheat the oven to 325°F/160°C.

Mix the ground almonds, flour, salt and cinnamon together and set aside.

The residue from powdered chocolate will give the cake a slightly muddy appearance, so sift any powder out from the grated pieces, making sure that you still have the correct weight left. Add to the flour and nut mixture.

Whisk the eggs and sugar together until thick and pale and the mixture falls off the whisk in a thick ribbon rather than a thin stream. Gently fold the flour mixture into the eggs. I find a balloon whisk better than a spatula – but don't whisk, just make light figure-eights with the whisk.

Add the melted butter and fold in with the whisk until there are no more streaks of butter evident in the batter. Don't overwork the mixture.

Transfer the batter to the prepared pan and smooth the surface with a scraper or spatula. Bake in a preheated oven for 45–55 minutes, or until light golden brown. A skewer inserted into the center of the cake should come out clean except for the odd smudge of melted chocolate.

Leave in the pan for about 5 minutes, then release the clip and transfer the cake to a wire rack to cool completely.

Well wrapped, the cake will keep for a few days at cool room temperature.

LAMINGTON SLICES

Strictly speaking, I should call these "Lamington-inspired slices," as I have taken a few liberties. This unwaveringly popular Australian favorite is made at home and by professional bakers, but the homemade version is much better than any commercial product. After numerous samplings in Queensland, I concluded that the latter can be uniform and unexciting in taste, albeit generous in size. The home baker, unhampered by troublesome things like profit margins, is fortunate to be able to create a far superior article. For the original, cubes of sponge cake are cloaked in chocolate and shredded coconut, creating an irresistible treat. A simple frosting is generally made from confectioner's sugar, cocoa and milk, and a layer of jam or butter cream is sometimes added. I prefer to use real chocolate and take the easy and lazy way out by glazing the entire cake before cutting it into slices, instead of fiddling around with coating each cube separately. However, instructions follow for those of you who prefer to do it the right way.

The origin of the name poses a bit of a puzzle. The most plausible explanation is that the cakes were named after Lord Lamington, Governor of Queensland from 1895 to 1901. The oldest known recipe was printed in *The Queenslander* newspaper in January 1902 and appeared for the first time in a cookbook a few years later, in the same region.

This is fairly quick if you make the slices, though cubes take longer. Allow enough time for the glaze to set before serving.

SPONGE CAKE

4½ oz/scant 1 cup all-purpose flour

1 oz/scant ¼ cup cornstarch

¼ tsp baking powder

¼ tsp salt

4 eggs

5½ oz/¾ cup superfine sugar

1 tsp vanilla extract

1¾ oz butter, melted and cooled slightly

GLAZE

7 oz dark chocolate, chopped

3½ fl oz/scant ½ cup milk

about 2–3 tbsp seedless raspberry preserve or
  jam

1¾ oz/generous ½ cup fine shredded
  (dry, unsweetened) coconut

EQUIPMENT:

8-inch square pan

Preheat the oven to 350°F/180°C. Grease the pan and dust with flour.

Sift the flour with the cornstarch, baking powder and salt, and set aside. Use an electric mixer to whisk the eggs, superfine sugar and vanilla extract until thick and pale. It should fall off the whisk in a ribbon rather than a thin stream. Gently fold in the flour mixture in two batches using a balloon whisk. Add the melted butter with the second batch of flour and mix just until there are no more streaks of flour or butter apparent in the batter.

Transfer the mixture to the baking pan and level the top. Bake for 20–25 minutes. When you press the top with a fingertip, the indentation you create should slowly regain its original shape. Transfer to a wire rack to cool.

For the glaze, put the chocolate and milk in a heavy-based saucepan over low heat. Stir gently to melt the chocolate. As soon as the mixture is homogenous, remove it from the heat and set aside to cool slightly and thicken. A spoonful dipped up and allowed to fall should do so in large blobs rather than a thin stream.

Cut the cooled cake in half and sandwich it with the raspberry preserve. Trim the sides if necessary. Brush the surface of the cake free of crumbs. Pour the glaze onto the middle of the cake and use swift, sweeping strokes to smooth it over the surface and the two long sides. Leave the glaze to set for about 15 minutes.

Scatter the shredded coconut over the top and gently press some against the sides of the cake. Leave to set completely in a cool place away from strong smells.

NOTE

To make "real" Lamingtons, omit the raspberry filling and cut the sponge into 16 cubes. You will need 2½–3 times the amount of chocolate glaze and coconut to coat 5 sides of each cube.

Use the glaze while it is still fairly liquid. Hold each cube on a fork over the bowl or pan of glaze and use a spoon or small jug to pour the glaze over the cake. That way, you can catch and re-use all spills.

When the glaze has almost set, put the coconut on a plate. Prick the unglazed bottom on a fork and lightly press each glazed side in the coconut.

NUT CAKES

SWISS WALNUT AND TOFFEE PIE
ENGADINER NUßTORTE

The Engadin valley in the southeastern Swiss district of Graubünden is justly famed for this pie, which is also known as *Bündner Nußtorte*. It requires a little more patience than most of the other recipes but is well worth the effort. It goes without saying that the walnuts should be of the best quality you can find; even a slight rancid taste will spoil the effect. Traditionalists use nothing but honey in the filling, and frown on substitutes. However, I find that light corn syrup or liquid glucose makes it easier to get a smoother filling, as either retards re-crystallization.

The pie is very rich, so serve it in small wedges. It will keep for at least 1 week in a cool place, well wrapped.

PASTRY

10½ oz/2 cups all-purpose flour

¼ tsp salt

5½ oz/generous 1¼ sticks butter, chilled and cubed

3½ oz/1 cup confectioner's sugar

1 egg, beaten

FILLING

9 oz/1¼ cups granulated sugar

2 tbsp water

2 tbsp honey, light corn syrup or liquid glucose

5 fl oz/⅔ cup heavy cream, warmed

9 oz/2¼ cups walnuts, coarsely chopped

EQUIPMENT:

9-inch springform pan

Make the pastry first. In a large bowl, mix the flour and salt. Rub in the butter until the mixture resembles fine breadcrumbs. Add the confectioner's sugar and rub in until well incorporated. Or simply put all the ingredients in a food processor and pulse until it resembles fine breadcrumbs, then transfer to a bowl.

Reserving 2 tsp egg, add the rest to the bowl and use your fingertips to bring it together. Add a few drops of water if necessary. Cover with plastic wrap and chill while you make the filling.

Have a pair of oven mitts standing by. Put the sugar, water and honey in a large heavy-based saucepan over medium heat. Stir gently to dissolve the sugar. Bring to a boil and let it continue to boil until it becomes a dark golden color. Stir from time to time.

Put on the oven mitts and pour the warm cream into the saucepan in a steady stream, stirring continuously. It will hiss and bubble ferociously, but the mitts should protect your hands and arms. Keep on stirring the mixture on medium heat until it is creamy and slightly thickened. To test, pour 1 tsp onto a cold saucer and tilt it after a few seconds. The mixture should spread slowly and not disintegrate into rivulets. Remove the saucepan from the heat and stir in the walnuts, coating them well. Set aside to cool.

Preheat the oven to 350°F/180°C. Grease the pan.

To assemble the pie, the pastry should be chilled but still malleable, or it will break when you roll it. Divide the pastry into two portions, one slightly larger than the other. Roll out the larger portion between two sheets of plastic wrap to a 12-inch circle and use it to line the pan. (Use the bottom sheet of plastic wrap to help move it, removing the sheet once the pastry is in place.) Press the edges of the pastry against the side of the pan.

Scrape the filling onto the pastry. Level the top as well as you can, but don't apply too much pressure, or you may tear the pastry and the filling will leak out. Fold the excess pastry inwards over the filling.

Roll the second piece of pastry to a neat 8½-inch circle. Trim if necessary. Moisten the edges of the pastry base in the pan with a little water and position the second pastry circle on top of this. Use a fork to crimp and seal the edges. Brush with the reserved egg and prick with a fork in several places. If you like, you can score a plaid pattern onto the surface with the fork.

Bake for 35–40 minutes, or until golden brown. Leave to cool until lukewarm in the pan, then loosen the sides, release the clip and carefully transfer the pie to a wire rack to cool completely.

Pictured on p. 169 and next pages.

NUTTY MERINGUE SLICES

This meringue is just the thing to make when you have a few egg whites left over from another recipe. It is a great standby to have in the freezer because it can be used to assemble a number of desserts in next to no time. Among other things, you can sandwich it with whipped cream or chocolate and serve it with seasonal berries; use it to garnish a bowl of ice cream; or simply break it into pieces and eat it on its own, straight from the freezer. I like to bake it at a higher temperature than is recommended for proper meringues: as it colors, it caramelizes a little, bringing out even more flavor.

3½ oz/1 cup ground almonds

1¾ oz/½ cup confectioner's sugar

2 tbsp cornstarch

⅛ tsp salt

3½ oz egg white (about 3)

3½ oz/½ cup superfine sugar

mixed berries, for serving

EQUIPMENT:
baking sheet 14 x 10 inches,
  lined with parchment paper*

FILLING

14 fl oz/1¾ cups whipping cream

sugar to taste

or

10½ oz dark chocolate, chopped

5 fl oz/⅔ cup whipping cream

Mix the ground almonds with the confectioner's sugar, cornstarch and salt, and set aside.

Preheat the oven to 325°F/160°C. Line the baking sheet with parchment paper.

Put the egg whites in a scrupulously clean bowl and whisk until foaming. Add the superfine sugar in a slow and steady stream while whisking, and continue to whisk until stiff peaks hold their shape. Using a balloon whisk, gently but thoroughly fold in the almond mixture. Stop as soon as all the white streaks have disappeared.

Transfer to the sheet and level the top as best you can, holding onto one edge of the paper to keep it in place. Bake for 30–35 minutes. Don't over-bake; the slight caramelization gives it extra flavor, but if you leave this for too long a bitter aftertaste may develop.

Remove from the oven and invert onto a wire rack. Carefully remove the parchment paper and leave to cool.

This will keep for several days, well wrapped, in a dry place or airtight container and also freezes well. It tends to soften a little as time goes by, but shouldn't become sticky. When you are ready to assemble the cake, cut the meringue sheet into three equal rectangles.

If you are making a chocolate filling, you can assemble the cake a few hours in advance. Put the chocolate and cream in a heavy-based saucepan and stir gently to melt the chocolate and incorporate the cream. Let it stand for a few minutes to cool and thicken a little, then use it to sandwich the three pieces of meringue together. Set aside for 1–2 hours to allow the filling to set.

If you would like to sandwich the meringue with whipped cream, do this just before serving, or the meringue will get soggy. Sweeten the cream to taste and whip it until soft peaks hold their shape. Then use it to sandwich the three pieces of meringue.

Serve with fresh berries.

* Cut the parchment paper generously at two opposing ends so that you have something to grab onto when spreading the meringue. If not, the sheet will slide back and forth, and the spreading will take forever.

STEEPED WALNUT CAKE
KARIDOPITA

Karidopita, sometimes referred to as Athenian Walnut Cake, is one of those typical Greek cakes born of a happy marriage between Eastern and Western ingredients and techniques. It has many remarkable features and defies categorization: it is a spice cake, nut cake and syrup cake rolled into one. Bread or rusk crumbs are used instead of flour, shortening the baking time a little. It is at its lightest on the day of baking, but the flavor mellows and the nuttiness becomes more evident after a day or so.

4½ oz/ 1 cup fine dried breadcrumbs
   or rusk crumbs

2 tsp baking powder

1 tsp ground cinnamon

¼ tsp ground clove

3½ oz/1 cup walnuts, finely ground

4 eggs

5½ oz/¾ cup superfine sugar

3½ oz/⅞ stick butter, melted and cooled slightly

5 fl oz/⅔ cup prepared sugar syrup
   (see recipe on p. 273)

EQUIPMENT:
9-inch round springform pan

Preheat the oven to 350°F/180°C. Grease the pan, then line the base with parchment paper and dust with flour.

Mix the breadcrumbs with the baking powder, cinnamon, clove and walnuts, and set aside.

In a large bowl, whisk the eggs and superfine sugar until thick and pale. When the whisk is lifted, the mixture should fall in a ribbon rather than a stream. Gently fold in the dry mixture using a balloon whisk. Add the butter and make sure it is well incorporated.

Transfer the batter to the prepared pan and bake for 30–35 minutes, or until a skewer inserted into the center of the cake comes out clean. The cake will shrink a little towards the end of the baking time.

Put the cake pan on a wire rack and loosen the sides from the pan with a spatula. Pour the syrup evenly over the top of the hot cake, starting from the outside and working your way towards the middle with a circular movement. Leave to cool.

When cool, release the clip and carefully turn the cake onto a flat surface. Remove the bottom of the pan and the paper and re-invert the cake onto a plate, then serve. Alternatively, store in an airtight container.

GERBEAUD SLICES
GERBEAUD/ZSERBÓ SZELET

Gerbeaud House occupies palatial premises on Vörösmarty tér, one of the finest squares in Pest, Hungary, where you can expect to be entertained by impromptu musical performances. On an average day, you might hear the deep and ominous rumble of a huge drum accompanied by what appear to be native bagpipes competing with violinists and breakdancers for the attention of passers-by and patrons. This dignified white building is a place of pilgrimage for lovers of cake and pastries, locals and tourists alike. It can seat several hundred guests, either in comfortably cushioned cane chairs on the terrace or in beautifully upholstered chairs in one of the stylish, classically decorated salons. (Sadly, this elegance and luxury is reflected in the bill.)

Emil Gerbeaud, on whose name the enterprise rests, came from a family of Swiss confectioners. After perfecting his art in several European capitals, including Paris, he went to Budapest at the invitation of Henrik Kugler. Himself the son and grandson of confectioners, Kugler had expanded his father's business, moving to the present location in 1870. Gerbeaud became the owner in 1884, when Kugler retired, and he proceeded to lift the already renowned patisserie to even more dizzying heights. He is credited with introducing Hungarians to the finer French-influenced flavors, which they could enjoy in sumptuous surroundings. Wars, occupation and nationalization took their toll, and for a brief period during World War I the building even housed horses instead of discerning pastry eaters. The communist era saw the proud name removed from the façade and the shop renamed after the square on which it stood. The Gerbeaud family are long gone, but the name has now been restored and its reputation remains undiminished.

Their signature cake, the Gerbeaud Slice, has become public property and is imitated by rival patissiers and home bakers alike, some of whom like to add a personal touch. Competitor Ruszwurm, housed in a microscopic but equally famous shop situated near Buda Castle on the other side of the Danube, makes a Gerbeaud Slice that appears to include apples. Having tasted it, I can't say that the apple does great things for the flavor or texture, but many locals prefer it to the original.

The following version, more in the style of the original, is simple to make at home. Even though the unusual pastry is yeast-based, the actual preparation time is quite short. The good thing about these slices – apart from the fact that they are irresistible – is that you can vary the sweetness to suit your taste, by using a different blend of dark chocolate or a jam or preserve that is either sweeter or tarter.

STARTER

1 tsp sugar

1 oz/scant ¼ cup all-purpose flour

1¼ tsp active dry yeast

1¾ fl oz/scant ¼ cup warm milk

PASTRY

8 oz/1½ cups all-purpose flour

¼ tsp baking powder

4½ oz/1 stick butter, chilled and cubed

1¼ oz/½ cup confectioner's sugar

¼ tsp salt

2 egg yolks

FILLING

3½ oz/1 cup walnuts, finely ground

3½ oz/½ cup superfine sugar

4½ oz/generous ⅓ cup tart apricot preserve or
   jam

GLAZE

4½ oz dark chocolate, chopped

1¾ fl oz/scant ¼ cup milk

EQUIPMENT:

8-inch square pan

For the starter, mix together all the ingredients in a small bowl. Cover with plastic wrap and set aside in a warm place for 10 minutes, or until bubbles appear on the surface.

For the pastry, mix the flour with the baking powder. Rub the cold butter into the flour with your fingertips until it resembles coarse breadcrumbs. Add the sugar and salt and combine well. You can also simply put it all into a food processor and pulse until it reaches the desired consistency, then transfer to a bowl for the next step.

For the filling, combine the walnuts with the superfine sugar and set aside.

Add the starter and the egg yolks to the other pastry ingredients and knead well to make a soft, pliable dough. Cover and let it rest for about 10 minutes, then divide into 3 portions.

On a lightly floured surface (a silicone mat is ideal), roll out a piece of pastry so that it is about ½ inch larger than the bottom of the pan on all sides. Grease the pan, then use the rolling pin to transfer the pastry carefully to the pan and to line it so that the excess pastry comes up the sides. This will prevent jam and sugar from seeping out and leaving ugly streaks.

Spread half of the jam on the pastry and sprinkle half of the walnut and sugar mixture over it.

Roll out a second piece of pastry and trim it if necessary so that it fits neatly over the filling. Spread the remaining filling over this layer, then top with the third piece of pastry and press gently to make the top and edges even. Cover with plastic wrap and leave at room temperature for about 1 hour. Don't expect to see it rise because it won't.

Preheat the oven to 340°F/170°C.

Use a fork or sharply pointed knife to prick several rows of holes on the surface of the pastry and bake for 25–30 minutes, or until golden brown. Remove the pan from the oven and allow it to stand for about 5 minutes, then invert the pastry onto a rack to cool.

When the pastry has cooled completely, make the glaze. Put the chocolate and milk in a heavy-based saucepan and heat it very gently, stirring to melt the chocolate and to combine it with the milk.

Pour the glaze over the top of the pastry (the smooth inverted bottom) and use swift strokes to spread it neatly.

When the glaze has set, trim two opposing sides of the pastry and make a cut down the middle at right angles to the trimmed sides. This gives neater slices. Slice each half into 6 or 8 pieces. This will keep at cool room temperature for a few days, but the pastry will soften a little as time goes by.

SEMOLINA AND ALMOND CAKE
BASBOUSA

Basbousa, known as *namura* in some countries, is a typical Middle Eastern cake that usually consists of semolina alone or semolina mixed with nuts like almonds, coconut or pistachio. Yogurt is sometimes added to the batter, and the cake is more often than not steeped in a sugar syrup when it is removed from the oven. Sometimes melted butter is also poured over the baked *basbousa*, but I find that this only makes the cake unnecessarily rich without enhancing the flavor. It does, however, remain a cake that is best served in small portions. I like to serve it for dessert after a spicy meal. I find it addictive and take a small portion – every time I pass the dish.

3½ oz/⅔ cup blanched almonds, finely ground

5½ oz/generous ¾ cup semolina

1 tsp baking powder

¼ tsp salt

5½ oz/¾ cup Greek-style (strained) plain yogurt

3½ oz/½ cup superfine sugar

4½ oz/generous 1 stick butter, melted and cooled slightly

7 fl oz/¾ cup prepared cold sugar syrup (p. 273)

EQUIPMENT:
9-inch springform pan

Mix the almonds, semolina, baking powder and salt together in a bowl. Set aside.

Preheat the oven to 350°F/180°C. Grease the pan, then line the base with parchment paper and dust with flour.

Beat the yogurt and sugar together until the sugar has become well incorporated. Add the butter and mix well. Add the dry ingredients and beat well to mix.

Transfer to the pan and bake for 30–35 minutes, or until a skewer inserted into the middle comes out clean and the cake is golden brown in color.

Remove the cake from the oven and use a sharp spatula or knife to make 6 parallel cuts. Do this carefully, with just one downwards movement; the cake is very fragile. Turn the pan slightly and cut a further 6 times so that you have diamond-shaped pieces. Pour the cold syrup over the hot cake. To bring out the flavor, leave to stand for a few hours before serving.

ALMOND CAKE
PASTEL DE SANTIAGO

Spaniards are fond of a sweet breakfast, when they bother with the meal at all.
As a student in Salamanca, it took me a while to get used to the fact that breakfast
consisted of a few Marie biscuits or a small Magdalena cake accompanied by a cup
of milky coffee or hot chocolate – and if you were really unlucky, a hot and cloyingly
sweet "chocolate" drink called ColaCao. Lunch was a far way off, at 2:30 pm, and
at mid-morning break there was a group sprint to the café across the road from the
lecture rooms. There we would attempt to quiet the protests of rumbling stomachs
with more *café con leche* and a pastry or a *bocadillo*, a crusty roll with potato omelet,
Manchego cheese or Serrano ham.

This cake is very popular in northern Spain, and, in true Spanish style, you can
expect to have it served at breakfast. However, it also makes an excellent dessert. It is
named after St James (Santiago in Spanish), whose remains were interred at Santiago
de Compostela in the ninth century. James, one of the apostles closest to Jesus, was the
first to be martyred when Herod Agrippa had him executed by sword. In the Middle
Ages, Santiago de Compostela ranked as one of the three most important places of
pilgrimage, coming only after Jerusalem and Rome, and it still draws large numbers
of pilgrims every year. The cake is sometimes decorated with a stencil of a sword or
a large scallop shell, symbols that are both associated with St James. The scallop shell
appears on his hat in depictions from the fourteenth century onwards, and the two
are linked in more than one language. Both Dutch and French, for instance, refer to
a scallop as a "St James" shell – *Sint Jakobsschelp* and *coquille St Jacques* respectively.

My recipe uses butter, but you will often find it made with olive oil in Spain.
Butter has a superior flavor and better creaming properties, but if you would like to
try it with oil, use the equivalent weight and heat the oil very slowly with a piece of
lemon rind, allowing it to cool completely before use. This Spanish technique tames
the strong and distinctive taste of the oil, making it more flavorful and suitable for
use in a cake. The eggs and sugar should then be whisked together and the oil added
last, after the flour.

7 oz/1¼ sticks butter, softened
12 oz/1¼ cups superfine sugar
5 eggs, lightly beaten
grated zest of 1 lemon
12 oz/2⅓ cups blanched almonds, finely ground
3½ oz/⅔ cup all-purpose flour

¼ tsp salt
confectioner's sugar, for dusting

EQUIPMENT:
9-inch springform pan

Preheat the oven to 350°F/180°C. Grease the pan and line with parchment paper.

Beat the butter until smooth. Add the sugar and continue to beat until lightened in color and fluffy. Add the egg in three batches, scraping down the sides of the bowl well after each addition. Add the lemon zest with the last batch of egg.

Mix the almonds, flour and salt together and gently fold into the creamed mixture.

Transfer the mixture to the prepared baking pan, then level the top and bake for 50–60 minutes, or until a skewer inserted into the center of the cake comes out clean. The cake should be moist but not under-baked. Leave to cool in the pan for about 5 minutes, then loosen the edges with a spatula and release the clip. Transfer to a wire rack to cool completely.

When the cake has cooled, dust lightly with confectioner's sugar.

YOM TOV TIK

In our house, this cake is called *Yom Tov Tik*, Dutch-Yiddish for "holiday food." It started when my son was a toddler and has now become part of the family vocabulary. I served it one evening during Passover while my father-in-law was visiting, and as he slowly savored a mouthful, he murmured appreciatively that it was "real *Yom Tov Tik*." Leon heard that and firmly held on to it as the name of the cake, which has remained one of his favorites.

Now for just a bit of background to explain things: although the Jewish population of the Netherlands has now been decimated, it was sizable before World War II. My own experiences of Jewish life here are obviously fairly recent, though they span almost three decades, but I have always listened with interest to the stories related by the friends and relatives who visited my in-laws. Tante Surry was a regular and welcome visitor. She and my mother-in-law were closely bound together by ties forged at places that are just names in history books to most of us: Dachau, Bergen Belsen, Sobibor and Auschwitz.

She was a cheerful, friendly woman who could talk on a wide variety of topics at great length. In addition to her ironic little jokes – like telling inquisitive strangers that the concentration camp number tattooed on her forearm was her phone number, as she was quite forgetful – she would offer spontaneous tidbits of information at the appropriate moment. She was about 20 when the war broke out, one of a large brood of children of a Hague greengrocer and his wife. She and her youngest sister were the only survivors. Sentence by sentence, she built up wonderfully vivid word pictures about pre-war life.

While not exactly poor, they had to do the necessary scrimping and saving to make ends meet. Added to that was the burden of having to pay more for Kosher food than for regular groceries. In general, only the very religious ate strictly Kosher throughout the year, buying solely those foods that had been approved by the rabbinate. But at Passover, all Jewish households ate not only Kosher but "Kosher for Passover," which is even more restrictive. Wheat flour, and any products that ferment, are banned during this period, which commemorates the flight of the Israelites from Egypt. Pursued by Pharaoh's men, Moses and his followers were compelled to keep moving, so there was no time to let their bread rise and they baked it in its unleavened state. Ever since then, Jews throughout the world have marked the occasion by replacing bread with matzohs and matzoh-based products for the eight days of Passover.

In Tante Surry's house, Passover was the great event of the year and money would be set aside regularly beforehand in order to be able to buy the special foods required. It was a very taxing time for the household budget. The thin matzohs need more topping than bread, and butter has a sneaky way of creeping into all the little undulations on the crackers' generous expanse. Treats like cake and cookies, normally made with flour, would now have to be made with matzohs, matzoh meal and nuts. In addition to that – and I speak from personal experience – matzohs are not very filling and one eats matzoh after matzoh before reaching the pleasant state of satisfaction that bread induces more quickly.

First, the house was cleansed of any lingering traces of *chametz*, polluting non-Passover food, and the Passover crockery was brought down from the attic. Then the buying started. In their household, that included several institutional-sized boxes of matzohs, pounds and pounds of butter, hefty chunks of salty, mature Gouda cheese and mounds of thinly sliced *pekelvlees* (corned beef), to be eaten with generous helpings of *krijn*, grated horseradish mixed with vinegar and sugar. Not all of the matzohs would be eaten in their original form. Instead of the usual vermicelli, *Shabbes* soup would now sport matzoh dumplings, delicious with more brain-searing *krijn*. *Gremselich*, pancakes made from matzoh crumbs, apple, raisins, nuts and egg, soaked up copious quantities of butter from the frying pan and would be devoured with alacrity as soon as they left it. Shortbread and sand cake made way for marzipan and lusciously rich nut cakes, compact without leavening, but absolutely mouth-watering – all simply delicious "*Yom Tov Tik*." How my father-in-law must have missed such food during the three lonely, holiday-less years he spent in an abandoned hayloft in the middle of an isolated field in eastern Holland, fearing that each approaching step might be made by an enemy boot.

FLOURLESS PASSOVER CAKE
OUR YOM TOV TIK CAKE

This is the type of cake that is usually eaten during the Jewish holiday season of Passover, or *Pesach*. For the eight days of Passover, the staple at this time is the matzoh, an unleavened bread that looks and tastes like a water cracker. The wheat for the matzohs is grown under strict supervision and is given no chance to ferment at any stage. Observant Jews remove all opened products from the pantry prior to Passover and replace them with fresh ones that are not simply Kosher, but are Kosher for Passover. On the day before Passover, there is a ceremony that greatly appeals to children: a candle is lit and used to track down any crumbs remaining in the house. Some people even have separate crockery especially for Passover in order to avoid accidental contact with fermented products.

This cake contains no meal of any kind and relies on finely ground nuts for body. And if the final product is a little less slick than most other cakes, be happy nevertheless: at Passover, it is a treat to have a cake that is (a) relatively light in texture, and (b) free of matzoh in any form! It is delicious as it is, but I also like to serve it for dessert any time of the year. Try it with raspberries macerated in *crème de cassis*, and a dollop of sweetened whipped cream on the side, or glaze it with chocolate.

If potato starch is hard to find and if you are not making it for Passover, you could use cornstarch instead. The potato starch does give it a more melt-in-the-mouth quality, though.

4 eggs

7 oz/1 cup superfine sugar

7 oz/1⅓ cups blanched hazelnuts
   or almonds, finely ground

¼ tsp salt

4 packed tbsp potato starch

4 oz/1 stick butter, melted

1 tbsp brandy or Kosher spirit of your choice

GLAZE

4 fl oz/½ cup cream, light or heavy

4½ oz/4½ squares dark chocolate, chopped

EQUIPMENT:

8-inch square pan

Preheat the oven to 350°F/180°C. Line the pan with parchment paper cut to come up about 1 inch above the top of the pan.

Use an electric mixer (or failing that, a strong wrist and a hand whisk) to whisk the eggs and sugar until the mixture falls off the whisk in a thick ribbon rather than a thin stream.

Mix the nuts, salt and potato starch together, then fold gently into the egg mixture with a balloon whisk. Add the melted butter and brandy and fold in with the whisk until there are no more streaks of butter evident in the batter. Don't overwork the mixture.

Transfer the batter to the prepared pan and smooth the surface with a scraper or spatula. Bake in the oven for 30 minutes, or until light golden brown. A skewer inserted into the center of the cake should come out clean. The top will billow out a bit towards the end, but will subside as it cools.

Remove the pan from the oven and leave to cool for about 5 minutes, then grip the paper lining on two opposing sides and lift the cake from the pan. Put it on a wire rack, ease down the paper sides and leave to cool completely.

When completely cool, re-invert the cake onto a serving plate and carefully remove the paper. If you plan to glaze the cake, do not re-invert it; the bottom is smoother and will give a better finish.

To glaze the cake, put the cream and chocolate in a small saucepan over a very low heat and stir until the chocolate has melted and the mixture is homogenous. Let it cool slightly, then pour over the top of the cooled cake and spread swiftly with a palette knife. Leave to set.

Slice into pieces, dipping a knife into hot water and drying quickly before each cut to avoid damaging the glaze.

COCONUT CAKES

COCONUT TEA BREAD

This tea bread, the kind favored in the Caribbean, is fairly compact with a simple, clean coconut taste, especially if you use fresh or frozen coconut (the latter will need to be brought to room temperature). It can be eaten as it is, or with butter. Simple and quick to make, it keeps well for a few days but is at its lightest on the day of baking.

7 oz/1⅓ cups all-purpose flour

1¾ tsp baking powder

¼ tsp salt

2 eggs

4½ oz/generous ½ cup superfine sugar

1 tsp vanilla extract

5½ oz finely grated coconut, fresh or frozen *or*

   3¼ oz/1 cup fine shredded

   (dry, unsweetened) coconut mixed with

   4 tbsp warm water

3½ oz/⅞ stick butter, melted

EQUIPMENT: *1-lb loaf pan*

If using shredded coconut, mix it with the water and leave to stand until needed. If using frozen coconut, allow it to come to room temperature.

Preheat the oven to 325°F/160°C. Grease the loaf pan, then dust with flour.

Sift the flour with the baking powder and salt and set aside.

Whisk the eggs, sugar and vanilla extract until thick and lightened in color. Add the flour mixture, coconut and melted butter and mix well.

Bake for 45–50 minutes, or until a skewer inserted into the center of the loaf comes out clean. Don't over-bake. Cool on a wire rack.

Serve in slices.

COCONUT CAKE

This cake is a little richer and lighter in texture than the Coconut Tea Bread (opposite) and makes a good dessert served with fruit and whipped cream or crème fraîche. Quick and easy to make, the cake will stay moist for a few days but is at its best a few hours after baking.

8 oz/1½ cups all-purpose flour

2¼ tsp baking powder

¼ tsp salt

8 oz/2 sticks butter, softened

8 oz/generous 1 cup superfine sugar

3 eggs, lightly beaten with

1 tsp vanilla extract

8 oz finely grated coconut, fresh or frozen

or 4¾ oz/1½ cups fine shredded (dry, unsweetened) coconut mixed with 3 fl oz/⅓ cup warm water

EQUIPMENT:

8-inch square pan

If using shredded coconut, mix it with the water and leave to stand until needed. If using frozen coconut, allow it to come to room temperature.

Preheat the oven to 325°F/160°C. Grease the pan, then dust with flour.

Sift the flour with the baking powder and salt, and set aside.

Beat the butter and sugar until creamy and lightened in color. Lightly beat the eggs with the vanilla extract and then add to the mixture, a little at a time, beating well after each addition. Gently fold in the flour in three batches, then fold in the coconut and mix it just enough to distribute the coconut throughout the cake batter.

Bake in the oven for 35–40 minutes, or until the cake is light golden brown and a skewer inserted into the center comes out clean. Cool on a wire rack.

Pictured on p. 189.

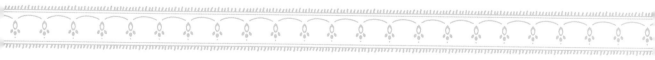

COCONUT AND CASSAVA PUDDING
CASSAVA PONE

If you are one of those people who likes to taste a bit of this and a pinch of that while cooking, try to restrain yourself with the cassava. You are unlikely to eat a lethal quantity, but even small amounts of the prussic acid formed when the tubers are cut and exposed to air might cause stomach upsets. However, prussic acid is soluble in water and dissipates when heated, so cassava is completely harmless once cooked. Cassava (*Manihot esculenta*), also known as manioc and yucca, is native to Central and South America and has been used since time immemorial by the indigenous peoples of the region. One of the most delicious products of cassava is *cassareep*, a dark and thick sauce, similar to soy sauce, which is used to flavor succulent stews like Pepper Pot, in which meat is cooked slowly with *cassareep*, sweet spices and a generous amount of fresh chilies.

A primitive form of flatbread is still a staple of many Amerindian tribes in Guyana. Indeed, one of the most popular picture postcards, which has been available for as long as anybody can remember, shows thin discs of cassava meal being sun-dried on the thatched roofs of huts in an unnamed place in The Interior, as the vast hinterland is referred to by locals. More hygienic and less picturesque methods are no doubt used today, but these cards have led many a foreign recipient to shake their heads in wonder. The bread is rather an acquired taste and is sold to only a limited extent else-

where in the country. It is unleavened and quite hard, and many people like it toasted and spread with butter, neatly combining heritage with colonial veneer in a single solid mouthful. The tubers are used in a variety of savory dishes, mostly stews and soups. They are also boiled and seasoned much as potatoes are in the West, and eaten as an accompaniment to meat or fish. One of the simplest and tastiest ways to prepare cassava is to sauté chunks of boiled cassava with flakes of salted cod, some onion and chilies to taste. Though the repertoire is fairly limited, cassava makes excellent sweet dishes too, such as the following recipe.

This fairly substantial but delicious pudding is a favorite snack in the Caribbean region as well as in Surinam, where it is known as "*bojo*" (pronounced "bo-yo"). Similar puddings are made in many Asian countries. My Filipino friends like to give it a slightly looser texture by adding shredded gelatinous young coconut instead of using only the firm flesh of older coconuts. They also line the baking dish with banana leaf for an added flavor dimension.

Cassava Pone is whipped up in next to no time and both cassava and coconut are available frozen and ready-grated from ethnic supermarkets. I have added a few eggs to lighten the mixture, but this is generally omitted in the Caribbean, where people prefer a closer, stickier *pone* with a hint of black pepper.

This is extremely simple and quick once the grated cassava and coconut are at room temperature.

14 oz finely grated cassava, fresh or frozen

9 oz finely grated coconut, fresh or frozen

3½ oz/⅞ stick butter, melted

2 eggs, well beaten

a generous pinch of freshly grated nutmeg

5½ oz/¾ cup sugar

OPTIONAL:

a pinch of finely ground black pepper

EQUIPMENT:

a shallow oven-safe dish, with a capacity of about 2 pints/5 cups

If frozen, allow the cassava and coconut to come to room temperature.

Preheat the oven to 350°F/180°C. Grease the oven-safe dish.

Mix all of the ingredients together until homogenous and then transfer to the oven-safe dish. Level the surface and bake for about 35–40 minutes, or until the top is golden brown and the mixture has set. Serve lukewarm or at room temperature, cutting squares directly from the dish.

CORN PONE AND FAT TOP

The word "*pone*" is derived from the Algonquin/Delaware Indian *appone* and *apan*, meaning baked. When Americans speak of corn *pone*, they generally mean a cornmeal quick-bread made with lard, milk, baking powder and perhaps an egg or two, and then baked in a pan in the oven or dropped in spoonfuls onto a skillet. In the Caribbean, corn *pones* are denser and often use a little coconut as well.

In Guyana, *Corn Pone* is instantly transformed into Fat Top by means of the optional topping, and its name will no doubt do very little to endear it to the uninitiated. Please don't let it put you off; people from my part of the world use salient physical characteristics liberally in their descriptions and often with brutal honesty. I know people called Lil Gal, Fat Boy, Hopalong, Finey ("fine" means thin) – and even Gold Boy, a name probably given by doting parents. Fat Top is a very homely dish, which combines a cornmeal base with a baked-on topping of coconut milk – the "fat" top. It can be made under the most primitive conditions: in the past, when earthen fireplaces, or *chulhas*, were a common means of cooking in the countryside, the mixture used to be poured into large oval sardine cans and placed directly over the embers. They were covered with whatever sheet metal was at hand, usually an offcut of galvanized roofing material, and coals were heaped onto the metal sheet. The cooking holes of the *chulha* were then covered to improvise an oven-like situation. Later, when metal box ovens became more widespread, they were baked in these contraptions, which were perched over the fireplace. Obviously, temperature regulation was next to impossible, so it was all a very hit-or-miss kind of affair. Modern ovens offer greater precision, but Fat Top remains the comfort food it has always been.

Note that purists, among them my sister Goutami, will never use a raising agent as I have done here. She and I have an ongoing debate about how to make proper *Cassava Pone* and Fat Top. Normally, she defers to me in baking matters, but in this case she stubbornly insists that her way – the authentic way – is better. As she waxes lyrical about the texture of the unleavened, un-egged corn and cassava *pones* so beloved by Guyanese, adjectives like "dry," "gummy," "rubbery," "substantial" and even "leaden" flit around my mind. I will concede that she has a point about the topping: the coconut milk topping will form a neat layer on top of an unleavened mixture and give a nice effect, but my way makes a moister and lighter Fat Top. To be truthful, I've never been a fan of the heavier, crumbly *Corn Pone*. However, if you would like to try it, the recipe gives instructions for both.

Pones and Fat Top are usually eaten as a snack, but warm Fat Top also makes an excellent pudding, especially in the colder months. The recipe is easily halved for smaller households and should be baked in a correspondingly smaller dish.

This is easy and fairly quick once the grated coconut is at room temperature.

BASE

6 oz/1 cup fine cornmeal

5½ oz/¾ cup granulated sugar

¼ tsp salt

¼ tsp freshly grated nutmeg

5¼ oz grated coconut, fresh or frozen

3½ oz/⅞ stick butter, melted

1¼ tsp baking powder*

5 fl oz/⅔ cup dairy or coconut milk

1 tsp vanilla extract

TOPPING FOR FAT TOP

14 fl oz/1¾ cups coconut milk

2¼ oz/generous ⅓ cup granulated sugar

½ tsp vanilla extract

EQUIPMENT:

a shallow oven-safe dish, with a capacity of about 2 pints/5 cups

If using frozen coconut, allow it to come to room temperature.

Mix the cornmeal, sugar, salt, nutmeg, coconut and melted butter together in a bowl and leave to stand for about 5 minutes.

Meanwhile, preheat the oven to 350°F/180°C. Grease the oven-safe dish.

Add the baking powder, milk and vanilla extract and beat well. Don't worry if a little milk seeps out at this point.

Transfer to the oven-safe dish and level the top.

For *Corn Pone*, bake for 35–40 minutes, or until golden brown and a skewer inserted into the center of the *pone* comes out clean. Remove from the oven and leave it in the dish.

Eat warm or cold on the day of making. This has a crumbly, crunchy texture.

For the Fat Top, bake the mixture as described above for 20 minutes.

Meanwhile, whisk the coconut milk, sugar and vanilla extract together until the sugar has dissolved. After 20 minutes, pour carefully over the top of the *pone* and continue baking for a further 25–30 minutes, or until a golden-brown skin forms over the top. Remove from the oven and leave it in the dish. The topping will have penetrated the *pone* and it will be moist and creamy.

Eat warm or cold on the day of making, and if you have leftovers, heat them up in the microwave for a few seconds to improve the texture.

* The baking powder may be omitted for a more dense version, in which the topping will remain on top and not penetrate the cake, as it does in my version.

OTHER CAKES

GREEN TEA CAKE

Powdered green tea, or *matcha* (the tea used for the Japanese tea ceremony), makes an excellent flavoring for cakes and fillings and is becoming increasingly popular in the West at the top end of the market. It transforms batter into a gorgeous moss green color – I could make this cake for that alone – and produces an equally delightful flavor. A word of warning, though: the tea has an extremely high caffeine content. Not for nothing was it drunk at regular intervals by Japanese monks who wanted to stay alert during rituals. Serving it with sweetened whipped cream will soften the kick a little. My friend Pia has been baking this cake ever since I shared the recipe with her several years ago and she sometimes sandwiches it with a layer of lemon curd.

Japanese shops and some specialist tea shops sell *matcha*. Make sure that you buy a very finely ground kind that has not been sweetened. Some *matcha* is sold sweetened, for making ice tea, and will not give a good result since it will be difficult to adjust the recipe accordingly.

5 eggs, separated

5½ oz/¾ cup superfine sugar

2¾ oz/½ cup all-purpose flour

1 oz cornstarch

1 tbsp unsweetened green tea powder (*matcha*)

EQUIPMENT:

8-inch square pan

Whisk the egg whites until frothy. Still whisking, add 1¾ oz/¼ cup sugar and continue to whisk until stiff peaks hold their shape.

Preheat the oven to 350°F/180°C. Grease the pan and dust with flour.

In another bowl, whisk the yolks with the remaining sugar until thick and pale.

Sift the flour with the cornstarch and green tea powder.

Carefully fold the whites into the yolks in three batches and add the flour mixture in two batches.

Transfer the mixture to the prepared pan and bake for 25 minutes, or until a skewer inserted into the middle of the cake comes out clean. Remove from the oven, then turn out onto a wire rack to cool.

Pictured on p. 199.

SEMOLINA SPONGE
REVANI

This lemon-flavored sponge, which is baked in Greece and Turkey, is the plainer but lighter cousin of the *basbousa* and *namura* of neighboring countries. This version has very little sugar in the batter, as it is steeped in syrup after baking. Use all the syrup because the cake needs it for moistness. This is simple and quick to make, especially if the syrup has been made beforehand.

4½ oz/scant 1 cup all-purpose flour

4½ oz/⅔ cup fine semolina

1½ tsp baking powder

¼ tsp salt

4 eggs

3½ oz/½ cup superfine sugar

pinch of lemon zest

¾ oz/scant ¾ stick butter, melted and cooled slightly

9 fl oz/1 cup prepared cold sugar syrup (see p. 273)

EQUIPMENT:

9-inch springform pan

Preheat the oven to 350°F/180°C. Grease the pan, then line the base with parchment paper and dust with flour.

Mix the flour, semolina, baking powder and salt together in a bowl. Set aside.

Whisk the eggs, sugar and lemon zest together until thick and light in color. Fold in the dry ingredients, then the butter, and mix well.

Transfer the mixture to the pan and bake for 30–35 minutes, or until a skewer inserted into the middle comes out clean and the cake is golden brown in color.

Remove from the oven, but do not turn the oven off. Use a sharp spatula or knife to cut the sponge into 6 parallel strips. Turn the pan slightly and cut a further 6 times so that you have diamond-shaped pieces. Pour the cold syrup over the hot cake and put it back in the oven for 5 minutes. Remove from the oven and leave to stand for a few minutes.

Eat lukewarm or cold.

TIPSY CORNMEAL CAKE

Having secured the island of Curaçao off the coast of Venezuela, the Spaniards gamely decided to try growing a few crops on the obviously arid land. They planted Valencia oranges, but instead of producing the delicious sweet fruit they anticipated, climatic conditions conspired to produce a bitter, inedible fruit, and the trees were left to run wild. Centuries later, a curious soul discovered that the oils in the skin made an excellent flavoring, and recipes were developed for the liqueur known as Curaçao. The first liqueurs were distilled on the island but European companies, Dutch ones in particular, began to make their own versions and still remain significant producers of Curaçaos. The most popular type is perhaps the deadly-looking blue one that is such a prized component of many cocktails.

The once despised bitter oranges, known locally as *lahara*, have now been dignified with the botanical name *Citreus aurantium currassuviensis*, and their juice and peel are a welcome flavoring in Curaçao cuisine. This recipe is loosely based on a local cake recipe that calls for both those things, neither of which are available outside the region. This is my own version, using orange zest and orange-based liqueur instead of the original bitter orange peel, juice and rum. I have chosen Triple Sec instead of Curaçao purely on the grounds of its color. Triple Sec is also made from bitter oranges, among other things, and is clear so it won't make the batter muddy-looking. You could also use Grand Marnier or Cointreau if that's what you happen to have in your liquor cabinet.

The batter fills the pan three-quarters full and will rise beautifully all the way to the top of the pan. The pan height should be at least 2½ inches. If you lack a suitable pan, or if such a close fit makes you nervous, use a 9-inch pan and start checking that it is done after 45 minutes. The cake has a slightly crunchy texture and is good eaten fresh, but is even better if wrapped in plastic wrap and left to mature for a day or two. It will keep for several days.

This is quick to make, but is best left to mature for a day.

4½ oz/generous ⅔ cup fine cornmeal

4½ oz/scant 1 cup all-purpose flour

¼ tsp salt

2 tsp baking powder

8 oz/generous 1 cup superfine sugar

3 eggs

zest of 1 orange, preferably organic

6 oz/1½ sticks butter, melted

7–8 tbsp Triple Sec

EQUIPMENT:

8-inch springform pan

Preheat the oven to 325°F/160°C. Grease the pan and dust with flour.

Mix the cornmeal, flour, salt and baking powder together and set aside.

Use an electric mixer to whisk the eggs and sugar with the orange zest until the mixture falls off the whisk in a thick ribbon as opposed to a thin stream. Remove any zest clinging to the whisk and return it to the eggs.

Gently fold in the cornmeal mixture with a balloon whisk. Add the butter and 5 tbsp Triple Sec and mix gently to incorporate.

Transfer the batter to the pan and bake for 1 hour, or until a skewer inserted into the center of the cake comes out clean.

Remove from the oven, then brush the top with half of the remaining Triple Sec. Let it stand for about 5 minutes, then loosen the sides and release the clip. Invert the cake onto a wire rack and brush the bottom with the remaining Triple Sec. Leave to cool completely on a wire rack.

CARAMEL SANDWICH CAKE
TARTA DE MANJAR

Caramel spread is popular in Latin America, where it is called by a number of different names: *manjar* in Chile, *dulce de leche* in Argentina, *arequipe* in Colombia and *cajeta* in Mexico. It is made from milk and sugar, boiled until the sugar caramelizes and the whole mixture is golden brown and thick. It tastes like cream toffee and is, as you would expect, very sweet. Chileans are extremely fond of it and its uses vary from spreading on bread to simply spooning it up like a pudding or using it in cakes such as this one. All kinds of cakes and pastries are filled with it, even prepackaged little cupcakes, and so highly do people rate it that the local Swiss Roll filled with *manjar* is known as *Brazo de Reina*, Queen's Arm – in contrast to a similar Spanish cake that goes by the name of *Brazo de Gitano*, or Gypsy's Arm.

Hardly anyone bothers to prepare caramel spread at home because it is very time-consuming to make and readily available in plastic packages, jars and cans. It is also becoming increasingly popular outside Latin America and is sold in supermarkets and delicatessens in many countries, most often as *dulce de leche* (literally "milk sweet"). Two recipes follow for those who wish to try making it at home.

The following recipe offers one way to use caramel spread, but use your imagination and add extras, such as dark chocolate chips. Or sandwich the cookies for Chocolate and Pistachio Sandwich Cookies (see p. 232) with the caramel.

This is very easy, but the base cake must be made in advance. Homemade *dulce de leche* takes a few hours to make.

CAKE
Use the base cake from Three-Milk Cake
   (p. 211) or Lamington Slices (p. 165)

1 lb jar *dulce de leche* (to make your own, see the
   recipes on the next page)
1¼ oz/½ cup walnuts, finely chopped

Cut the base cake in half vertically or horizontally and spread the *dulce de leche* on one half. Sprinkle the walnuts over this and top with the second half. It's that easy! If you have a very sweet tooth, you could use more caramel to coat the top, or you might also like to top it with one of the glazes from the Chocolate section.

Finished cake pictured on pp.112–13.

TO MAKE YOUR OWN FILLING:

Recipe 1
14 oz condensed milk

Pour the condensed milk into the top of a double boiler. The water in the bottom should be just simmering. If you don't have a double boiler, improvise one with a pot, a heatproof bowl that fits snugly over it and a cover that will stay in place on top of the bowl. Aluminum foil, in multiple thickness, can always be substituted for the cover. It is more important that no steam escapes from the pot. Cover and cook for about 1¼–1½ hours. The color darkens to a lovely golden brown. Stir from time to time to prevent the outer edge from cooking too quickly. To test for doneness, treat the *dulce de leche* much as you would jam: pour a little of the *dulce de leche* onto a cold plate. Hold the plate up. If the *dulce de leche* moves very slowly, it is finished. If it runs out easily, it needs further cooking.

As soon as the *dulce de leche* is ready, plunge the bottom of the pot or bowl into a large bowl of water and beat the *dulce de leche* well. It is essential to cool it in this way because hot caramel mixtures continue cooking for some time as they retain heat.

Transfer the *dulce de leche* to a bowl and leave to cool. You can keep it in an airtight jar in the refrigerator for up to 2 weeks.

Recipe 2
10½ oz/1½ cups granulated sugar
17 fl oz/generous 2 cups milk
½ vanilla pod (bean)

Put the sugar and milk in a large pot. Scrape out the insides of the vanilla pod and add both pod and scrapings to the milk. The mixture seethes quite a bit while boiling, so make sure the pot is at least four times larger than the contents.

Bring to a boil slowly, stirring continuously to dissolve the sugar. Let it simmer, uncovered, until it is golden brown. Test that it is done as described in Recipe 1. Then finish off as described. This method requires much more attention than the previous one because the mixture is exposed to direct heat. It is enough to stir the mixture from time to time in the beginning, but as soon as it starts to color, it must be stirred continuously. It should take about 1 hour to cook, but start testing early.

If you do accidentally overcook this, it won't be suitable as a filling, but you can mix in the nuts and pour it into a container to cool for a kind of fudge.

BUTTERY SHORTCAKE
BOTERKOEK

This is another of those Dutch specialties that defy precise translation. You can readily buy whole rounds or small squares of this delicious, buttery shortcake or shortbread in any bakery or supermarket, but the homemade version beats them all hollow. It is usually baked in a shallow round pan with a built-in cutter at the bottom, known as a sandwich pan in most English-speaking countries; in Holland it is called a *boterkoekvorm*, or butter shortbread pan. The flavors are pure and simple, intensified by the overnight ripening of the unbaked dough, and as its name suggests, butter is one of the principal ingredients. The plain version, sometimes topped with blanched almonds, is the most popular. Preserved ginger used to be a popular flavoring, particularly in the Jewish community, but seems to have fallen from grace in recent years. I ran the cake stall at the village school's annual bake sale for several years and *boterkoek*, offered in five variants, was my bestseller. Older villagers preferred the plain ones, but younger generations were easily convinced to try something new, and my own favorite walnut version soon ran a close second.

This is quick and simple, but the dough must ripen overnight.

5½ oz/¾ cup superfine sugar

9 oz/1⅔ cups all-purpose flour

¼ tsp salt

zest of ¼ lemon

7 oz/1⅞ sticks butter, softened

1 egg yolk

a little beaten egg, for glazing

FLAVORINGS (OPTIONAL)

2 oz/½ cup walnuts, finely chopped

3½ oz preserved ginger, drained
   and chopped

2¾ oz/generous ¾ cup fine shredded
   (dry, unsweetened) coconut

2 oz/⅓ cup blanched whole almonds

2 oz/⅓ cup skinned hazelnuts

EQUIPMENT:

9-inch round pan

Mix the superfine sugar, flour, salt and lemon zest together in a large bowl. Add the softened butter and egg yolk and knead until everything is well mixed in. If you are using walnuts, ginger or coconut, knead them in now. Shape the dough into a ball and put it in a sealed plastic bag in the refrigerator overnight.

Next day, remove the dough from the refrigerator and leave to come to room temperature. Preheat the oven to 350°F/180°C. Grease the pan and dust with flour.

Knead the dough very briefly, then shape it into a large disc and put it in the pan. Use your hand to flatten it as evenly as possible to fit the pan. Brush with beaten egg. If you are using almonds or hazelnuts, press them into the surface. Otherwise, score a plaid pattern onto the surface with a fork.

Bake in the oven for 20–25 minutes. *Boterkoek* should never be hard or crisp, so this should be baked only until just done. It will be soft when it comes out of the oven. Leave to cool until lukewarm in the pan, then carefully turn it out onto a wire rack to cool completely.

Store in an airtight container in a cool place so that the butter doesn't go rancid. It will keep for at least 1 week but is at its best after 24 hours. Serve in small squares.

YOGURT CAKE
YOGURTLU KEK OR YAOURTOPITA

Turkish *Yogurtlu kek* and its Greek counterpart *Yaourtopita* are homely cakes with an appealing tang. The cake browns quickly, so test carefully that it is done because it is easy to remove it from the oven too soon, leaving an uncooked, wet bit at the bottom. Greeks like to top it with a generous dusting of confectioner's sugar. In Turkey, it is either eaten as it is, or honey or a sugar syrup is poured over the hot cake. This cake may be eaten as soon as it is cool, but the flavor improves after a day or two.

This is quick to make, and it benefits from maturation.

9 oz/1⅔ cups all-purpose flour

1½ tsp baking powder

½ tsp baking soda

¼ tsp salt

7 oz/1⅞ sticks butter, softened

9 oz/1¼ cups superfine sugar

3 eggs

1 tsp vanilla extract

7 oz/scant 1 cup Greek-style (strained) plain
    yogurt, at room temperature

EQUIPMENT:

9-inch springform pan

Preheat the oven to 325°F/160°C. Grease the pan, then line the base with parchment paper and dust with flour.

Sift the flour, baking powder, baking soda and salt together, and set aside.

Cream the butter and sugar until lightened in color and fluffy. Lightly beat the eggs with the vanilla extract, then add in three batches, whisking well and scraping down the sides of the bowl after each addition. Add the yogurt with the last batch and don't worry if it goes slightly grainy at this stage.

Fold in the flour and transfer to the prepared pan. Bake for 1 hour, or until a skewer inserted into the center comes out quite clean. Leave in the pan for 5 minutes, then loosen the sides, release the clip and transfer to a wire rack to cool. Wrap it well in plastic wrap as soon as it is cool.

THREE-MILK CAKE
TORTA DE TRES LECHES

This cake is immensely popular in Latin America, where each country claims to have "invented" it. The eponymous milks come in varying combinations of condensed milk, evaporated milk, cow's milk, goat's milk, sour cream and whipping cream. Mexican variants also feature *cajeta*, the popular milk caramel spread known in various regions of Latin America as *dulce de leche*, *manjar* and *arequipe*.

For this cake, everyone has their favorite degree of saturation: some prefer it to be just moistened, others are not satisfied unless the cut cake oozes generous amounts of milky goodness. This recipe uses a whipped cream topping, but a popular alternative is an egg white and sugar mixture whisked *au bain-marie* to a meringue.

CAKE
3 eggs
5½ oz/¾ cup superfine sugar
1 tsp vanilla extract
5½ oz/1 cup flour
1 tsp baking powder
pinch of salt
3 tbsp milk

MILK MIXTURE
7 oz condensed milk

4 fl oz/½ cup sour cream
5 fl oz/⅔ cup evaporated milk
4½ fl oz/½ cup whole milk

TOPPING
9 fl oz/1 cup whipping cream
2–3 tsp granulated sugar

EQUIPMENT:
8-inch square pan, with sides at least 1½ inches high

Preheat the oven to 350°F/180°C. Line the pan with parchment paper.

Use an electric mixer to whisk the eggs, superfine sugar and vanilla extract until thick and pale.

Sift the flour, baking powder and salt together, then fold into the mixture. Next, gently but thoroughly mix in the milk. Scrape the batter into the baking pan and level the top. Bake in the oven for about 25 minutes, or until dark golden brown. It will be cooked through before that, but the extra browning – slight overbaking – adds to the flavor in this case.

While the cake is baking, combine the condensed milk and sour cream thoroughly. Add the other two milks and set aside.

Turn the baked cake out onto a cooling rack and immediately cover the bottom and sides generously with aluminum foil. Re-invert into the baking pan so that the aluminum foil lines the pan. Prick several holes in the cake with a skewer and slowly pour the milk mixture over the warm cake, from the center outwards. Do this in three batches, allowing the previous additions to be absorbed. It will look like too much liquid, but don't be alarmed: the cake will soak it all up. Leave to cool. Chill until ready to serve.

Serve in squares at room temperature with sweetened whipped cream.

CHEESECAKES

The Ancient Greeks appear to have been quite fond of cheesecakes, which they made with the curd cheeses at their disposal. When the Romans conquered Greece, they enjoyed the cakes to such an extent that they took them home and experimented with them, developing a variety of sweet and savory kinds, which later spread to their possessions across Europe. The cakes were baked or fried. Based on curd cheese, they were mixed with eggs and rye or wheat flour, and honey was used in sweet variants. Various flavorings were added, such as in the sweet cakes ascribed to Apicius: these contained aniseed, cumin, grated laurel bark and wine must, and were baked on bay leaves. It may sound like a very strange combination, but I have eaten cakes made from a similar recipe at a Roman banquet hosted by the Oxford Symposium on Food and Cookery, and they were delicious, aromatized by the bay leaf and with a subtle sweetness.

By the seventeenth century, recipes had begun to resemble those we would recognize today. In addition to the traditional flavors of rose water, saffron and other spices, almond, orange and lemon cheesecakes were also popular. In Britain at least, the mixture was now being baked in "*coffyns,*" substantial pastry cases. Sugar, still a luxury product at that time, was used sparingly, but gradually took a more prominent place, pushing honey into the background. Nowadays, though most baked cheesecakes use sugar as a sweetener, curd cheeses and honey still form a delicious fresh dessert combination in many European countries.

In Europe, many cheesecakes continue to be made with local curd cheeses, ranging from German quark to Italian ricotta, with several Eastern European variants in between. In the English-speaking world, American-style cream cheesecakes have now ousted their ancestors. In 1872, two Americans trying to make French Neufchâtel cheese accidentally created another product that was soon marketed as cream cheese, and recipes showed people how to use it. Even the European immigrants who had been making their traditional cakes with curd cheeses soon found this a delicious alternative and the American-style cheesecakes set out to conquer the world.

RICOTTA TART

Traditional Italian baking uses ricotta to create wonderfully light but succulent cheesecakes and tarts. I use a fairly flat pan to make mine because I like to serve it as a base for berries and tropical fruit. If you prefer a higher cheesecake, use a springform pan with higher sides and use one-and-a-half times the quantity of filling.

This is quick and easy to make. It keeps well but must be chilled if not served immediately.

CRUST

2¾ oz/½ cup all-purpose flour

2¾ oz/generous ¾ cup finely ground almonds

1 tsp baking powder

3 tbsp superfine sugar

¼ tsp salt

2¾ oz/scant ¼ stick butter, chilled
  and cubed

1 egg, well beaten (as needed)

FILLING

1 lb 2 oz/2½ cups ricotta

5½ oz/¾ cup superfine sugar

2 tbsp all-purpose flour

2 eggs

1 tsp vanilla extract

EQUIPMENT:

9-inch fluted flan pan, 1 inch deep

For the crust, put all ingredients except for the egg in a food processor and pulse until the mixture looks like fine breadcrumbs. Transfer to a large bowl. If you have to do this by hand, mix together the dry ingredients, then rub in the butter with your fingertips until you get the same texture. Add enough egg to moisten the dry ingredients (you may not need the whole egg) and knead lightly to form a dough. Shape the dough into a ball, then cover with plastic wrap and put it in the refrigerator to rest for about 10 minutes while you make the filling.

Put all of the filling ingredients in a large bowl and mix until you get a homogenous mass. Better yet, put everything in a food processor and whiz until homogenous.

Preheat the oven to 325°F/160°C. Grease the pan, then dust with flour and place on a baking sheet.

Roll the dough out between two sheets of plastic wrap to about 12 inches and use it to line the baking pan. Neaten the edges if necessary.

Pour the filling into the prepared pan and bake for 50–60 minutes, or until set and golden brown. If you give the pan a slight shake, there should be no movement in the center of the cheesecake. Place the pan on a wire rack and leave to cool until lukewarm, then loosen the edges carefully and transfer to a serving plate.

Serve at room temperature with a generous helping of berries or other soft fruit, or with a sweetened fruit purée or coulis.

MANGO CHEESECAKE

This recipe is simplicity itself and is put together in a matter of minutes. Although food snobs around the world look down on condensed milk, it helps to give a lovely texture in cheesecakes. If you can get really ripe and flavorful mangoes, use them. If you use canned mangoes, try to get an Oriental brand, as the mangoes generally seem riper and sweeter. However, do not expect a blast of mango flavor. This is more of a subtle fruity background tang that cuts the richness of the cream cheese. My crust is slightly cakelike, but if you prefer a firmer crust, omit the baking powder. For a special occasion, serve it with a chocolate sauce made from equal quantities of dark chocolate and cream and left to cool a little to thicken. For a slightly more virtuous special dessert, serve with lightly sweetened passion fruit pulp.

CRUST

5½ oz/1 cup all-purpose flour

1 tsp baking powder (optional)

¼ tsp salt

2¾ oz/¾ stick butter, chilled and cubed

1 egg, well beaten

FILLING

14 oz/2 cups cream cheese, softened

10½ oz sweetened condensed milk

3 tbsp all-purpose flour

3 eggs

1 tsp vanilla extract

9 oz mango pulp

EQUIPMENT:

8-inch springform pan, greased
and floured

For the crust, put all ingredients except for the egg in a food processor and pulse until the mixture looks like fine breadcrumbs. Transfer to a large bowl. If you have to do this by hand, mix the dry ingredients, then rub in the butter with your fingertips until you get the same texture. Add the beaten egg and knead lightly to form a dough. Shape it into a ball, then cover with plastic wrap and put it in the refrigerator to rest while you make the filling.

Put all of the filling ingredients in a large bowl and mix until you get a homogenous mass. Better yet, put everything in a food processor and whiz until homogenous.

Preheat the oven to 325°F/160°C. Grease the pan and dust with flour.

Roll out the dough between two sheets of plastic wrap to about 11 inches and use it to line the baking pan.

Pour the filling into the prepared pan and bake for 50–60 minutes, or until set and golden brown. If you give the pan a slight shake, there should be no movement in the center of the cheesecake. Loosen the sides with a spatula and leave to cool in the pan in the oven with the door ajar.

Chill for at least 4 hours before serving. Bring individual portions to room temperature before serving. The cheesecake will keep for up to four days in the refrigerator. Keep well covered and away from strong-smelling products, as it will absorb any unpleasant odors.

SMALL CAKES, PASTRIES & SAVORIES

Tiny treats, sweet and savory, to please every palate and ornament any occasion

MAKING PASTRY

Pastry is not as difficult to make as people seem to think. What is undoubtedly true, though, is that shortcrust pastry can be slightly temperamental compared to its more relaxed cousins. There are a few basic rules and once you pay attention to these, the pastry will practically make itself.

Shortcrust pastry does not like to be handled more than strictly necessary. Made from a basic ratio of half fat to flour, the fat must be rubbed in to coat the flour well before liquid is added. This technique also introduces air into the mixture and will lighten the texture. Fingertips make an excellent tool, but there are also metal pastry blenders with five or six parallel rows of curved cutters that can do the job equally well – and even better if you happen to have "hot hands." Some people have better blood circulation than others and their hands are so warm that the butter starts to melt before it can be rubbed in properly. Hot-handed folk make good bread, though, if that is any consolation. The ingredients must be as cold as possible. Butter must be chilled and cut into cubes beforehand and the liquid (usually water) will need to be chilled in warmer climates. Once the liquid has been added to the butter and flour, the pastry should be given a few brief strokes to bring it together because overworking will encourage the gluten to develop and stretch. While this is desirable in the case of bread, it will not do your pastry any good: the finished product will not be "short" and loose, but tough. The fat that is used will also influence the texture of shortcrust pastry. Butter gives the best flavor but, much as it pains me to say this, vegetable shortening can provide a looser texture. As shortening has no obvious flavor, it is best used in combination with butter.

Pastries with sugar, or other ingredients such as semolina or nuts, will allow themselves to be handled more without apparent ill effects. Work quickly and follow the instructions given in the recipe.

FOOD PROCESSOR

Most pastry can be made in the dry stage in a food processor, which gives excellent results, shortening the preparation time considerably. I always use the metal blade for this purpose. Some bakers add the liquid to the food processor and finish the pastry off right in there. In most cases, I prefer to do just the dry stage in the food processor and turn the mixture into a bowl, adding the liquids by hand. It makes it easier to control the process that way, and prevents the pastry from being overworked by the machine.

RESTING PERIOD

Most kinds of pastry, especially shortcrust pastry, benefit from a resting period. This allows the pastry to relax and makes it less likely to shrink in the oven, which is what would happen if you try to use it straight away. It is usually chilled or put in a cool place at this stage, allowing it to firm up and making it easier to handle. Always wrap the pastry well before putting it in the refrigerator. If you chill it too long, it will have to be left at room temperature for a short time until it becomes malleable again. If not, it will crack when you try to roll it out.

WORK SURFACE

Pastry is best rolled on a cold surface. Marble slabs and stainless steel or granite countertops are perfect. Wood is also fine, as long as the pastry has been chilled properly beforehand. Silicone mats are great for rolling out pastry because only a minimal amount of dusting flour will be needed. Some also come with pre-drawn circles, making it easy to check the diameter. When you roll out pastry, try not to add too much flour because this will also have a slightly toughening effect.

MESS-FREE ROLLING

My favorite way to roll out pastry, on whatever surface, is to use two large sheets of tightly stretched plastic wrap to enclose it. This has multiple advantages. It is mess-free, it won't stick to the surface, it needs no extra flour and the bottom sheet of plastic wrap can be used to transport the pastry to its destination without breakage. You simply turn it upside down when the pastry is above the pan that needs to be lined and press it into the desired shape, removing the plastic wrap only when everything is in place.

TRIMMING EDGES

If your pan is non-stick, use a plastic scraper to cut off excess pastry, or at the very least, the back of a knife. If not, you may end up damaging the coating.

KEEPING AND STORING

Pastry-based articles are always best eaten fresh. The pastry starts to soften when left to stand, especially if the filling is moist. Tarts and pastries with a filling of meat or cream cheese usually need to be chilled, but all other pastries should be left on a plate, covered with plastic wrap, at room temperature. If you do not plan to eat them by the next day, freeze them for later. Wrap them appropriately in plastic wrap and put them in freezer bags or suitable containers.

LEMON SHORTBREAD COOKIES
GOUDSE MOPPEN

The city of Gouda in the Netherlands is famous for its caramel-filled wafers, or *stroopwafels*, and has also lent its name to these cookies. These, and similar buttery treats, or *koekjes*, were taken by Dutch immigrants to the New World and they subsequently metamorphosed into what are known as cookies. This is a recipe to make when you want to give people the – false – impression that you have been slaving away in the kitchen for their benefit. Prepare the dough in advance and bake the cookies just before your guests are expected, and a warm and instant welcome will emanate from your oven.

9 oz/1⅔ cups all-purpose flour

½ tsp baking powder

⅛ tsp salt

5½ oz/scant 1½ sticks butter, softened

3½ oz/½ cup superfine sugar

1 egg yolk

zest of ½ lemon

MAKES ABOUT 30 COOKIES

Mix the flour with the baking powder and salt and set aside.

If possible, use the paddle attachment of a mixer to cream the butter and sugar together until lightened in color. If you don't have a mixer, use a wooden spoon and be very thorough. Beat in the egg yolk and lemon zest. Add the dry ingredients and knead lightly until it all comes together and stays together.

Transfer to a large sheet of parchment paper or parchment paper and shape into a "sausage." Use the paper to help you roll the "sausage" into a neat cylinder about 11–12 inches long. Chill the dough in the paper for at least 1 hour, or until firm enough to slice. You can leave it overnight if necessary.

Preheat the oven to 350°F/180°C. Line 2 baking sheets with parchment paper.

Remove the dough from the refrigerator and unwrap it. Use a sharp knife to cut rounds ½ inch thick. Neaten the edges with your fingers and space them evenly and well apart on the baking sheets.

Bake one sheet for 15 minutes, or until the outer edges are golden brown. Remove from the oven, and use a thin spatula to transfer the biscuits to a wire rack to cool and firm up. Cook the second batch.

Store in an airtight container.

BUTTER SHORTBREADS
GHORABIYAH

These melt-in-the-mouth shortbread biscuits are made in many countries, from
Northern Africa to the Balkans and India, and names and ingredients may vary.
Their common characteristic is a pale creaminess and buttery flavor. Butter,
plain or clarified, is the single constant and while all-purpose flour is generally used,
fine semolina is also often added for a crunchier texture. They may be flavored
with rose water, cardamom, cinnamon or chopped nuts.

Moroccan Jews make a walnut version for Purim. In Greece, where they
are known as *kourabithes*, they are traditionally eaten at Christmas and a clove
is sometimes stuck into the top to symbolize the gift of spices from the Three
Wise Men.

4½ oz/scant 1 cup all-purpose flour

1 oz/scant ¼ cup cornstarch

¼ tsp salt

3½ oz/⅞ stick butter, softened

2¾ oz/¾ cup confectioner's sugar, sifted, plus
extra for dusting

FLAVORING

16 blanched almonds

or 1 oz/¼ cup walnuts, finely chopped

or one of the flavorings listed above, to taste

MAKES 16 SHORTBREADS

Sift the flour with the cornstarch and salt, and set aside.

Beat the butter until smooth. Add the confectioner's sugar a little at a time, beating until
light and fluffy. Add the flour mixture a little at a time with your choice of flavoring (unless
you are using blanched almonds, which should be added later). Continue to beat until
everything is well incorporated. An electric mixer fitted with a paddle (not a whisk) works
very well.

Preheat the oven to 300°F/150°C. Grease a baking sheet.

Divide into 2 portions and shape each one into a short "sausage." Cut each "sausage"
into 8 equal pieces. Squish each piece once or twice in your hand to compact it, then roll into a
ball between your palms. Place on the baking sheet and flatten slightly with your fingers;
don't worry about small cracks. Repeat with the rest of the dough and arrange the
shortbreads with some space in between, as they spread a little while baking. If using
blanched almonds, press an almond into the center of each shortbread.

Bake for 25 minutes. These shortbreads stay creamy white; only the almond should
color a little. They will be soft and will firm up as they cool. If dusting with confectioner's
sugar, do this while they are still on the baking sheet. Then use a spatula to remove the
shortbreads carefully and let them cool completely on a wire rack.

TOASTED FLOUR PASTRIES
POLVORONES

A *polvorón* will melt on the tongue and likely leave you clutching more than a few crumbs as the outer layer disintegrates. It lives up to its name: *polvo* is Spanish for "dust." This treat is particularly associated with the Christmas season, and the best are made by the dwindling communities of Spanish nuns who carry on the ancient custom of producing sweets and baked delicacies to sell to the appreciative public.

The flour is toasted, giving the pastries a slightly nutty flavor. The method for shaping these pastries is a little unorthodox since there is a bowlful of crumbs to be dealt with instead of dough. Once you get over the initial surprise, though, it's smooth sailing. Commercial versions are often molded mechanically and are usually wrapped in colored squares of thin parchment paper to keep them from falling apart. Lard is generally used in Spain, but butter gives an even better result, and chopped almonds or hazelnuts and other flavorings such as cinnamon or lemon zest are sometimes added.

The Filipinos borrowed the recipe from the Spanish colonists and changed it into a local sweet. The toasted flour is mixed with butter, sugar and powdered milk and pressed into little spring-loaded molds for easy release. The result is eaten unbaked.

9 oz/1⅔ cups all-purpose flour

4½ oz/1¼ cups confectioner's sugar

¼ tsp salt

4½ oz/generous 1 stick butter, softened

confectioner's sugar, for dusting

MAKES ABOUT 20 PASTRIES

Put the flour in a dry wok or similar vessel and toast it over medium heat. Use a wooden spatula to keep on moving the flour gently so that it doesn't burn. The flour should only just darken to a creamy color. This will take about 10 minutes. Remove from the heat, then stir it a little to decrease the temperature, and allow to cool.

Put the flour in a bowl and stir in the confectioner's sugar and salt. Add the softened butter and mix well with both hands to a sandy mixture. All of the flour should be well coated with butter.

Preheat the oven to 350°F/180°C. Grease a baking sheet.

Scoop up a small handful of the mixture with your fingers and compress the crumbs into a firm, ridged oval. Place it on the baking sheet and make the other cookies in the same way. Resist the temptation to neaten the inevitable untidy edges, or the whole thing may fall apart.

Bake for 10–12 minutes, or until just colored. Remove from the oven and leave on the sheet to cool. As they cool, the *polvorones* will become firm, but the outer layer will retain the "dusty" consistency it should. Some cooks sprinkle confectioner's sugar over them, and this helps conceal irregularities. I find them to be sweet enough as they are and the cragginess has its own appeal.

Store in an airtight container. They will keep for several days.

DATE-FILLED PASTRIES
MA'AMOUL

In the Middle East, dates are consumed in great quantities. They are eaten fresh; dried; stuffed with delicious tidbits such as nuts; and of course, in pastries such as *ma'amoul*. The pastry can be made from semolina or a mixture of semolina and flour, as in this recipe. The pastry case sometimes contains rose water and eating one fresh from the oven, when the rose aroma is at its strongest, is marvelous. If you cannot get really good rose water, omit it and replace it with an extra tablespoonful of water. Fillings for *ma'amoul* range from dates to nuts and mixtures of the two. Cinnamon is usually used with stronger-tasting fillings like dates and walnuts, while more delicate flavors like almonds and pistachios might be heightened by a judicious addition of rose water.

Wooden molds, looking like large scoops with a pattern carved into the bowl, are sold for molding the pastries and these produce a lovely pattern, much like traditional Scottish shortbread (see picture on p. 12). The molded kinds need to have a thick layer of drier pastry to retain their beauty. This recipe is for freeform pastries; it contains too much butter for a pattern to keep its shape well after baking. Eat them as soon as they have cooled or store in a cool place for up to a week.

FILLING

12 oz/2 cups dates, chopped

3½ fl oz/scant ½ cup water

1 tsp ground cinnamon

PASTRY

9 oz/1⅔ cups all-purpose flour

3½ oz/generous ½ cup fine semolina

6 oz/1½ sticks butter, chilled and cubed

4 tbsp water

1 tbsp rose water

MAKES 24 PASTRIES

Make the filling first. Place the dates and water in a saucepan. Simmer gently until all of the water is absorbed. Remove from the heat. Add the ground cinnamon and mix well. Set aside.

For the pastry, mix the flour and semolina in a large bowl. Rub in the butter with your fingertips. Add the water and rose water and use your fingertips to bring it together in a ball. Leave to rest in a cool place until the filling is cool.

Preheat the oven to 325°F/160°C. Grease a baking sheet.

Divide the pastry into 24 pieces. Shape each piece into a ball and flatten between your palms. Pinch the edges with your fingers to make them thinner than the rest of the circle. This will ensure that the finished pastry has an even thickness. Place a spoonful of the filling in the center. Pleat and pinch to seal the pastry for rounds, or fold over and press the edges to seal for half-moon shapes. Fill and seal the other pastries in the same way.

Arrange on the baking sheet and bake in the oven for about 25 minutes. The pastries should remain pale. Transfer to a wire cooling rack.

ALMOND PASTE ROUNDS
AMANDEL RONDO'S

The Dutch are passionate about almond paste and use it in a wide variety of cookies, pastries and breads. These little cakes are absolutely delicious and very simple to make. I generally bake them in large batches and freeze them, individually wrapped, for lunchbox or teatime treats. Use coarse almond paste, preferably not the sticky canned stuff. You can make it yourself too, from equal quantities of ground almonds and granulated sugar with a pinch of lemon zest and enough beaten egg to bind the mixture. Leave in a covered jar in the refrigerator for a day or two to mature before using it.

PASTRY

9 oz/1 ⅔ cups all-purpose flour

1½ tsp baking powder

¼ tsp salt

zest of ½ lemon

4½ oz/½ cup superfine sugar

5¾ oz/1½ sticks butter, chilled and cubed

1 egg, beaten (reserve 1 tbsp)

10½ oz almond paste

12 blanched almonds

EQUIPMENT:

12-hole muffin pan

MAKES 12 ROUNDS

Check the almond paste to see if it is malleable. If not, add some extra beaten egg (not the reserved tbsp). Divide into 12 portions and set aside.

Put all the dough ingredients, except for the egg, in a food processor. Pulse for a few seconds until it looks like fine breadcrumbs, then transfer to a bowl. Alternatively, sift the flour, baking powder, salt and lemon zest together. Mix in the sugar and rub in the butter with your fingertips.

Reserve 1 tbsp beaten egg, then knead in the rest to make a supple dough. You may need to add a drop or two of water in cooler weather. If the weather is warm and the dough feels sticky, you can chill it briefly so that it becomes more manageable.

Preheat the oven to 350°F/180°C. Grease the muffin pan and dust with flour.

Divide the dough into 12 portions. Roll each portion swiftly between your palms, using a dusting of flour as necessary, to form balls. Flatten each ball to a diameter of 2½–2¾ inches and put a portion of almond paste in the center. Coax the dough around the almond paste and pinch to seal. If the dough breaks or tears, simply patch it with your fingers. The dough must contain the almond paste completely. Flatten slightly and place in the muffin pan, sealed-side down. Shape the rest in the same way. Flatten the cakes in the pan so that the tops are fairly flat.

Brush with the reserved egg and press an almond into the center of each cake. Bake in the preheated oven for 20–25 minutes, or until golden and cooked through. Leave to rest in the pan for about 5 minutes. If you have greased and floured your pan well, a quick twist with your fingers should loosen the cakes. Transfer to a wire rack to cool.

CHOCOLATE AND PISTACHIO SANDWICH COOKIES
ISCHLER TÖRTCHEN

These tartlets seem to have originated in Bad Ischler in Austria and are extremely popular in both that country and Hungary. They are made plain or with various kinds of nuts and the jam in the filling can vary, but they are always covered with a delicious chocolate glaze. They are not hard to make, but you do need patience and a gentle touch. Freshly made, they will be crisp but will start to soften after a few hours. Both textures have their charms. You could also bake the cookies in advance and assemble the tartlets shortly before serving, to preserve the crispness. Remember to leave enough time for the chocolate to set.

8 oz/1½ cups all-purpose flour

⅛ tsp salt

2¾ oz/¾ cup confectioner's sugar

5½ oz/scant 1½ sticks butter, softened

3½ oz/⅔ cup pistachios, ground

about 4 tbsp apricot jam, strained

12–14 whole pistachios for garnishing

GLAZE

5½ oz dark chocolate, chopped

4 tbsp milk

MAKES 12–14 SANDWICH COOKIES

Sift the flour with the salt and confectioner's sugar. Add the butter and knead lightly to make a dough. Knead in the ground pistachios and shape the dough into a disc. Cover with plastic wrap and leave to rest for about 1 hour at cool room temperature.

Preheat the oven to 350°F/180°C. Line 2 baking sheets with parchment paper.

Roll the dough out on a lightly floured surface to a thickness of ⅛ inch and use a 2½-inch cutter to cut out 24–28 rounds. If the dough breaks while rolling, just press it back together again. Use a metal spatula or a thin plastic scraper to lift the rounds so that they stay in one piece and retain their shape. Arrange the rounds on the lined baking sheets. Re-knead the trimmings lightly and roll out again, as necessary.

Bake for 8–10 minutes, or until they just begin to turn golden brown around the edges. Carefully lift them off the baking sheet with a metal spatula and transfer to a cooling rack. They will still be quite soft but will firm up as they cool. Bake the second sheet of rounds as before.

When both batches have cooled, make the glaze. Put the chocolate and milk in a saucepan with a thick base over low heat and stir very gently until the chocolate has melted and the mixture is homogenous. Sandwich the cookies with the jam and glaze the top of each pair generously with the chocolate mixture. Garnish with whole pistachios.

PINE TARTS

These are really Guyanese jam tarts – triangles filled with pineapple jam. (The locals call this fruit "pine," hence the name.) In addition to being a homemade favorite, they are a pastry shop staple and the quality can vary greatly. You can whip them up in next to no time, so you have absolutely no excuse to buy an inferior product. If you make a double amount of pastry, you can bake a batch of Cheese Rolls (see p. 252) at the same time. See the recipe for Quick Pineapple Jam (opposite) if you feel like making your own.

9 oz/1⅔ cups all-purpose flour

¼ tsp salt

/4½ oz/1 stick butter, chilled and cubed

about 4 tbsp cold water

12 tbsp pineapple jam (see recipe opposite)

beaten egg, for glazing

MAKES 12 TARTS

For the pastry, put the flour and salt in a large bowl. Rub in the butter until the mixture resembles fine breadcrumbs. This can also be done in a food processor: pulse until well blended, then transfer to a bowl.

Add enough water to make the ingredients all come together. Do this with your fingertips and don't overwork the pastry. Shape into a ball, then wrap it in plastic wrap and let it rest in a cool place for about 30 minutes.

Preheat the oven to 400°F/200°C. Grease a baking sheet.

Divide the pastry into 12 pieces and shape them into balls. Roll each ball out to a 5-inch circle. Don't worry if the edges are rough. Brush around the circumference of the pastry with water and put 1 tbsp jam in the center of each circle. Fold the sides inwards to form a triangle, completely enclosing the jam. Gently press to seal well, or the jam will flow out and burn. Crimp the points of the triangle with a fork for a decorative and effective seal.

Brush with beaten egg and bake for 20 minutes, or until the tops are golden brown. Cool on a wire rack.

Eat within a day or freeze, well wrapped.

QUICK PINEAPPLE JAM

Special gelling sugar is often sold in supermarkets, especially during the summer months when fruit surpluses abound. It makes life easy as it contains added pectin which helps thicken and set jams and jellies in a relatively short period of time. The only drawback is that you seldom get the clarity and depth of color produced by using granulated sugar that requires a longer cooking time. If you are unable to buy gelling sugar, use granulated sugar. Canned pineapple will take about fifteen minutes once a rolling boil is reached and fresh pineapple should take about twenty minutes – but is well worth the wait. Check for setting toward the end of the times indicated. Pour half to one teaspoonful of jam onto a cold plate. It should spread slowly. Leave it for a few seconds, then push it with your fingertip. If it has reached the right consistency, the surface will wrinkle very slightly but stay together. Overcooking will mean that you end up with a hard and sugary mass. As more moisture evaporates during the longer cooking time, the second jar may not be completely full. Allow this one to cool uncovered and keep it in the refrigerator.

Fresh pineapple makes the tastiest jam, but canned gives an acceptable result. If you are using canned fruit, pineapple canned in its own juice is better than pineapple canned in syrup. The latter tends to be overly sweet.

1 lb 2 oz fresh or canned pineapple

1 lb 2 oz gelling sugar (with added pectin) or
   granulated sugar

juice of ½ lemon

MAKES ABOUT 2 X 1 LB JARS

Wash 2 jam jars and their lids thoroughly. Dry them well and place them on a folded dish towel on the countertop.

Chop the fruit coarsely, then purée it in a food processor. If you have a handheld blender, put the fruit in the pan and purée it there. Put the puréed pineapple, sugar and lemon juice in a large heavy-based saucepan and heat gently. Stir constantly to dissolve the sugar, then turn up the heat and bring the mixture to a boil. Keep stirring. Let it boil for 5 minutes, or according to the instructions on the package of gelling sugar; or 15 minutes if using granulated sugar. The mixture will thicken – but not to a jamlike consistency; that happens after it has cooled.

Pour the hot jam into the clean, dry jam jars, filling them right up to the top. Screw on the lids and turn the jars upside down for 5 minutes, then turn them back the right way up and leave to cool completely. This takes several hours and the jam sets while it cools.

Store in a cool, dark place and keep opened jars in the refrigerator.

MOON CAKES

For the festival of the Harvest Moon, which usually falls in August, Chinese all over the world exchange moon cakes. Huge amounts of the delicious little cakes are busily ferried back and forth to family, friends and colleagues. They may be presented in boxes of 4, representing the moon's phases – although some people consider 4 to be an inauspicious number, since it sounds like the Chinese word for "death." Alternatively, they are presented in mounds of 13, representing the months of the lunar year.

A square piece of paper is often put on the bottom of the box or under the cakes. This is a reminder of the prominent role moon cakes played in overthrowing the Mongol Yuan dynasty. As the legend goes, a group of Chinese activists hatched a plot to revolt on the 15th night of the 8th month. They needed to get word out without arousing suspicion, so pieces of paper with messages were hidden in the moon cakes, which were sent to the appropriate people. The unsuspecting Mongols were caught unawares and the Yuan dynasty brought to an abrupt end.

Traditional moon cakes are made with a special rich, thin pastry usually referred to as a "skin." The pastry is filled and then molded before being baked. Industrial bakeries use fully or semi-automated processes, but most small bakeries have their own distinctive and intricately carved wooden molds, which may indicate the name of the bakery and the filling. The molds can be round or rectangular, straight-sided or fluted and are generally about 2 inches in diameter or length. The variety of fillings is truly astounding and often reflects the affluence and geographic location of the customer. The more traditional types are widespread and include red, yellow and black beans; Chinese red dates; lotus seed; and winter melon, often with shreds of pork and chopped nuts added. A salted duck egg yolk – a very acquired taste – is tucked into the center to represent the moon, and baked cakes are usually quartered so that each piece has a visible bit of yolk. Malaysian Chinese prefer a less sweet cake than Hong Kong Chinese and the people of Shanghai go for a really sweet red bean cake. Malaysians use local and foreign ingredients to create their own specialties, and while the older generation may still prefer traditional flavors, screwpine leaf, durian and pineapple are also popular. Trends come and go, and in mainland China shark's fin is becoming popular at the top end of the market. A ganache-filled cake has also made an appearance.

FLAKY CHINESE BEAN CAKES

I confess to a lifelong addiction to bean cakes and never miss an opportunity to sample the offerings of Chinese bakeries anywhere. These bean cakes are made with a fantastically flaky pastry using a unique technique. They can be found wherever Chinese immigrants have settled and have become mainstream in places like Guyana and the Philippines. Fillings have been adapted to local tastes and availability, but the pastry has always retained its essential character. The pastry for each cake is assembled individually and can house traditional favorites like lotus seed, adzuki bean, black bean or red date paste, as well as taro and glutinous rice. In Guyana, a filling of black-eyed peas is standard; and in the Philippines, mung beans, yellow split peas and purple yam are popular. The purple yam, *ube*, is a shock to the uninitiated. Its natural color is so vibrant that it suggests artificiality. Lard is generally the Chinese fat of choice, but I find it overpowering. And though I am usually one of the most fervent advocates of butter, I must admit that shortening is quite acceptable in this case. Butter makes a flavorful but closer-textured pastry, while shortening gives flakier layers, like the original lard would.

If you plan to make your own filling, you will need to start the day before. Note too, that the pastry for each cake needs to be shaped and rolled individually, so be sure to set aside enough time.

FIRST PASTRY

2 oz/½ stick soft butter *or* 4 tbsp sunflower or
   corn oil

9½ oz/scant 2 cups all-purpose flour

2 tbsp superfine sugar

about 8 tbsp cold water

SECOND PASTRY

7 oz/1⅓ cups all-purpose flour

4½ oz/generous 1 stick butter
   or vegetable shortening, softened

egg yolk, for glazing

FILLING

1 lb 2 oz–1 lb 5 oz canned sweetened red bean
   paste
   or one of the following:

BLACK-EYED PEA PASTE

9 oz/1¼ cups dried black-eyed peas

4½ oz/generous ½ cup granulated sugar

2 oz/½ stick butter *or* 4 tbsp sunflower
   or corn oil

LOTUS SEED PASTE

6 oz/scant 1¼ cups dried lotus seeds

7 oz/1 cup granulated sugar

1¾ oz/scant ½ stick butter *or*
   3 tbsp sunflower or corn oil

MAKES 16 CAKES

If you're not using canned paste, start making the filling the day before. These pastes can even be made a few days in advance and can also be frozen.

For black-eyed pea paste, rinse the peas and put them in a large bowl. Cover generously with water and leave for at least 8 hours, or overnight.

Drain the peas, then put them in a large pot with about 3½ pints/8 cups water and bring to a boil. Cover and simmer until very tender – about 1 hour, depending on how fresh the peas are. Check the water level regularly so that the peas don't boil dry.

Strain off the liquid and pass the peas through a strainer – I use a rotary Moulinex vegetable purée-maker fitted with a medium disc. If you've done a thorough job, you should be left with only a few tablespoons of skins in the strainer.

Mix the peas with the sugar and butter and put in a heavy-based saucepan over medium heat. (I use a non-stick wok.) Keep stirring and cook for 15–20 minutes, or until it forms a thick paste. Set aside to cool. Stir before using.

For the lotus seed paste, rinse the seeds, put them in a large bowl and cover generously with water. Leave for at least 8 hours, or overnight.

Drain the seeds, then split them open and remove any green shoots (which are bitter).

Put the seeds in a large pot and cover with at least 2¾ pints/6¼ cups water. Lotus seeds have a more pungent smell and a far longer cooking time than black-eyed peas. They will need about 2½ hours to become very tender.

To prepare the paste, proceed as for black-eyed pea paste.

Make the first pastry. If using butter, rub it into the flour, then add the remaining ingredients. Knead just long enough to make a smooth dough. Shape it into a ball, then cover with plastic wrap and set aside for about 15 minutes at room temperature.

For the second pastry, mix the flour and soft fat together and knead lightly to make a loose dough. Divide this into 16 pieces and shape them into balls. Cover and set aside.

Divide the first pastry into 16 pieces. Press each piece flat in your palm to a rough circle about 3½ inches and fill with a pastry ball. Pleat and press edges to seal the second pastry into the first. You should have a small ping-pong ball. Make 15 more balls in this way.

Flatten the balls and roll each one out on a lightly floured surface to a rough circle with a diameter of about 5 inches. Fold the top third of the pastry towards the middle and fold the bottom third over this. Fold this strip in thirds too so that you get a small square.

Preheat the oven to 350°F/180°C. Grease 2 baking sheets.

Roll out the squares to make 4–5 inch square-ish shapes and fill with the paste of your choice. Moisten around the circumference with a finger dipped in water and pleat and pinch the edges to seal well. Flatten each cake with the rolling pin to about 3 inches and arrange on a baking sheet. Make the other cakes in the same way.

Brush with beaten egg yolk and make two parallel rows of holes in the top with a fork. Bake for 20–25 minutes, or until the tops are golden. Cool on a wire rack.

These are crisp when just made, but are equally delicious as they soften.

Pictured on next page.

STEAMED RICE CAKES

In Asian countries, delicacies made from rice abound. Market stalls and roadside vendors often have several rice-based treats on display: intriguing balls, discs, cylinders and more, wrapped in banana leaves or parchment paper, rolled in shredded coconut, sprinkled with aniseed, some with a filling inside the rice and others left plain. Most are made from glutinous rice that is soaked and then pounded to the right consistency and the variety of rice is a key element. Locals seem to prefer chewiness to lightness, but Western palates tend to feel more comfortable with a less chewy product.

For this recipe, non-glutinous rice flour will give a light and fluffy result. It was inspired by a recent trip to the Philippines, where such cakes are described as *puto* and can be made in slabs or as individual cakes. Made with rice flour, they are quick and easy and not too sweet. Serve freshly made, with some shredded or grated coconut on the side. They can be eaten as a breakfast cake, snack or dessert, or even an accompaniment to an Asian gravy-based dish.

You will need a steamer for this recipe, preferably one that holds 8 foil muffin cases or small metal molds. Have the boiling water ready for steaming, because the batter is whipped up in next to no time.

4½ oz/scant 1 cup non-glutinous rice flour

3¼ oz/scant ½ cup granulated sugar

⅛ tsp salt

1½ tsp baking powder

7 fl oz/generous ¾ cup coconut milk

1 egg, beaten

shredded or grated coconut, for serving

MAKES 8 CAKES

Prepare the steamer and make sure that the water is boiling. If you're not using disposable foil cases, grease and flour the molds.

Mix the dry ingredients together in a bowl. Whisk in the coconut milk and egg, then beat until all the dry ingredients are well incorporated.

Pour the batter into the cases or molds. If using disposable cases, these will be about three-quarters full.

Steam for 10 minutes, or until cooked.

Serve with some coconut on the side.

STEAMED CORNMEAL PARCELS
CONKIE

Conkie and its relatives are popular all over the Caribbean and in neighboring Latin American countries. Made from seasoned cornmeal, boiled or steamed in banana leaves, they come in countless variants and under a variety of names, each reflecting the local population and the way it has adopted the recipe. In the English-speaking Caribbean alone, there are several names pointing to an African heritage. *Conkie* is itself an Anglicization and the alternative pronunciation of *kanki* is also popular in Guyana, suggesting Assante and Fante linguistic origins. By the same token, *dokono*, *dukuna* and even *duckanoo* – all popular in the smaller islands, Jamaica and Belize – have West African equivalents that refer to maize bread, particularly sweet ones. Jamaicans often use the graphic description "blue drawers," as the banana leaf changes from green to blue while cooking.

The basic *conkie* may be made from cornmeal, raisins, spices and sugar, and Caribbean inventiveness has yielded mixtures of cornmeal with sweet potato, banana, coconut and pumpkin. Banana leaves are the usual packaging, or corn husks, and a few islanders use the leaves of the sea grape (*Coccoloba uvifera*) to create a *dolma*-like parcel. Climbing up the culinary ladder, one soon finds *pastelles* and *hallacas*, as well as the whole range of *tamales*. *Tamales*, exceedingly popular in Mexico, can be found in countless sizes and types. There are tiny *norteños*, *sacahuiles* 40 inches long, and *tamales* with plain bread-like fillings, spicy meat or poultry centers or even sweet ones; they are usually steamed or boiled in corn husks, but regional variants use banana or other leaves. In addition to the plain *pémi* (from French *pain de mie*), Trinidad boasts an elaborate meat-filled *pastelle* (from Spanish *pastel*, cake), which resembles the Venezuelan *hallaca*.

Venezuelans would have us believe that the *hallaca* is the queen of its type. It is a festive dish, eaten on holidays, especially during the Christmas period. It is enormously time-consuming to prepare, especially if the cornmeal is to be freshly ground with a mortar and pestle, and many families make an event of it, involving everyone in some way. The cornmeal is kneaded into a dough with stock, often tinted red with annatto. The *guiso*, or filling, consists of several kinds of meat and poultry, onion, peppers, hard-boiled eggs and various other seasonings along with what would originally have been imported European luxury products: capers, stuffed olives, prunes, gherkins and almonds. It has taken on an almost religious significance for Venezuelans living abroad, and much as diaspora Jews will say "Next year in Jerusalem" at the Passover table, many a Venezuelan expatriate will sigh a similar sentiment when eating *hallacas* at Christmas.

This recipe is for the plainer Guyanese *conkie*. I generally use aluminum foil as a wrapping and it works very well, particularly as I'm not a fan of the leafy flavor. Many ethnic grocers stock frozen banana leaves, so if you would like to try that, make neat parcels with strips of leaf and tie them up with string.

You will need a steamer. If you don't have one, you can also boil the parcels, but make sure that they are completely sealed so that the filling won't get soggy.

10½ oz pumpkin (or slightly under-ripe banana),
   chopped into small pieces

3½ oz grated coconut

5½ oz/scant 1 cup fine cornmeal

3½ oz/½ cup granulated sugar

1 tsp vanilla extract

¼ tsp finely ground black or white pepper

2 oz/½ stick butter, melted

3½ fl oz/scant ½ cup milk

2¾ oz/½ cup raisins or sultanas
   (golden raisins)

MAKES 16 PARCELS – BUT THE
QUANTITY IS EASILY HALVED

Put all the ingredients, except the dried fruit, in a food processor and pulse until everything is well mixed, then mix the dried fruit in with a spoon.

Cut aluminum foil into 16 pieces about 10 x 8 inches and fold in half so that you get a thicker sheet 8 x 5 inches.

Put 2 generous tablespoons of the filling in the center and fold the edges over several times to seal well.

Steam or boil for 20 minutes. Eat warm or cold as a snack.

PLAIN STEAMED BUNS
MANTOU

Scholars speculate that steamed buns may have been borrowed from neighboring countries to the west of China, but they have been a standard part of the Chinese culinary repertoire for at least 2,000 years, since the early Han dynasty. They were originally indigenous to northern China, where rice was considered a luxury and wheat products were more common.

The buns are now eaten all over China and are made in a variety of shapes. The recipe below is for the simplest shape, with a few alternative suggestions. They can also be made into intricate patterns, such as Snails and Silver Thread Rolls. The Snail requires shreds of dough to be rolled and stretched into slender ropes and then massed together and twisted around a finger to create an elongated coil. Silver Thread Rolls use similar ropes, enclosing them in an outer layer of dough to create a distinctively textured and structured roll. The filled rolls come in yet more shapes, among them the Peach, signifying longevity.

These buns can be eaten warm as an accompaniment to Asian or Western food. The slight sweetness balances salty and sharp flavors well.

Remember that this dough needs to rise twice.

DOUGH

10½ oz/2 cups all-purpose flour

1 tbsp sugar

1½ tsp active dry yeast

1½ tsp baking powder

1 tbsp oil

about 5 fl oz/⅔ cup warm water

MAKES 6 LARGE OR 12 SMALL BUNS

Make a firm dough from all the ingredients. Knead well, then shape into a ball and leave in a covered bowl in a warm, draft-free place until doubled in size.

Cut 6 or 12 squares from parchment paper.

Punch down the risen dough and knead again very briefly, then divide into 6 or 12 portions. Shape each portion into a neat round bun and place on a small square of parchment paper, then place in the steamer basket. Leave in a warm, draft-free place until almost doubled in size.

If you don't have enough steamer capacity to steam all at the same time, leave some in a slightly cooler (but draft-free) place to delay the rising process.

Steam the small buns for 10 minutes and the large ones for 15 minutes, or until cooked through.

OTHER SUGGESTIONS

Folded roll

Divide the dough into 6 pieces and flatten or roll each piece out to a diameter of about 5 inches. Fold in half, then fold again so that you have a quarter circle. Fanlike spokes can be made by pressing a pattern into the dough with a chopstick or fork. Arrange on squares of parchment paper and proceed as above.

Lotus leaves

Divide the dough into 6 or 12 pieces, depending on the size you prefer. Flatten or roll each piece to a diameter of about 5 inches (half that for smaller ones) and pinch to make a small protrusion somewhere at the edge of the circle. Consider this the stem of the leaf and use a chopstick or fork to make a veined pattern in the leaf. Arrange on squares of parchment paper and proceed as above.

Flower rolls

Divide the dough into 6 pieces and roll each piece out to a thin, narrow rectangle. Size is not really important. What is important is that the dough is thin so that it will create a many-petaled effect. Roll up the rectangle from one narrow end to form a squat cylinder. Press a chopstick or the handle of a wooden spoon down the middle of the cylinder so that the spiraled sides tilt slightly upwards. Arrange on squares of parchment paper and proceed as above.

STEAMED SWEET RED BEAN BUNS

The same basic dough for Plain Steamed Buns can be used to make Sweet Red Bean Buns. Many Asian supermarkets sell good-quality, canned, sweetened red bean paste. One quantity of basic dough and one 16 oz can of paste will make 16 buns, but this can easily be halved. Sweet buns often have a red dot to distinguish them from savory ones, but that is optional and necessary only if you plan to serve several kinds at once. Eat warm, accompanied by small cups of fragrant tea.

DOUGH
1 quantity dough for Plain Steamed Buns
  (p. 246)

FILLING
16 oz can sweetened red bean paste

MAKES 16 BUNS

Knead the dough well, then shape into a ball. Put in a bowl and cover with a dish towel, then leave in a warm, draft-free place until doubled in size.

Cut 16 small squares from parchment paper.

Punch down the risen dough and knead again very briefly, then divide into 16 portions. Take one portion and shape it into a rough ball, then roll it out to a 4-inch circle. Moisten around the circumference with a finger dipped in water. Put a dessertspoonful of filling in the center and pleat the dough around this, pinching to seal. Place it on a square of parchment paper in the steamer basket with the seal at the bottom. Alternatively, press the pleats together, without pinching to seal, and arrange in the steamer with the pleats upwards. Repeat to make the remaining buns.

Leave to rest for about 20 minutes in a warm, draft-free place. They should be puffed up but not yet quite doubled in size. If you don't have enough steamer capacity to steam all at the same time, leave some in a slightly cooler (but draft-free) place to delay the rising process.

Steam for 10 minutes, or until the dough has set and is cooked through.

STEAMED SAVORY BUNS
BAOZI

Sweet and savory buns and dumplings, served with endless steaming cups of tea, form the popular Chinese dim sum lunch or snack meal. Chinese chefs are artists, and their deft fingers fly back and forth, transforming basic ingredients into magnificent works of art that you almost hesitate to spoil by eating. It is a skill that needs lots of practice to master, but any home cook can produce delicious, if more modest, buns with this simple recipe. If you vary the composition of the filling, you can even create an assortment with very little extra effort. Shrimp or ground pork can be used instead of the chicken in this recipe and the seasoning can be adapted, or slices of vegetables such as Chinese mushrooms, bamboo shoots or water chestnuts can be added. They can be dipped in a simple uncooked sauce of soy sauce, rice vinegar, spring onion and chili with a pinch of brown sugar added.

DOUGH
1 quantity dough for Plain Steamed Buns
    (p. 246)

FILLING
10½ oz raw boneless chicken
1 scallion
1-inch piece fresh ginger root
1 garlic clove

1 green chili (optional)
2 tsp sesame oil
2 tsp oyster sauce
2 tsp soy sauce
2 tsp Shaoxing or other rice wine
salt, if desired

MAKES 12 BUNS

Knead the dough well, then shape into a ball. Put in a bowl and cover with a dish towel, then leave in a warm, draft-free place until doubled in size.

For the filling, chop the chicken into small pieces. Slice the scallion, ginger, garlic and green chili and put them into a food processor. Pulse until fine. Add the chicken pieces and the remaining ingredients and pulse until finely ground. Divide the mixture into 12 portions and set aside until needed. (This filling can be made several hours ahead of time and stored in an airtight container in the refrigerator. Remove from the refrigerator about 30 minutes before needed.)

Cut 12 small squares of parchment paper.

Punch down the risen dough and knead again very briefly, then divide it into 12 portions. Take one portion and shape it into a rough ball, then roll it out to a 4-inch circle. Moisten around the circumference with a finger dipped in water. Put one portion of filling in the center and pleat the dough around this, pinching to seal. Place it on a square of parchment paper in the steamer basket with the seal at the bottom. Repeat to make the remaining buns.

Leave to rest for about 20 minutes in a warm, draft-free place. They should be puffed up but not yet quite doubled in size. If you don't have enough steamer capacity to steam all at the same time, leave some in a slightly cooler (but draft-free) place to delay the rising process.

Steam for 15 minutes, or until the dough has set and the filling is cooked through.

COCKTAIL CHEESE BISCUITS

These tiny biscuits are whipped up in next to no time and tend to disappear from the plate just as quickly. The dough can be made in advance and chilled until you're ready to bake the biscuits. The recipe is easily halved.

9 oz/1⅔ cups all-purpose flour

pinch of ground cayenne or chili pepper

salt to taste, if needed

5½ oz/scant 1½ sticks butter, softened

9 oz very mature (sharp) cheese (Gouda, Edam, Cheddar), finely grated

1 tbsp cold water, or as needed

MAKES SEVERAL DOZEN — DEPENDING ON THE SIZE YOU ROLL THEM

Mix the flour, cayenne and salt together in a bowl. Add the remaining ingredients and knead to form a dough. Add more water if necessary.

Preheat the oven to 350°F/180°C. Line 3 baking sheets with parchment paper.

Make hazelnut-sized balls from the mixture and arrange on the baking sheet.

Bake the first baking sheet for 12–15 minutes, or until pale golden brown. Don't overbake, or the cheese will become bitter. Remove from the oven. (If you have only one baking sheet, prepare the second and third batches while the first batch is cooking, placing them on 2 sheets of parchment paper. When the first batch is done, pick up the paper to lift off the first batch, then replace with the second sheet.)

Enjoy fresh with your favorite drink.

CHEESE ROLLS

For a Guyanese living abroad, a "cheese roll" is not a bread roll with a slice of cheese but an elongated pastry rich in nostalgia. These savories are made with the same pastry as Pine Tarts (p. 234), and I often make a double batch of pastry and whip up both at one go. Some people make a paste of the filling ingredients and then spread them onto the pastry. My way is quicker and less prone to leakage and torn pastry.

9 oz/1⅔ cups all-purpose flour

¼ tsp salt

4½ oz/1 stick butter, chilled and cubed

about 4 tbsp cold water

about 1 tbsp sharp mustard

2¾ oz mature (sharp) cheese (Cheddar, Edam or
   Gouda), grated

ground cayenne pepper

beaten egg, for glazing

MAKES 12 PASTRIES

For the pastry, put the flour and salt in a large bowl. Rub in the butter until the mixture resembles fine breadcrumbs. This can be done in a food processor: pulse until well blended, then transfer to a bowl. Now add enough water to make the pastry come together. Do this with your fingertips and don't overwork the pastry. Shape into a ball, then wrap it in plastic wrap and let it rest in a cool place for about 30 minutes.

Divide the pastry into 12 pieces and shape them into balls. Roll each ball out to a 4½- inch circle. Don't worry if the edges are rough.

Preheat the oven to 400°F/200°C. Grease a baking sheet.

Brush around the circumference of the pastry with water and smear a dab of mustard over the pastry. Sprinkle one-twelfth of the cheese and a pinch of cayenne pepper over this. Fold the top ¾ inch of the pastry downwards and continue to fold so that you get a flattened log shape. Pinch the seam to seal and place seam-side down on the baking sheet. Crimp the ends with a fork and brush with beaten egg. Prick three rows of holes in the pastry with a fork.

Bake for 20 minutes, or until the tops are golden brown. Cool on a wire rack.

Eat within a day or freeze, well wrapped.

QUICK CHEESE AND PARSLEY BUNS
POĞAÇA

Hungary was one of the ports of call of the rampaging Turks and both countries have a small round roll called *pogáca* and *poğaça* respectively. At the same time, the Albanians have *pogaçe*; the Bulgarians and Macedonians *pogacha*; Romanians *pogacea*; the Serbs, Croatians and Slovenians *poğaça*; the French *fougasse*; and the Italians *focaccia*. The name appears to derive from the Latin *panis focacius*, "hearth bread." With the exception of the Turkish and Hungarian rolls, all other variants are flatbreads and the Balkan versions were originally unleavened and baked in the embers of the hearth.

In her excellent book *The Melting Pot: Balkan Food and Cookery*, Maria Kaneva-Johnson suggests that both the Hungarians and Turks borrowed the breads from the Balkans. She sees the original Balkan breads as a pre-Christian product that was used in pagan rituals, which is one of the reasons why they were never taken to church to be blessed nor were they cut with knives. This last piece of information is particularly interesting, because it explains why the Hungarian *pogáca* has a deeply-cut cross-hatched pattern on its surface. If a bread could not be cut, it had to be broken, and the cuts would help. Although the roll now resembles a scone more than anything else, the tradition seems to have stayed.

In Hungary, you will find these in the humblest bakery as well as the most sophisticated pastry shop. They vary in size, from a walnut to an orange. The larger ones are eaten as snacks or as an accompaniment to stews, while the dainty little ones are often enjoyed with a glass of wine or *palinka* brandy. They can be plain or enriched with a number of ingredients including potato, cheese (particularly sheep's cheese) and pork or goose cracklings. Fond of their pork, many Hungarians like their *pogáca* to be made with lard, and connoisseurs will tell you that it adds to the flakiness.

Poğaça are sold on practically every street corner in Turkish towns, enticingly stacked in glass-fronted handcarts. This recipe is for a quick homemade version that can be eaten warm or cold as a snack or even as an accompaniment to soup. The simple cheese filling is one that is used in many flatbreads, rolls and pastries in Turkey.

DOUGH
9 oz/1⅔ cups all-purpose flour
½ tsp baking soda
¼ tsp salt
2¾ oz/scant ¾ stick butter, softened
3½ oz thick Greek-style (strained) plain yogurt
1 egg, beaten (reserve 2 tbsp)

FILLING
4½ oz feta cheese*
small handful flat-leaf parsley or cilantro,
    finely chopped

MAKES 12 BUNS

Knead together all of the ingredients for the dough and set aside while you make the filling.

For the filling, crumble the feta and mix it with the chopped herbs.

Divide the dough into 12 pieces and flatten or roll out one piece to a 4-inch circle. Try to get the edges thinner than the rest of the surface area.

Preheat the oven to 400°F/200°C. Grease a baking sheet.

Put 1 tbsp of the filling in the center and pleat and pinch the edges to seal into a ball. Place it on the baking sheet and flatten slightly with the palm of your hand. Repeat with the remaining 11 pieces of dough and the filling.

Brush twice with the reserved egg and bake for 12–15 minutes, or until golden brown.

* Feta cheese can be very salty. Soaking the whole piece in water for about 2 hours before use will help remove some of the salt. However, in this recipe, I find that the dough acts as good foil for the cheese, so no soaking should be necessary.

CHICKEN PATTIES

These mini chicken pies, a colonial legacy, make a delicious lunch, afternoon or cocktail hour snack. Proper patty pans, the really shallow kind, have become something of a rarity and the patties offered here are very chunky compared with the authentic Guyanese versions, which are usually less than half the size. Those, of course, date from an age when hired help was always on hand to create a mouth-watering array of delicacies, without pausing to check the time or to complain of the effort. They take a bit of patience to put together, but the good news is that this can be done in easy stages. You can make the pastry in advance and chill it while you cook and cool the chicken, and then assemble the patties just before baking. Or you could opt for the simpler Jamaican method and make large turnovers instead.

Feel free to adjust the seasoning to your taste. In the Caribbean, a generous piece of chili is used, usually Habanero, which is known as Scotch bonnet in Jamaica and Ball o' fire (for obvious reasons) in Guyana. We always added a herb referred to locally as "thick-leaf thyme," which has succulent, rather hairy leaves with toothed edges and a remarkable flavor. Its botanical name used to be *Coleus aromaticus* and has now been changed to *Plectranthus amboinicus*. It is sometimes called Spanish or Mexican thyme, and in the Philippines, where it grows in profusion, they refer to it as "native oregano." Regular thyme, oregano, flat-leaf celery and cilantro all make flavorful alternatives.

For a shrimp version, substitute an equal amount of chopped raw shrimp for the chicken.

PASTRY
12 oz/2⅓ cups all-purpose flour
generous ¼ tsp salt
6 oz/1½ sticks butter (or half butter and half
    vegetable shortening)
6–7 tbsp cold water, as needed

FILLING
1 lb boneless raw chicken, mixed thigh and
    breast meat
2–4 tsp mild curry powder
¾ tsp salt, or to taste
a piece of Habanero chili, finely chopped

1 tsp dried thyme *or*
    about 2 tbsp finely chopped flat-leaf celery,
    cilantro, or oregano
1 onion, finely chopped
1 tbsp corn or sunflower oil

egg for glazing

EQUIPMENT:
12-hole bun/muffin pan, greased

MAKES 12 PATTIES

Make the pastry first. Put the flour in a large bowl and mix in the salt. Add the butter and use a pastry blender to cut the fat into the flour, or rub it between your fingertips until it looks like coarse breadcrumbs. This can also be done in a food processor: pulse until it looks like coarse breadcrumbs, then transfer to a bowl. Add the water and bring the pastry all together with a few swift strokes of your fingertips to form a large ball. Cover and chill until needed.

Chop the chicken into very small pieces, about the size of a grain of corn or a tiny pea. Put into a bowl and add the salt, curry powder, chili and thyme or other herbs. Mix together and set aside.

Heat the oil in a wok or heavy skillet and add the chopped onion. Sauté the onion until softened, then add the chicken and stir-fry until cooked through. Set aside to cool, then use straight away or chill until needed.

Allow the chilled pastry to come to room temperature. Dust your work surface with flour and roll out to a thickness of about ⅛ inch. Do this in two batches if your work surface is small.

Preheat the oven to 375°F/190°C. Grease the muffin pan.

Cut 12 4-inch circles and the same number of 3-inch circles. Line the muffin pans with the larger circles. If you have a pastry tamper, use it – it makes life a lot simpler. If not, just use a small ball of pastry or your fingers. Press the pastry against the sides of the pan, bringing it up neatly to cover the entire cavity.

Fill with chicken mixture. Moisten the circumference of the smaller circles with water and press on top of the chicken. It should be resting on top of the larger pastry circle. Use a fork to crimp the edges. This is both a decorative and practical touch, as it seals the patties. Brush with beaten egg and make three rows of holes with the fork.

Bake for 25–30 minutes, or until the tops are light golden brown.

Eat warm from the oven or at room temperature. These are best eaten fresh.

TURNOVERS

Divide the pastry into 6 pieces and roll out to a saucer-sized circle. Put a sixth of the filling slightly off-center, moisten the circumference with a finger dipped in water and fold over to form a semi-circle. Crimp the edge to seal, then brush with beaten egg and prick with a fork in a few places.

PASTRIES STUFFED WITH LAMB
SAMSA

Indian *samosas* and Middle Eastern *sambusik* are related to the *samsa* that are a much-loved snack in Uzbekistan and neighboring countries. As so often happens, each country claims to have invented the original version and to have dispersed it into world cuisine. *Samsa* are both street food and homemade delicacy, and the pastries can be slapped onto the side of a tandoor oven to bake in the fierce heat or simply baked in a domestic oven. In keeping with local tastes, these Uzbek pastries are mildly spiced. Lamb or mutton, often with extra mutton fat, form one of the most popular fillings, but they can also be stuffed with green herbs, pumpkin, potatoes or chickpeas.

Shapes are generally geometrically inclined – ovals, triangles and squares – but skilled bakers are able to produce four-petaled flowers and the like in the twinkling of an eye. The dough is usually very lean and in this version, leaf pastry is brushed with butter and layered, transforming it into something resembling puff pastry. However, the amount of fat used is minimal so these should be eaten warm, before the layers compact too much and harden.

PASTRY

9 oz/1⅔ cups all-purpose flour

1 tsp baking powder

¼ tsp salt

1 egg, well beaten

about 4 fl oz/½ cup lukewarm water

¾ oz/scant ¼ stick butter, melted

FILLING

9 oz lamb, very finely chopped

1 medium onion, very finely chopped
   (about 3½ oz)

½ tsp salt, or to taste

1 tsp ground cumin

black pepper or chili flakes, to taste

small handful cilantro, finely chopped

MAKES 8 PASTRIES

For the pastry, sift the flour, baking powder and salt together in a bowl. Reserve 1 tbsp beaten egg, then add the remaining egg and enough water to make a fairly firm dough. Knead by hand until smooth and elastic. Shape into a ball, then return to the bowl and cover with plastic wrap. Leave to rest at room temperature for about 15 minutes.

Knead the rested dough again lightly; the texture will have improved. On a silicone mat or a surface lightly dusted with flour, roll the dough out with a rolling pin or dowel to a very thin sheet, about 14 x 14 inches. Brush with melted butter and roll up to form a cylinder. Wrap with plastic wrap and chill for at least 30 minutes.

To make the filling, thoroughly combine all ingredients in a bowl, then cover and set aside. If you make this several hours in advance and need to keep it chilled, use a good airtight container, or the onion will make everything else in the refrigerator smell.

When you are ready to assemble the pastries, remove the chilled roll from the refrigerator and cut it into 8 equal pieces.

Preheat the oven to 350°F/180°C. Grease a baking sheet.

Flatten a piece and roll it out to 5–5½ inches. It will be slightly square. Put one-eighth of the filling in the center of the pastry, then bring two opposing sides together and pleat the edges, pinching to seal it in the middle. If you're not very proficient, you may need to roll the pieces a little bigger to give you more pastry to work with. However, bear in mind that the smaller you keep the margin outside the meat, the less chance there is of getting a large, uncooked piece at the bottom. Place the pastry on the baking sheet and flatten it with the palm of your hand. Shape the other pastries in the same way.

Brush with the reserved egg and bake for 25–30 minutes, or until light brown and shiny. Leave them to cool for a few minutes, then serve warm.

LEAF & THREAD PASTRIES

Old Ladies' Necks, Palace Rolls and Nightingales' Nests:
Baklava and its intriguing relatives

HOW TO HANDLE PHYLLO PASTRY

Phyllo is a member of the leaf pastry family and this is its Greek name. Turks call it *yufka*, Austrians and many other Europeans call it "strudel dough." North African variants are made by a different technique and include *warqa* or *ouarka*, *dioul* and *masluqa*.

Phyllo is sold frozen in most supermarkets and is extremely easy to work with as long as you follow three simple rules:
- always store it well wrapped to prevent freezer burn;
- if frozen, allow it to thaw completely before trying to unfold or separate the sheets;
- keep the unused sheets covered with a slightly damp cloth or a sheet of plastic wrap at all times.

If you fail to follow these guidelines, there is every chance that the paper-thin sheets will dry out, edges first, and become brittle. These will then need to be trimmed and you will lose a lot of pastry in the process. Follow the advice, though, and phyllo is pure pleasure to use.

There is no standard size or thinness. For one brand, an 8¾ oz pack will give you 10 sheets measuring 10 x 10 inches, while another brand may have double that number of sheets, and may even be slightly larger. So don't be discouraged if you cannot find sheets precisely the size and weight of the ones I specify. You can always cut or trim larger sheets to the right size or simply consider how best to use the filling to suit your pastry. Very thin sheets can be used in double, instead of single, thickness. The recipe will never fail purely on the basis of the size of the sheets; it will simply have a slightly different character. The result may be a little crisper or chewier, larger or smaller, depending on the pastry, but it will always be delicious.

The sheets are usually kept separated by cornstarch or another starch. They will not stick to each other unless there is excess moisture – for example, in the form of ice crystals. It is not ideal to find ice crystals on your phyllo, but it happens. If you find any on your phyllo, just brush them off and use a piece of paper towel to absorb the residue.

The sheets can be cut or trimmed to size with a pastry or pizza wheel, a pair of scissors or the very obvious sharp knife. Do be careful where you do this, so that you don't end up slicing your favorite silicone mat in half or scratching your countertop.

I use a fairly wide pastry brush (2 inches) for brushing the sheets of phyllo with butter. This cuts down considerably on the preparation time. Natural bristle is best.

A silicone mat is very handy for working with phyllo because it limits the mess to a very small area and has the added advantage that the sheets will be less likely to stick.

Crisp leaf pastry products are best kept at cool room temperature, suitably covered. Storing them in the refrigerator will soften the texture. I often freeze part of a batch, straight after cooling. This is taboo in baklava-producing communities, but the result is not too bad and surely better than leaving it to go stale. The softer types suffer no ill effects.

SOME TURKISH DELIGHTS

The Turkish origins of baklava has been hotly debated by neighboring countries, but convincing arguments have been put forward by food historian Charles Perry, placing baklava as we know it in Turkey. Although there is evidence that the Nomadic peoples of central Asia made primitive kinds of layered breads and pastries, it is undeniable that these were refined by the palace pastry cooks of the Ottoman period, from the fifteenth century to the early twentieth century. Some of the best artisans from all corners of the extensive empire were attracted to the palace kitchens. It is possible that they had an exciting time learning from each other, but the truth is more likely to be that each jealously guarded his secret. From such competition came mouth-watering delicacies for the delectation of palace officials and harem ladies – among them the leaf pastry, nut and syrup confections that shelter under the umbrella of baklava.

In the past, these sweet morsels were produced once a year for the Janissaries, the Sultan's elite corps formed in the mid-fourteenth century and disbanded in 1826. The occasion was the Mantle of the Prophet Procession, in the middle of Ramadan, when palace pastry cooks prepared trays of baklava, covering them with cloths and placing them in readiness outside the kitchens. As there was one tray for every 10 Janissaries and auxiliaries, the process was quite a production and came to be known as the Baklava Procession. The soldiers marched from the palace to their barracks under the interested eye of the local population, with the trays swaying in the carrying cloths suspended from poles. The empty trays would be returned the next day, but occasionally, untouched trays were taken back as a mark of discontent, presumably a gesture that was politically, and not gastronomically, inspired.

By the end of the nineteenth century, baklava had begun to ease its way out of the palace kitchens. As the first of many pastry shops were opened in Istanbul, it became available to the aspiring middle classes. It later spread to Greece and various Middle Eastern and Central Asian countries, or developed there along parallel lines, and regional variants surfaced. Cashews and pine nuts, for instance, are popular in the Middle East, and Greeks are fond of almond fillings, often combined with cream. While the coarser Azerbaijani *Pakhlava* may appear to have more in common with its Nomadic predecessors, the Persians set to work to create a sweet of subtle elegance. Here, pastry is a mere formality and is used in sparing quantities, barely containing the rich rose-scented almond or pistachio filling. Dexterous hands all over the region continue to press, roll, fold and coax a whole range of sweets, cleverly creating a fabulous diversity from the same basic ingredients.

Labor shortages, economic crises, family ties and a spirit of pure adventure took the original baklava eaters to all parts of the world. Bakeries soon sprang up wherever there were enough customers to warrant their presence. Unfortunately, in most cases, the lack of good competition, as well as a reluctance on the part of struggling immigrant communities to pay for a quality product on a regular basis, has meant that few people outside its native area have been privileged to eat baklava at its best.

Knowing that there was a treasure to be uncovered, and frustrated by the prevailing monotony of the phyllo pastries in Western Europe, I decided to go to its cradle, so to speak – Konya, a Turkish province in Central Anatolia. This is where my friend Nevin Halıcı lives, and I was sure she would be able to help me find the nuances I so desperately sought. Not only is she a wonderful friend and hostess, she is also a respected Turkish food historian. My idea was that Nevin would explain what was what while I made copious notes. It turned out differently: we went from shop to shop, tasting and re-tasting pastry after pastry and reflecting on the flavor, ingredients and composition, and only then did I feel able to make those notes. It was an experience that justified the trip. These were not the pallid, sickly sweet pastries that are the norm in immigrant communities, where some bakers, untroubled by conscience, even resort to dyeing coconut green in the hope that someone will eat it and be fooled into thinking it's pistachio. Even with the country in the throes of an economic crisis, I found there was excellent baklava to be tasted.

After tasting my way through countless pastries, I found my baklava Mecca at Biroğlu's. *Antepli* ("from Gaziantep," the baklava paradise in eastern Turkey) and *tereyağlı* ("made with butter") are two of the most coveted predicates for any good baklava shop – and needn't necessarily be strictly true. Our rotund, swarthy Antepli Mr Biroğlu had hung his framed license in a prominent place to erase any doubt in his customers' minds about his origins, and tasting his wares was the only proof needed concerning the butter content. It was a modest-looking but spotlessly clean establishment, with three tables at the back. The plates of pastries were still slightly warm from the oven and came with hygienically sealed glasses of cold mineral water. Mr Biroğlu came to talk to us and, with Nevin as my interpreter, I learned that he used only the best-quality ingredients and had his pistachios sent from Gaziantep, where they grow some of the best. If the nuts are harvested during the three-week peak period, they retain their lovely green color as well as all the flavor. He was very proud of his products and when I remarked that he looked as if he enjoyed his wares, he immediately retorted that he'd like to see me after a month or two in Turkey!

One of the first things I noticed was that when the pastries were lifted from the baking trays, only a droplet or two of syrup stayed behind. How different from the relentless saccharine lakes of previous experience. A good baklava-maker does not use glucose (which prevents crystallization) in his syrup, and even if a particular pastry calls for a heavier type of syrup, it is rarely cloying. The cold syrup is usually poured over the hot pastry and the amount must be carefully dosed. Classic baklava will absorb differently from a roll, and a roll lying on its side will absorb less readily than one with the cut side exposed. Looking at the take-away containers of baklava shops can give a clue about the syrup content of the pastries. Those who flood their pastries tend to go for plastic containers; the waxed cardboard boxes used by their superior competitors would ooze all over the place.

Phyllo pastry – or *yufka*, as it is called in Turkey – is, of course, the basis of baklava. The commercial type is usually fairly straight: bread flour, salt, a little butter or oil and water. Homemade types often include eggs and perhaps an acid agent to help increase elasticity.

I was rather surprised to see ashy water listed as an ingredient in one of Nevin's books. I asked her about it, assuming that this was a mistake caused by poor translation. It was, in fact, nothing of the kind. Ashy water is made by mixing the ashes from a wood fire with water, leaving it overnight and then draining off the water for use. Cooks in previous generations often used it as a tenderizer, although modern cooks tend to use milk instead – or they just buy ready-made *yufka*.

Supermarket phyllo usually comes in one or two standard thicknesses, but a professional baklava-maker will use pastry of varying thickness. This, together with the placement of the nuts, the amount and kind of nuts used, the shape of the resulting pastry and the amount of syrup, gives each pastry its unique character. Classic baklava, for example, is very crisp and is golden brown. A roll made by spreading finely ground nuts on an entire sheet of pastry remains pale in color and tender to the bite. This pastry is generally slightly thicker than that used for baklava. The same roll, shortened and placed with the cut side upwards, will have a different texture because it will absorb a little more syrup. And it goes without saying that pastries made with oil and margarine can never have the same flavor as those made with pure butter.

LEAF PASTRY

Leaf pastry is not difficult to make and requires more patience than proficiency. That said, it is tricky for the home cook to roll or stretch it out as thinly as the commercial product, and the baked result may not be as crisp. However, it is ideal in recipes where the pastry must offer some resistance to the sheer abundance of filling, such as Palace Rolls (p. 283) and strudels. The baking powder in this recipe acts as a tenderizer. Old Turkish recipes specify "ash(y) water" (*küllü su*) as an ingredient (see Some Turkish Delights, p. 267). Unorthodox though it may sound, this is actually an effective primitive form of leavening, which commonly goes by the name "potash."

    This recipe will make two sheets at least 8 x 18 inches, or a larger number of smaller sheets. It is also easily halved, for instance for Apple Strudel (p. 306). You will need a large, cool surface for rolling out the pastry.

9 oz/1⅔ cups bread flour

½ tsp salt

1 tsp baking powder

2 tbsp neutral-tasting oil, such as corn, sunflower
   or peanut oil

1 tbsp vinegar

about 4 fl oz/½ cup lukewarm water

cornstarch, for dusting

EQUIPMENT:
a dowel at least 24 inches long

The quickest way to make this pastry is using a food processor fitted with a plastic kneading blade. Put all the ingredients in the food processor and knead until smooth. Alternatively, knead by hand until smooth. Be quite rough with the pastry, throwing it from time to time onto your work surface. This improves the texture. Shape into a ball, then oil lightly and cover with plastic wrap. Set aside for about 1 hour.

    Divide the pastry into portions for rolling out, according to what you want to make. If you would like to make Apple Strudel, for instance, divide the dough into two pieces and use the second piece for another dish, or simply make up half the recipe and roll out the whole thing at once. For Palace Rolls, you will need to divide it into 5 portions.

    Use the coldest surface you can find, such as a marble or granite countertop, to roll out the pastry. If you use a silicone sheet, make sure that it is large enough to accommodate the finished size of the sheet.

    Dust the work surface and the pastry (or portion of pastry) with cornstarch and flatten it. Roll out to the desired size. This is a gradual process and the best way to do it is to roll the dowel back and forth, moving the position of your hands several times so that you can exert even pressure in all places. Try to roll in several directions to ensure evenness, and rotate the pastry twice or so, wrapping it around the dowel and then unrolling it so that you give it a quarter turn each time. Dust with cornstarch as needed and try to make the sheets as thin as possible.

Keep each finished sheet on a surface dusted with cornstarch. Dust the top and cover with a sheet of plastic wrap. Add the subsequent sheets to this pile, always making sure that there is enough cornstarch to separate the layers.

Use the pastry within a few hours, or it will start to dry out and become brittle.

SUGAR SYRUP

Heavy, cloying syrups can ruin baklava, and syrups that are too thin make it soggily unappetizing. Unless otherwise specified, this medium syrup is suitable for all the recipes in this book. Use it at your discretion, depending on how sweet you like your pastries and cakes. It is very easy to make and can be stored in an airtight container in the refrigerator for several weeks. It is also a useful standby for other purposes such as fruit salads and even cocktails. Lemon juice prevents the sugar from re-crystallizing and also serves to cut the sweetness a little, while remaining subtly in the background. If you would like to flavor the syrup, it is best to do so with just the portion that you are going to use so that the rest of the batch can be used for other purposes.

1 lb 2 oz/2½ cups granulated sugar

13 fl oz/generous 1½ cups water

2 tsp lemon juice, strained volume

rose water or orange flower water, to taste

Put the sugar, water and lemon juice in a heavy saucepan over medium heat. Bring to a boil, stirring all the time to dissolve the sugar. Then lower the heat and simmer for 5 minutes. Remove from the heat and set aside to cool.

If using, stir rose water or orange blossom water into the cold syrup, a few drops at a time, until you get the desired flavor.

PURE PERFECTION

Gaziantep, in south-eastern Turkey, is a worthwhile place of pilgrimage for baklava lovers. The city boasts dozens of shops, and traditional methods, some of them specific to the city, are used to create a staggering array of local specialties. A true Antep baklava-maker is proud to set high standards, and healthy competition has brought the art of baklava-making as close to perfection as it is likely to get.

A cool kitchen, free of drafts and direct sunlight, is the starting point, and the ideal work surface is marble. In the past, it was a great struggle to keep temperature and humidity down in the hot summer months. Laborious but efficacious cooling solutions were found – for instance, rubbing the floor with blocks of ice at regular intervals. While modern cooling techniques may be used today, some traditionalists still require employees to shower every two hours during the summer, in an attempt to control body temperature and create the perfect atmosphere for baklava production.

The ingredients must be the very best. Hard, gluten-rich durum wheat flour is used. And though baklava-makers in other regions are content to use cornstarch as a dusting medium for rolling out and separating the layers, wheat starch is used in Gaziantep. Some of it is inevitably incorporated into the rolled sheets of pastry, which helps to define the texture of the finished product. It is produced to local pecifications and, in addition to certain physical qualities, it has magical properties: it speaks to the baker. Rubbing it between the fingers, the baker listens for the rustling whisper *cıyır cıyır* ("juh-yur juh-yur"), which announces that the correct consistency has been reached. When the dough is ready, it is portioned and a seemingly careless flick of the wrist dusts it with what is nevertheless a precisely dosed amount of wheat starch. Too little would make the pastry stick and too much would make it dry. Deft hands wield thin, long dowels with easy expertise, flying back and forth over the marble slab. As the sheet gets thinner, the pastry is wound loosely around the dowel and rolled at the same time, encouraging it to stretch even more to produce translucent sheets, so thin that up to 40 layers can make one batch of baklava.

Pistachio nuts are a speciality of the area, but not just any kind will do, no matter how high the quality or how green the color. The color reflects the chlorophyll content, and pistachios have a color spectrum that ranges from rich cream to vivid green. The greener nuts are particularly prized by bakers and sweet-makers all over the world. In Gaziantep, a special variety called *beyaz ben* (white speckle) or *boz* is used. This is harvested a little before complete maturation, when the oil ratio has reached its peak and the flavor is at its finest.

Clarified sheep's milk butter is the most prized fat of all. In order to retain the purity of taste, which can be influenced by a factor as simple as the weeds, shrubs and grasses on which the animals grazed, the milk of sheep from different flocks is not usually mixed. Şanlıurfa, Pazarcık and Kahramanmaraş are particularly renowned for their sheep's milk butter, which has a more pronounced flavor than its cow's milk counterpart, and good baklava-makers will go to the trouble of sourcing their own butter in these districts. It is poured in copious quantities over the uncooked baklava and left to stand to allow maximum absorption. As soon as it comes out of the oven, some of the excess butter is drained off and boiling syrup is poured over the hot baklava. This is a key difference between Gaziantep and other areas: it is more usual to pour cold syrup over hot baklava or hot syrup over cold baklava.

All of these factors combine to produce a sweet that must be tasted to be believed. One of the most popular kinds is simply referred to as Gaziantep baklava; it is similar in appearance to classic baklava, but while the classic version has a filling of ground walnuts, the Antep variant is filled with the exquisite local pistachios, made even more rich and delicious by an addition of *kaymak*, the silky-textured clotted cream.

Making Gaziantep baklava

CLASSIC BAKLAVA

Classic baklava is one of the easiest kinds to make and usually has one layer
of walnuts between several sheets of pastry. Though generally served in small
squares, rectangles or rhomboids, it can also be cut into more fanciful shapes such
as a blunt-bottomed wedge resembling a carrot. This is known in Turkey as *Havuç
Dilimi*, or Carrot Slice, but its shape is the only thing that distinguishes it from the
classic version.

6–7 oz/1½–1¾ sticks butter, melted

1 lb 2 oz phyllo pastry (20 sheets 10 x 10 inches)

5½ oz/1½ cups walnuts, finely ground

9–10 fl oz/1–1¼ cups prepared cold sugar syrup
  (p. 273), or to taste

EQUIPMENT:

8–9 inch square pan

MAKES 25–36 SQUARES

Preheat the oven to 350°F/180°C.

Brush the baking pan with melted butter. Place one sheet of phyllo in the pan to fit as
neatly as possible. Allow the excess pastry to come up the sides of the pan. Brush with more
melted butter. Continue this layering and brushing with butter until you have used up 10
sheets of pastry.

Scatter the ground walnuts over the buttered pastry and continue the layering and
buttering until you have used up all 20 sheets. Use a sharp knife to cut right through to the
bottom of the pastry layers. (Use a plastic spatula with a cutting blade if your pan is a non-
stick one.) Make 4 or 5 parallel rows of cuts, then make 4 or 5 more rows of cuts at right
angles to the first.

Bake for 30–40 minutes, or until golden brown and crisp on top. Remove from the oven
and pour the cold syrup evenly across the surface, allowing it to run into the cuts. Leave to
cool in the pan.

PERSIAN BAKLAVA

Persian baklava is richer than its Turkish and Middle Eastern cousins with lots of nuts and very little pastry, and is more like a piece of marzipan than a traditional baklava. The filling, usually made of almonds, is sweetened and spiced with cardamom and the syrup is scented with rose water, giving a delicate flavor that lingers on the tongue.

SYRUP
2½ oz/generous ⅓ cup granulated sugar
5 fl oz/⅔ cup water
1½ tbsp rose water

FILLING
9 oz/2⅔ cups finely ground almonds
4½ oz/½ cup superfine sugar
½ tsp ground cardamom

1¼ oz/½ stick butter, melted
6 sheets phyllo pastry, 10 x 10 inches

EQUIPMENT:
8-inch square pan

MAKES 36 SQUARES

For the syrup, put the sugar and water in a saucepan and bring to a boil, stirring all the time to dissolve the sugar. Lower the heat and allow it to simmer for 5 minutes. Remove from the heat and set aside to cool. When cool, stir in the rose water.

Combine the ground almonds, sugar and cardamom in a bowl and set aside.

Preheat the oven to 350°F/180°C. Meanwhile, brush the baking pan with melted butter. Place one sheet of phyllo in the pan and allow excess pastry to come up the sides of the pan. Brush with more melted butter and continue to layer and brush with butter until you have used up 3 sheets of pastry. Scatter the filling over and press with your hands to make a smooth and compact layer. Top with the remaining 3 sheets, layering and buttering as before.

Use a sharp knife to cut right through to the bottom of the pastry layers. (Use a plastic spatula with a cutting blade if your pan is a non-stick one.) Make 5 parallel rows of cuts, then make 5 more rows of cuts at right angles to the first. You may need to keep one hand on the pastry as you cut, as it will be very loose on top of the dry filling. Don't worry about this dryness; the syrup will take care of that later.

Bake for about 20 minutes, or until golden brown and crisp on top. Remove from the oven and pour the cold syrup evenly across the surface. Leave to cool in the pan.

VARIATION

A two-nut version can be made with almonds and pistachios, separated by a layer of pastry. Use 4½ oz/1⅓ cups ground almonds and 2 oz/¼ cup granulated sugar to make one filling and the same weight of sugar and ground pistachios to make the second filling. Spice both fillings with cardamom. You will also need 3 extra sheets of phyllo pastry and an additional ¼ stick butter to separate the fillings.

PAKHLAVA

As its name suggests, this cake is a relative of baklava, but the resemblance does not extend beyond the walnut filling and layering technique. Popular in the former Soviet countries to the east of Turkey, such as Azerbaijan, it is made with a rich butter and sour cream pastry. Nowadays it often has only two or three layers of filling, but old recipes have up to eight. It is not usually syruped, except in Armenia. This recipe is a breeze if you use a food processor, and the sour cream pastry is wonderfully supple to roll.

FILLING
4½ oz/generous 1 cup walnuts
2¾–4½ oz/generous ⅓–scant ⅔ cup granulated
   sugar
2 egg whites

PASTRY
½ oz/2 cups all-purpose flour
¼ tsp salt

½ tsp baking powder
4½ oz/generous 1 stick butter, chilled
   and cubed
4 fl oz/½ cup sour cream
2 egg yolks

EQUIPMENT:
9-inch springform pan, greased

Put the walnuts and sugar (to taste) in the bowl of the food processor and pulse until the nuts are very fine. Transfer to another bowl, then add the egg whites and combine well. Set aside.

Wipe the bowl of the food processor to remove the worst of the mess and add the flour, salt and baking powder. Pulse a few times to mix. Add the butter in cubes and pulse until the mixture resembles fine breadcrumbs. Add the sour cream and egg yolks and pulse until the pastry comes together. If there are any streaks, you can knead them out by hand. Put the pastry in a plastic bag and chill for about 15 minutes.

Preheat the oven to 350°F/180°C. Grease the pan.

Divide the pastry into 4 portions. Roll out one portion ¾ inch larger in diameter than the pan. Drape it over the rolling pin and transfer to the bottom of the pan. Press into place, with the excess pastry pressed against the sides of the pan. Spread a third of the filling onto the pastry. Repeat the rolling and layering process so that you have 3 layers of filling and 4 layers of pastry. Trim the top sheet of pastry neatly, then moisten the outer edges and press around the circumference of the pan to seal.

Bake for 45 minutes, or until pale golden brown.

PALACE ROLLS
SARAY SARMASI

This irresistible treat is tender rather than crisp and you need to be very generous with the pistachios: a good layer of nuts will contribute to both tenderness and flavor. It is very aptly named, as it is not one of the cheaper types to make; it was probably invented by the palace chefs in Istanbul.

9 oz phyllo pastry – 10 sheets, 10 x 10 inches

4½ oz/generous 1 stick butter, melted

7–9 oz/1⅓–1⅔ cups pistachios, very finely ground

7 fl oz/generous ¾ cup prepared cold sugar syrup (p. 273), or to taste

EQUIPMENT:

a thin dowel (with a diameter of about ¼ inch), at least 12 inches long

MAKES 20 PASTRIES

If you don't trust your ability to divide the nuts equally "by eye," weigh out 5 portions onto pieces of parchment paper or plastic wrap and set aside.

Place 2 sheets of phyllo side by side on your work surface with the ends overlapping each other by about ½ inch. Brush with melted butter. Leaving a margin of about ½ inch free along both long sides and one short side, and ¾ inch along the other short side, sprinkle one-fifth of the ground pistachios over the butter, trying to distribute the nuts as evenly as possible.

Position the dowel at the short side of the pastry on top of the free ¾-inch margin and roll up to form a fairly tight cylinder. With the cylinder resting on your work surface, gently ease out the dowel. Brush the pastry with butter and set it aside. Repeat this procedure for the next 4 pairs of sheets.

Preheat the oven to 350°F/180°C. Butter the pan.

Place the 5 cylinders next to each other on a cutting board and trim the ends to neaten them. Cut each cylinder into 4 rolls and arrange them in the pan. The cut ends should just touch each other and the rows of rolls should also just touch each other. There will be some room left over in the pan, but this slight crowding gives a more tender texture to the finished pastries.

Bake for about 15 minutes; they should not color too much.

Pour the cold syrup evenly over the hot pastries and leave to cool in the pan.

NOTE

If you use a really thin dowel and nuts ground almost to powder, you will be able to produce tight and compact rolls with a very professional look and an even more succulent texture.

BIRDS' EYES
KUŞ GÖZÜ

It is not hard to see how these pastries got their name. Garnished with a dollop of cream and a whole pistachio, they look like a bird's beady eye. They are made like Palace Rolls (see p. 283) but are cut and arranged differently before being decorated, and are slightly crisp compared with the tender Palace Rolls. Having a wider expanse of cut surface, they also absorb a larger amount of syrup.

4 tbsp *kaymak* or crème fraîche

1 tbsp sugar

4 tbsp fine semolina

9 oz phyllo pastry – 10 sheets, 10 x 10 inch

4½ oz/generous 1 stick butter, melted

7–9 oz/1⅓–1⅔ cups pistachios, very finely ground

40 whole pistachios

9 fl oz/1 cup prepared cold sugar syrup (p. 273), or to taste

EQUIPMENT:
a thin dowel (with a diameter of about ¼ inch), at least 12 inches long;
8-inch square pan

MAKES 40 PASTRIES

Mix the *kaymak*, sugar and semolina together, and set aside.

Preheat the oven to 350°F/180°C.

Meanwhile, use the method described for making Palace Rolls (p. 283) to make the cylinders – but this time, cut each cylinder into 8 pieces. Arrange the slices cut side up on the buttered baking pan. Use two teaspoons (or a piping/pastry bag fitted with a small plain nozzle/tip if you have one) to spoon a neat dollop of cream mixture onto the center of each roll. Stick a pistachio into the cream.

Bake for about 15 minutes, or until lightly colored at the edges.

Pour the cold syrup evenly over the hot pastries and leave to cool in the pan.

NIGHTINGALES' NESTS
BÜLBÜL YUVASI

There are claims that this pastry originated in the Istanbul Palace kitchens at the end of the nineteenth century, but a similar pastry of unknown date is also popular in northern Syria and southern Turkey. Before it is rolled up, the pastry sheet is sometimes sprinkled with ground almonds or pistachios, this apparently being the palace refinement. The unfilled version makes a delicious change and gives a crisper finish. In some parts of the Middle East, a Nightingale's Nest is made from thread pastry (*kadayif* or *kunafeh*, available in international food stores) and whole pistachios are used for garnish, giving quite a realistic depiction of a bird's nest.

9 oz phyllo pastry – 10 sheets, 10 x 10 inches

3½ oz/⅞ stick butter, melted

3½ oz/generous 1 cup finely ground almonds or pistachios (optional)

5 oz/⅔ cup prepared cold sugar syrup (p. 273), or to taste

1¼ oz/⅓ cup pistachios, finely ground

MAKES 10 PASTRIES

Preheat the oven to 350°F/180°C.

Place a sheet of phyllo on your work surface and brush with melted butter. If using the ground almonds or pistachios as a filling, sprinkle one-tenth of it over the butter. Roll up the phyllo pastry into a loose cylinder. With the seam at the bottom, coil the cylinder loosely to form a spiral, pushing gently from either end, concertina-style, to pleat it a little and prevent the pastry from breaking. Put the finished coil on a baking sheet and continue to shape the remaining 9 in the same way. Brush the shaped pastries with butter and sprinkle some of the ground pistachio into the center of each coil.

Bake for 12–15 minutes, or until crisp and golden brown. Pour the cold syrup evenly over the hot pastries and leave to cool in the pan.

PISTACHIO AND CREAM TRIANGLES
ŞÖBİYET

These crisp triangles are filled with pistachio paste and cream and need a very moderate amount of syrup. You could even get away with just brushing on a little syrup to make a shiny glaze, as the pistachio paste is already sweetened. Some of the preparation can be done the day before. Superfine sugar will give the filling a little crunch, while confectioner's sugar will make a smoother paste.

PISTACHIO PASTE

1¾ oz/⅓ cup pistachios, very finely ground

1¼ oz/scant ¼ cup superfine sugar;

    or generous ¼ cup confectioner's sugar

about 2 tbsp prepared cold sugar syrup (p. 273)

CREAM MIXTURE

3 tbsp *kaymak* or crème fraîche

2 tbsp very fine semolina

1 tbsp superfine sugar

9 oz phyllo pastry – 10 sheets, 10 x 10 inches

3½ oz/⅞ stick butter, melted

3½ fl oz/scant ½ cup prepared cold sugar syrup

    (p. 273), or to taste

MAKES 10 PASTRIES

For the pistachio paste, mix all of the ingredients until you get a malleable paste. Divide it into 10 pieces and shape each piece between your palms into a small squat "sausage" or pellet about 1½ inches long. Cover with plastic wrap and set aside until needed. This can be done the day before.

To make the cream mixture, simply mix all the ingredients together to a smooth paste. Cover and set aside for about 1 hour to allow the semolina to swell. This can also be done a day in advance. Keep it well covered in the refrigerator and allow it to come to room temperature as you assemble the other ingredients.

Preheat the oven to 350°F/180°C.

Place one sheet of phyllo on your work surface and brush with melted butter. Divide it into three with your eye and fold the left third over the middle third, then the right third over this. Brush lightly with butter. Position a pistachio pellet diagonally in the bottom left corner and add one scant teaspoon of the cream mixture (1). Lift the pastry up by the point and fold it over to make a closed triangle of pastry encasing the filling (2). Now keep on turning over this triangle on the remaining pastry, so that every "somersault" encloses it in another layer of the pastry (3). Towards the end, you'll be left with just a small strip of pastry. Snip this off neatly with a pair of scissors and place the triangle on the baking sheet (4). Brush lightly with butter. Repeat to make 9 more pastries.

Bake for 15–20 minutes, or until crisp and golden brown. Remove from the oven, put the baking sheet on a heat-resistant surface and crowd the pastries together so that they touch. Pour about 3½ fl oz/scant ½ cup cold syrup evenly over the triangles.

When they have cooled, arrange them on a wire rack to allow excess syrup to escape. Keep the baking sheet underneath the rack to catch the drips. They don't need too much syrup, as the filling is also sweetened. Adjust the amount of syrup to suit your taste.

WALNUT AND CREAM COILS
SAÇARASI

This is an Anatolian homemade speciality. Before the advent of domestic ovens in average homes, it used to be cooked between two griddles, hence the name, which literally means "between two griddles." (A *saç* is a sheet iron griddle that is slightly convex or concave, depending on how you position it over the heat source.) The *kaymak* gives it a tender and yielding texture on the inside and the traditional way to serve these pastries is with a dusting of confectioner's sugar, but they can also be lightly syruped.

9 oz phyllo pastry – 10 sheets, 10 x 10 inches

2¾ oz/scant ¾ stick butter, melted

4½ oz/generous 1 cup walnuts, chopped
   medium-fine

1 small container *kaymak* (about 6 oz)
   or 6 fl oz/¾ cup crème fraîche

5 fl oz/⅔ cup prepared cold sugar syrup
   (p. 273), or to taste
   or confectioner's sugar, for dusting

MAKES 5 LARGE PASTRIES

Preheat the oven to 350°F/180°C.

Place two sheets of phyllo next to each other on your work surface, one piece overlapping the other by about ¼ inch. Brush with melted butter and spread about 2 tbsp *kaymak* over the butter, leaving about 1 inch free on all sides. The back of a spoon is useful for this purpose and the layer need not be perfectly even.

Scatter one-fifth of the walnuts over this, then roll the pastry into a loose cylinder, starting at one long side. With the seam at the bottom, coil the cylinder loosely to form a spiral, pushing gently from either end, concertina-style, to pleat it a little and prevent the pastry from breaking. Put the finished coil on a baking sheet and shape the remaining four in the same way.

Brush the shaped pastries with butter and bake for 25–30 minutes, or until the tops are crisp and golden brown.

If using syrup, pour it evenly over the hot pastries and leave to cool. If using confectioner's sugar as a garnish, wait until they cool before dusting to taste.

WALNUT CIGARS

These walnut cigars are the result of experiments to recreate a pastry I ate and greatly enjoyed in the food court of an American mall, of all unlikely places. As I passed the Greek takeout, my eyes fell on the huge trays of baklava and paused on the golden-brown cigars. Being a sucker for baklava, I had to try one. It turned out to be a crisp and buttery pastry filled with delicious cashews. The close-lipped owner cautiously volunteered that she used a lot of butter and good nuts, but I had already figured out that much for myself. The taste stayed with me and I set to work in my own kitchen, eventually coming up with this version. I decided to substitute walnuts for the cashews because, no matter how hard I tried to bring out their flavor, the cashews still insisted on tasting like plaster. These cigars do not need to be syruped since the filling is already sweetened.

FILLING

2¾ oz/scant ¾ stick butter

3½ oz/½ cup (solidly packed) soft light brown
  sugar

4½ oz/generous 1 cup walnuts, finely chopped

9 oz phyllo pastry – 10 sheets, 10 x 10 inches*

3½ oz/⅞ stick butter, melted

MAKES 20 CIGARS

Make the filling first. Put the butter and sugar in a saucepan and stir slowly over low heat to melt the butter and dissolve the sugar. Increase the heat a little and keep stirring. Once the first bubbles appear, keep on stirring for 1 minute more, then remove the saucepan from the heat and stir in the walnuts. Stir well to coat evenly. Set aside to cool.

Preheat the oven to 350°F/180°C.

Cut the sheets of phyllo in half. Place a half sheet on your work surface, keeping the rest covered. Brush each half sheet with melted butter and place 1 tablespoonful of the filling at one short end, leaving about ¼ inch free on three sides. Fold the long sides inwards from the point where there is no filling, so that each long side overlaps the filling by ¼ inch. Bring the short edge over the filling and roll up into a cigar shape. Put it on the baking sheet and repeat until all of the pastry and filling have been used up.

Brush the cigars lightly with any leftover butter and bake for 15–20 minutes, or until golden brown and crisp. Cool on a wire rack.

* The phyllo sheets that I use for this recipe measure 10 x 10 inches. If your sheets are vastly different, cut them as best you can and portion the filling accordingly. The size of the cigars is not really important. What is important is that you end up with a rectangle that can be rolled up to make a cigar.

ALMOND FLUTES
FLOGERES ME AMIGDALA

Greeks are very fond of almond and cream combinations, and these pastries are easy to make – and irresistible. Use as much or as little syrup as you like, but remember that the filling also contains sugar. They are quite good without syrup too, with a dusting of confectioner's sugar.

FILLING

4½ oz/1⅓ cups ground almonds

2 tbsp semolina

2 egg yolks

3½ fl oz/scant ½ cup cream, light or heavy

1¼ oz/¼ cup granulated sugar

zest of ½ lemon (optional)

9 oz phyllo pastry – 10 sheets, 10 x 10 inches

4½ oz/generous 1 stick butter, melted

6 fl oz/¾ cup prepared cold sugar syrup
  (p. 273), or to taste

MAKES 10 PASTRIES

Make the filling first. Combine all of the ingredients for the filling and mix to a smooth paste. Set aside for at least 1 hour to give the semolina time to swell. If not, it will swell while baking and will burst through the delicate pastry.

Preheat the oven to 350°F/180°C.

Place one sheet of phyllo on your work surface. Brush it with melted butter. Place a generous tablespoon of filling near the bottom of the sheet and use the spoon to help shape it into a rough "sausage," leaving about 1½ inches space at the bottom and 2½ inches at each side. (You can use a piping/pastry bag if you're a perfectionist.) Fold the bottom flap over the filling. Fold the two sides inwards over the filling. Roll up the pastry loosely but neatly and place on the baking sheet. Use up the rest of the sheets in the same way.

Brush the flutes with any remaining butter and bake for 25 minutes, or until crisp and golden brown.

As soon as you remove the baking sheet from the oven, crowd them together on the sheet and pour half, even all of the cold syrup over them. Leave to cool, then remove from the syrup and drain on a wire rack.

These will keep at cool room temperature for up to three days, but will obviously be crispest on the day of baking. They may also be frozen for up to two months. Thaw at room temperature.

ALMOND COIL
M'HENCHA

M'hencha is a large pastry spiral that is typical of the Berber people of North
Africa. The name *m'hencha* means "serpent," and the shape is intended to convey
the impression of a coiled snake. This shape is common in the Middle East and
North Africa and was used in Egypt as far back as the reign of Ramses.

Traditionally, a wafer-thin pastry called *ouarka* or *dioul* is used. A batter is made
from fine semolina and flour and this is scooped up with the hand and patted onto
a hot griddle, with quick, deft strokes. It takes considerable skill – not to mention
heat-resistant hands – to make these sheets, and good *ouarka* is thinner than most
kinds of phyllo. However, phyllo makes a very good substitute. The filling is
invariably based on almonds and sugar, sometimes flavored with orange flower water,
rose water or cinnamon, or a combination of these. Unlike most pastries of its type,
m'hencha is not drenched in syrup and its sweetness comes from the filling. To make
it even more attractive, dust with confectioner's sugar, or scatter a few slices of lightly
toasted almonds on top – or do both.

FILLING

5½ oz/1 cup blanched almonds, finely ground

5½ oz/¾ cup superfine sugar

1 egg, well beaten

9 oz phyllo pastry – 10 sheets, 10 x 10 inches*

3 oz/¾ stick butter, melted

1 tbsp rose water or orange flower water
  or ½ tsp ground cinnamon

confectioner's sugar, for dusting, and/or toasted
  almond slices

MAKES 1 COIL, WITH A DIAMETER
OF ABOUT 8 INCHES

For the filling, combine the ground almonds, sugar and egg – but reserve 1 teaspoon of
the egg. If desired, add one of the suggested flavorings. Mix well to combine. Divide into
5 equal portions and set aside.

Place two sheets of phyllo next to each other on your worktop, one piece overlapping the
other by about ¾ inch. Brush generously with melted butter and place two more sheets on top
in the same way, brushing again with butter.

Take one portion of filling and roll it between your fingers to make a "sausage" that fits
the width of one pastry sheet. Don't worry if it breaks. Simply lay it on the pastry and bring
it together again with your fingers. Make a second "sausage" in the same way to fit the second
sheet and pinch the ends of both "sausages" together to attach the two. The filling should be
positioned about 1 inch from the bottom with ½ inch free at either end. Bring the

1-inch strip up over the filling and roll into a cylinder. Don't roll too tightly, as the filling will expand while baking and may then burst through the pastry. Coil this cylinder into a closed spiral, with the seam at the bottom, and put it on a greased baking sheet.

Repeat this procedure to make another cylinder. Pinch one end of the cylinder and dab a little of the reserved egg on it. Insert this into the open end of the coil on the baking sheet, then press to secure.

Preheat the oven to 350°F/180°C.

Use up the last sheets of pastry and filling in the same way. You will now be making a tube half the length of the two previous ones. Dab with the egg, then insert into the open end of the coil and complete the coiling. Pinch the end and tuck it under the completed coil.

Brush with any remaining butter and bake for about 25 minutes, or until it is golden brown and crisp on the outside. Leave the coil to cool on the sheet before transferring it carefully to a serving plate.

Well wrapped, this will keep for a few days at cool room temperature and can also be frozen. Serve by cutting lengths off the coil so that you preserve the shape for as long as possible.

* My sheets of phyllo measure 10 x 10 inches and there are 10 sheets to a pack. You don't need to have sheets with exactly the same dimensions, but you should have an even number of sheets. Adapt the instructions to suit your pastry. If your pack has 12 sheets, for instance, divide the filling into 6 portions instead of the 5 specified by this recipe. If your sheets are much wider than mine, there might be no need to join two sheets together.

OTHER VARIATIONS

OLD LADIES' NECKS
KOCAKARI GERDANI

Old Ladies' Necks is not a name that sounds very appetizing, which is probably why some people prefer to call it *Oklavadan Çekme*, literally "pull from rolling pin." In fact, it a delicious, slender walnut roll that is rolled very tightly around a dowel so that it wrinkles as it is pulled off, hence its unprepossessing name.

Use the recipe for Palace Rolls (p. 283), substituting ground walnuts for the pistachios and using one sheet of pastry at a time to make a slimmer roll. When rolling the sheet of pastry around the dowel, try to do this as tightly as possible: you are aiming for a wrinkled effect as you subsequently pull it out.

CARROT SLICES
HAVUÇ DİLİMİ

A classic baklava is made in a large round tray, then a circle is cut from the center and portioned into wedges. The remaining pastry is cut into "carrots": wedges that taper to a blunt edge instead of a point.

SULTAN'S ROLLS
SULTAN SARMASI

This is another variation on classic baklava, but while the classic version has only a single layer of walnuts in the middle, Sultan's Rolls have walnuts between every layer of pastry, making them more rich and tender.

GAZIANTEP ROLLS
ANTEP DÜRÜM

Gaziantep, in the east of Turkey, is famous for its fine pistachios. If the nuts are harvested at their peak during the brief three-week season, they will retain their beautiful green color all year. Outside this period, they tend to turn yellow as time progresses. Any pastry with the prefix "Antep" is likely to contain pistachios. These rolls are similar to Palace Rolls but with fewer nuts, so that the pastry to nut ratio is a little higher.

ROSE
FRENK BAKLAVA OR WARDE

Reputedly created in the eighteenth century by a French chef in Istanbul, this pastry is known as *Frenk baklava* (European baklava) in Turkey and *Warde* (flower) in many Arabic-speaking countries. A multitude of exceedingly thin pastry squares enclose one or more layers of nuts and the pastry is folded into a simple envelope shape, with all the points touching in the center. As it bakes, the points open up to expose the filling, with the result that it does look a little like a flower with curled petals.

A FINE WEB OF THREADS

Thread pastry (*kadayıf*, *kataif*, *konafa*, *kunafeh*) looks exactly like a tangled skein of coarse, creamy white threads. It is used as the basis for a number of sweet delicacies all over Turkey, the Middle East and North Africa. The threads are sometimes allowed to retain their pale color and soft texture but can also be baked until very crisp and brown, and in some places the pastry is even fried beforehand to ensure this. Vacuum packing improves its shelf life and reduces the volume considerably, and thread pastry can be bought in bags from many international food stores or specialty food stores. When you open the package and start separating the threads, they will regain their original buoyancy and start to expand, so always use a large bowl.

Thread pastry is a specialist product and is made by a handful of bakers with the right equipment and expert staff. Invited by a friendly Turkish baker to watch the process, I thought at first that it looked amazingly easy. My optimism was soon dampened. Closer scrutiny revealed that one needs to be very finely tuned to the character of both the batter and equipment, since the whole operation takes only half a minute, from the time that the batter distributor is filled to the production of the threads. Only one man in the large bakery was skilled enough to make the pastry, and after finishing the daily batch he went back to work alongside his colleagues, producing more mundane items like *yufka ekmek*, the popular paper-thin griddle breads.

The batter was kept in a large barrel standing on the floor next to a copper-clad griddle. This copper plate was about 7 ft in diameter and revolved over three gas flames, the largest at the outer edge and the smallest in the center. The batter distributor, called a *kıf*, was suspended on a metal arm above the griddle. It looked like a deep copper saucepan with a V-shaped extension running along the bottom, neatly pierced in several places to allow a carefully dosed amount of the thin batter to trickle onto the griddle. The *kıf* was positioned above the outer edge of the griddle and held fast while the griddle revolved, spinning a fine web of threads. Once the first batch of batter had set into threads, the *kıf* was refilled and repositioned very slightly so that the second batch of batter could fall in between, but not on top of, the threads that had already been formed. It requires a great deal of skill to release the batter so that it does not cover the first lot and the density of batter has to be gradually decreased as the *kıf* moves inwards. As soon as he reached the center, the baker swiftly extended two nimble fingers and dexterously swept the filaments together into one large handful. The snowy threads were hung on wooden racks to cool and then bundled together and packaged for the customers, who were by now popping in and out.

WHITE NUT-LAYERED THREAD PASTRY BALLOURIEH

Once you have bought the thread pastry, this is one of the simplest sweets to prepare. It is baked at a very low temperature so that it stays pale and tender, the creamy whiteness contrasting beautifully with the green layer of pistachios.

9 oz thread pastry

3½ oz/⅞ stick butter, melted

7 oz pistachios, finely ground

7 fl oz/generous ¾ cup prepared cold sugar
    syrup (p. 273), or to taste

EQUIPMENT:

8-inch square pan

Preheat the oven to 300°F/150°C.

Put the thread pastry in a large bowl and pull apart to loosen the filaments. Pour the melted butter over it. Gently massage the butter into the pastry, turning the threads constantly and letting every thread pass through your hands.

Use half of the pastry to line the bottom of the pan. Scatter the nuts evenly over this layer and top with the rest of the pastry. Press down well with your hands to compact it.

Bake for about 25 minutes. The color should barely change from creamy white to light cream. As soon as you remove the pan from the oven, pour the cold syrup over the pastry.

Use a plastic spatula with a sharp edge to cut into 16 squares. Leave to cool in the pan.

CRISP THREAD PASTRY LOGS
BURMA

Almost the same ingredients are used here as for Thread Pastry Squares, but in a different way, creating a crisp and golden sweet. The name comes from the Arabic word *mabrouma*, meaning to twist or whirl, and this refers to the technique used to shape the pastries. It takes a little practice to roll neat logs, but they are still delicious even if they do turn out less slick than pastry shop versions.

9 oz thread pastry

3½ oz/⅞ stick butter, melted

3½ oz/⅔ cup whole pistachios

7 fl oz/generous ¾ cup prepared cold sugar
   syrup (p. 273), or to taste

EQUIPMENT:

a dowel at least 12 inches long;

8-inch square pan

Put the thread pastry in a large bowl and pull apart to loosen the filaments, but try not to break them, as it is easier to roll up longer threads. Pour the melted butter over it. Gently massage the butter into the pastry, turning the threads constantly and letting every thread pass through your hands. Divide the pastry into four portions.

Spread a large sheet of plastic wrap on your work surface and put one portion of pastry on this. Use your fingers to make a square "sheet" roughly 8 x 8 inches from the pastry.

Preheat the oven to 350°F/180°C.

Place the dowel at one end, about 1¼ inches from the bottom. Arrange a quarter of the whole pistachios just above the dowel. Now fold the threads at the bottom over the dowel, then roll up the rest of the sheet as tightly as you can. Use the plastic wrap to help you along, if necessary.

Grease a baking pan. Gently pull the dowel from the roll and put the roll in the pan. Press any stray threads onto the log. Repeat with the remaining three portions of pastry and nuts.

Bake for about 30–35 minutes, or until the top is crisp and golden brown. For a darker effect, leave for longer. As soon as you remove the pan from the oven, pour the cold syrup over the pastry. After about 15 minutes, turn the rolls over so that the syrup becomes more evenly distributed. Leave to cool in the pan before cutting into portions.

FAIRLY EASY APPLE STRUDEL
APFELSTRUDEL

It is likely that the Turkish invaders introduced leaf pastry to Austria, just as they did in the Balkans. Then local bakers added their own touches, creating a simple but spectacular strudel that forever after came to be associated with Austria. There is a great variety of fillings – apricot, cherry, curd cheese and dried fruit, to name a few – but apple strudel remains by far the most popular. The pastry itself may sometimes be enriched with egg, and the technique used to create a paper-thin layer is what really sets it apart: leaf pastry is rolled out very thinly, usually on a floured tablecloth. Then the maker uses the back of the hand, dusted with flour, to coax the already thin layer into a sheet so transparent that a newspaper can be read through it. Needless to say, this technique takes time and practice to master and the recipe given here is much simpler, using homemade leaf pastry that is rolled as thinly as you can manage. This strudel is also modest in size, unlike the typical Austrian versions, which are so long that they are curved into a horseshoe shape to fit onto the baking sheet.

1 lb 2 oz apples (peeled weight; about 4)

1 tsp ground cinnamon

½ quantity Leaf Pastry (p. 272)

2 oz/½ stick butter, melted

4 tbsp dried breadcrumbs

1¾ oz/¼ cup superfine sugar

about 3 tbsp raisins or sultanas (golden raisins)

cornstarch, for dusting

EQUIPMENT:
a dowel at least 24 inches long

Peel the apples, cut them into quarters and remove the core. Slice very thinly and put into a bowl with the cinnamon. Set aside.

Spread a large sheet of plastic wrap, or two smaller sheets, on your work surface so that at least 24 x 18 inches is covered. Dust the pastry ball with cornstarch and roll out with a dowel to a very thin large sheet about 14 x 22 inches. If you press your hands on the middle of the dowel (above the spot you are rolling), you'll be able to exert a more even pressure than if you keep them at the sides, as with a conventional rolling pin.

Preheat the oven to 350°F/180°C. Grease a baking sheet.

Brush the sheet of pastry with butter, leaving a free space of about 7 inches at one short end. Sprinkle the breadcrumbs over the butter and arrange the apples evenly on top, leaving a margin of about 2 inches free at the other end. Sprinkle the sugar and raisins over the apples. Use the plastic wrap to help lift up the 2-inch margin and roll the strudel up by keeping the plastic wrap tautly raised. Make sure that the seam is at the bottom of the roll.

Transfer the strudel carefully to the baking sheet and brush with melted butter. Bake for about 35 minutes, or until golden brown. Eat warm or cold.

SWEET CHEESE STRUDEL

This strudel is very easy to make as long you are not alarmed by the consistency of the uncooked filling and are bold enough to follow the instructions. Curd cheeses with a low moisture content are usually used in Austria and Central Europe, but ricotta makes a good alternative. The strudel can be served warm or cold, on its own or with prepared seasonal fruit as a dessert. You can add all kinds of extras to taste, such as chocolate sauce, vanilla sauce, and whipped cream.

FILLING
9 oz/generous 1 cup ricotta
2 oz/¼ cup superfine sugar
2 egg yolks
2 tbsp fine semolina
generous pinch of lemon zest

2 tbsp sultanas (golden raisins), optional

about 7 oz phyllo pastry – 8 sheets, 10 x 10
  inches, or similar
1 oz/¼ stick butter, melted

Put the filling ingredients in a bowl and mix until homogenous. Cover with plastic wrap and leave for about 1 hour to give the semolina time to start swelling, absorbing some of the moisture into the bargain.

Spread a really long piece of plastic wrap – about 40 inches – on your work surface. Position four sheets of phyllo pastry on top of this (working left to right), slightly overlapping each other to obtain a long, narrow sheet roughly 35½ x 10 inches.

Spoon the cheese mixture lengthwise over the middle of the first (left-hand) sheet, leaving about 1 inch free at the top and bottom and 2 inches at the sides. Fold the top and bottom inwards so that the margin now covers some of the filling. Bring the left flap of pastry over the filling and then roll up the strudel loosely, using the plastic wrap to help create a roll. It will flop into place as you keep on moving the plastic wrap.

When you reach the end, cut the plastic wrap so that the roll sits on its own piece of wrap. Position the four remaining sheets of phyllo to form a large square on the expanse of plastic wrap that has become available again, using an extra piece to make up the shortfall. Allow the edges of the pastry to overlap slightly. Brush this square with butter, reserving about 1 teaspoon.

Preheat the oven to 350°F/180°C. Grease a baking sheet.

Now use the small piece of plastic wrap on which the roll is lying to help carry, turn and position the roll on the left of the square, so that there is equal empty space at the top and bottom and about 4 inches free at the left. Carefully remove and discard the small piece of plastic wrap. Fold the left flap of pastry over the roll and fold the top and bottom inwards to enclose it. Use the large sheet of plastic wrap again to roll up towards the right, tucking the top and bottom edges in as you go. When you reach the end, lift the roll with the film and place it on the baking sheet, seam-side down if possible. Remove the film and brush the roll with butter.

Bake for 35 minutes, or until crisp and golden brown. Serve warm or cold.

SAVORY CHEESE STRUDEL

This is put together in next to no time and makes a good appetizer, served in thin slices because of the saltiness of the cheese.

2¾ oz feta cheese*

small handful parsley (preferably flat leaf), finely chopped

4½ oz phyllo pastry – 5 sheets, 10 x 10 inches

1 oz/¼ stick butter, melted

Crumble the feta in a bowl. Add the parsley, mix and set aside.

Spread a large sheet of plastic wrap, or two smaller sheets, on your work surface so that at least 32 x 31 inches are covered. Place 3 sheets of phyllo pastry side by side on your work surface, slightly overlapping each other to obtain a large, narrow sheet roughly 27 x 10 inches.

Sprinkle over the feta mixture, leaving about ¼ inch free on all sides. Fold the two long sides inwards so that the ¼-inch margin now covers some of the filling. Starting from one short side, roll up to form a cylinder. Don't roll too tightly, or the pastry may then burst while baking. Stop rolling just before you reach the ¼-inch margin that remains. Move the roll to one side and place the two remaining sheets of phyllo on your work surface, slightly overlapping. Brush with melted butter.

Preheat the oven to 350°F/180°C. Grease a baking sheet.

Position the cylinder so that the end flap of pastry on the cylinder rests on the edge of the freshly buttered pastry on your work surface. Fold the long sides of the buttered pastry inwards so that the size is now the same as the cylinder. Continue rolling, enclosing the cylinder in layers of the buttered pastry.

Place the cylinder on a baking sheet, seam-side down, and bake for 20 minutes, or until the outside is golden brown. The crust will be crisp and the inner layers that have been in contact with the cheese will be softer and more yielding.

Serve warm or cold, sliced into small pieces.

* Feta cheese can be very salty. Soaking the whole piece in water for about 2 hours before use will help to remove some of the salt.

MEAT CIGARS OR CIGARILLOS

These savory cigars are flavored in various ways in the Middle East and make a good appetizer. They can be assembled a few hours in advance, or even the day before, and baked at the last minute. Cutting the sheets in half and making more slender sausages with the filling will give you twice the number of daintier, smaller cigarillos to serve with drinks.

FILLING

10½ oz/2½ cups ground lean beef or lamb

1 tbsp dried breadcrumbs

2 tbsp finely chopped cilantro

½ tsp salt, or to taste

¼–½ tsp chili flakes

¼ tsp ground cumin

½ tsp ground coriander

1 small egg, well beaten

2 tbsp pine nuts

9 oz phyllo pastry

1½–2 oz/⅜–½ stick butter, melted

MAKES 10 CIGARS/20 CIGARILLOS

Combine all the filling ingredients well. For regular-sized cigars, divide the filling into 10 portions and shape each one into a "sausage" about 4½ inches long. For the cigarillos, divide the filling into 20 portions and shape each one into a "sausage" about 3 inches long.

Preheat the oven to 350°F/180°C.

If making cigars, lay a sheet of phyllo on your work surface, taking care to keep the rest covered. Place a "sausage" in the center of the sheet about ¾ inch from the bottom. Fold the pastry inwards at either side so that the ends just touch each other in the middle. Brush the pastry with melted butter. Bring up the ¾-inch bottom flap and roll to form a cigar. Place on a baking sheet and repeat to make another 9 cigars.

For cigarillos, cut the sheets of phyllo in half on your work surface. Place a "sausage" at one short end, leaving about ¾ inch free on three sides. Fold the long sides inwards from the point where there is no filling, so that each long side overlaps the filling by ¾ inch. Bring the bottom edge over the filling. Brush the pastry with melted butter and roll up into a slim cigar or cigarillo shape. Put it on the baking sheet and repeat until all of the pastry and filling have been used up.

Brush the cigars or cigarillos with butter and bake until golden brown and crisp, about 15 minutes for cigarillos and 25 minutes for cigars. Cool on a wire rack.

* The phyllo sheets that I use for this recipe measure 10 x 10 inches, and there are 10 to a pack. If your sheets have different dimensions, the "sausage" should be half the width of the sheet for cigars. For the cigarillos, measure the width of the sheet and subtract 1½ inches for margins (¾ inch on either side) to obtain the correct length for the "sausage."

INDEX

BIBLIOGRAPHY

Alexiadou, Vefa. *Greek Pastries and Desserts*. Thessaloniki: Vefa Alexiadou, 1991.

Algar, Ayla. *Classical Turkish Cooking*. New York: HarperCollins, 1999.

Almenábar, Laura. *Repostería*. Santiago de Chile: Ed. Zig-Zag S.A., 1992.

Ayto, John. *The Diner's Dictionary*. Oxford: Oxford University Press, 1993.

Batmanglij, Najmieh. *New Food of Life: Ancient Persian and Modern Iranian Cooking and Ceremonies*. Washington D.C.: Mage Publishers, 1998.

Brizova, Joza. *The Czechoslovak Cookbook*. New York: Crown Publishers Inc., 1965.

Chinese Dim Sum. Taipei: Chin Chin Publishing Co. Ltd., 1999.

Dalby, Andrew. *Dangerous Tastes: The Story of Spices*. London: British Museum Press, 2000.

David, Elizabeth. *English Bread and Yeast Cookery*. London: Penguin, 1982.

Davidson, Alan. *The Oxford Companion to Food*. Oxford: Oxford University Press, 1999.

Der Haroutounian, Arto. *Patisserie of the Eastern Mediterranean*. London: Macdonald & Co., 1988.

Gergely, Anikó. *The Traditional Hungarian Kitchen*. Budapest: Vince Kiadó, 2000.

Gran Libro de la Cocina Chilena. Santiago de Chile: Ed. Bibliogr. Chilena Ltd., 1993.

Halıcı, Nevin. *Nevin Halıcı's Turkish Cookbook*. London: Dorling Kindersley, 1989.

Hanneman, L.J. *Bakery: Bread and Fermented Goods*. London: Butterworth-Heinemann, 1990.

Hartley, Dorothy. *Food in England*. London: Futura, 1985.

Heiner. *Süßes Backen*. Geneva: Lechner Verlag, -.

Hillman, Howard. *Kitchen Science* (rev. ed.). Boston: Houghton Mifflin, 1989.

Hösükoglu, Filiz. "The Secret World of Baklava," paper presented at the International Congress on Mediterranean Cuisine in Mersin, 1995.

Hsiung, Deh-Ta. *De Chinese Keuken*. Baarn: Bosch & Keuning, 2000 (trans.).

Huijstee, Martin van. *Het Indonesisch Kookboek*. Weert: Uitgeverij M & P, 1993.

Jaine, Tom. *Making Bread at Home*. London: Weidenfeld and Nicolson, 1995.

Kaneva-Johnson, Maria. *The Melting Pot: Balkan Food and Cookery*. Totnes: Prospect Books, 1995.

Kellerman, Monika. *Das Große Sacher Backbuch*. Weyarn: Verlag Seehamer, 1994.

Kofranek, Albert. *Die gute Wiener Küche*. Vienna: Kreymar & Scheriau, 1961.

Kramer, René et al. *Confiseries et Pâtisseries d'Aujourd'hui*. Paris: VILO, 1994.

Larousse Gastronomique. Paris: Librairie Larousse, 1984.

Lim-Castillo, Pia. "The Coconut: Fruit and Nut; Food and Fat" in *The Fat of the Land*, Proceedings of the Oxford Symposium on Food and Cookery 2002, ed. Harlan Walker, Footwork, 2003.

Manden, A. C. *Recepten van de Haagsche Kookschool*. 's-Gravenhage: De Gebroeders van Kleef, 1899.

Mayer, Eduard and Schumacher, Karl. *Wiener Süßspeisen*. Linz: Trauner Verlag, 1968.

McGee, Harold. *On Food and Cooking*. London: HarperCollins, 1991.

Minifie, Bernard. *Chocolate, Cocoa and Confectionery*. New York: Van Nostrand Rhinehold, 1989.

Mirodan, Vladimir. *The Balkan Cookbook*. Wheathampstead: Lennard Publishing, 1987.

Neuber, Wolf. *Der K.u.K. Mehlspeisenhimmel*. Vienna: Verlag Carl Überreuter, 1994.

Pagrach-Chandra, Gaitri. "Damra Bound: Indian Echoes in Guyanese Foodways" in *Food and the Memory,* Proceedings of the Oxford Symposium on Food and Cookery 2000, ed. Harlan Walker. Totnes: Prospect Books, 2001.

Pagrach-Chandra, Gaitri. *Windmills in My Oven: A Book of Dutch Baking*. Totnes: Prospect Books, 2002.

Perry, Charles. "The Central Asian Origin of Baklava" in *Second International Food Congress/Ikinci Milleterarası Yemek Kongresi*. Konya: Konya Kültur ve Turizm Vakfı, 1989.

Roden, Claudia. *A New Book of Middle Eastern Food*. London: Penguin, 1986.

Sax, Richard. *Classic Home Desserts*. New York: Chapters, 1994.

Serrano, Blanca. *Cocina Española*. Madrid: Susaeta Ediciones, 1991.

Shaida, Margaret. *The Legendary Cuisine of Persia*. Henley-on-Thames: Lieuse Publications Ltd., 1992.

Simonds, Nina. *Classic Chinese Cuisine*. New York: Houghton Mifflin, 1994.

Sultan, William. *Practical Baking* (5th ed.). New York: Van Nostrand Reinhold, 1990.

Sweet Old Fashioned Favourites. Sydney: Australian Women's Weekly Home Library, 1992.

Swiss Confectionery. Lucerne: Richemont Craft School, 1985.

Symons, Michael. "'The Cleverness of the Whole Number': Social Invention in the Golden Age of Antipodean Baking, 1890–1940 in PPC 85." Totnes: Prospect Books, 2008.

Williams, R. O. and R. O. Jnr. *The Useful and Ornamental Plants of Trinidad and Tobago* (rev. 4th ed.). Port of Spain, 1951.

ACKNOWLEDGEMENTS

Few large projects can be undertaken single-handedly and this one was no exception. I owe many thanks to family, friends, kind strangers and others, particularly those listed below.

Sri and Roger Owen who brought my project to the attention of the right publisher; Pia Lim-Castillo for her unflagging support and practical help; my husband Henk and children Judy and Leon whose appetites helped shape this book; my agents Charlotte Bruton and John McLaughlin who took all the burden of worrisome details off my shoulders; Yvonne Gouveia; Tom Jaine; Bee Wilson; Frans Douwes and Loes de Jong.

My Turkish friends and acquaintances who have been so kind and generous in very many ways. In Konya: Nevin Halıcı, Örnek Bakery, the squad of specialist baking ladies at Köşk Restaurant and the nameless bakers and vendors who cheerfully and patiently answered my endless flow of questions. In Ankara: Aylin Öney Tan; in Gaziantep: Filiz Hösükoğlu, Harun Akköz and the Gaziantep Chamber of Industry.

The people at Pavilion: Emily Preece-Morrison who commissioned the book and enthusiastically saw it through all its stages; copy editor Caroline Curtis; designer Louise Leffler; cover designer Georgina Hewitt; production manager Rebekah Cheyne. The combined efforts of props stylist Wei Tang, food stylist and home economist Jane Suthering and photographer Vanessa Courtier produced the most gorgeous photographs.

PHOTO ACKNOWLEDGEMENTS

p. 11: © Royal Asiatic Society, London, UK/The Bridgeman Art Library

p. 40–41: © Nevada Wier/CORBIS

p. 85: © Rijksmuseum Amsterdam

p. 95: © Gaitri Pagrach-Chandra

p. 146: © Photononstop/Alamy

p. 237: © dbimages/Alamy

p. 266: © Imagestate Media Partners Ltd – Impact Photos/Alamy

p. 301 (x 4 images): © Gaitri Pagrach-Chandra

pp. 270–1, 275, 276–7, 299: by kind permission of the Gaziantep Chamber of Industry Archive

Artworks throughout: © Heidi Kalyani/HiDesignGraphics/ iStock